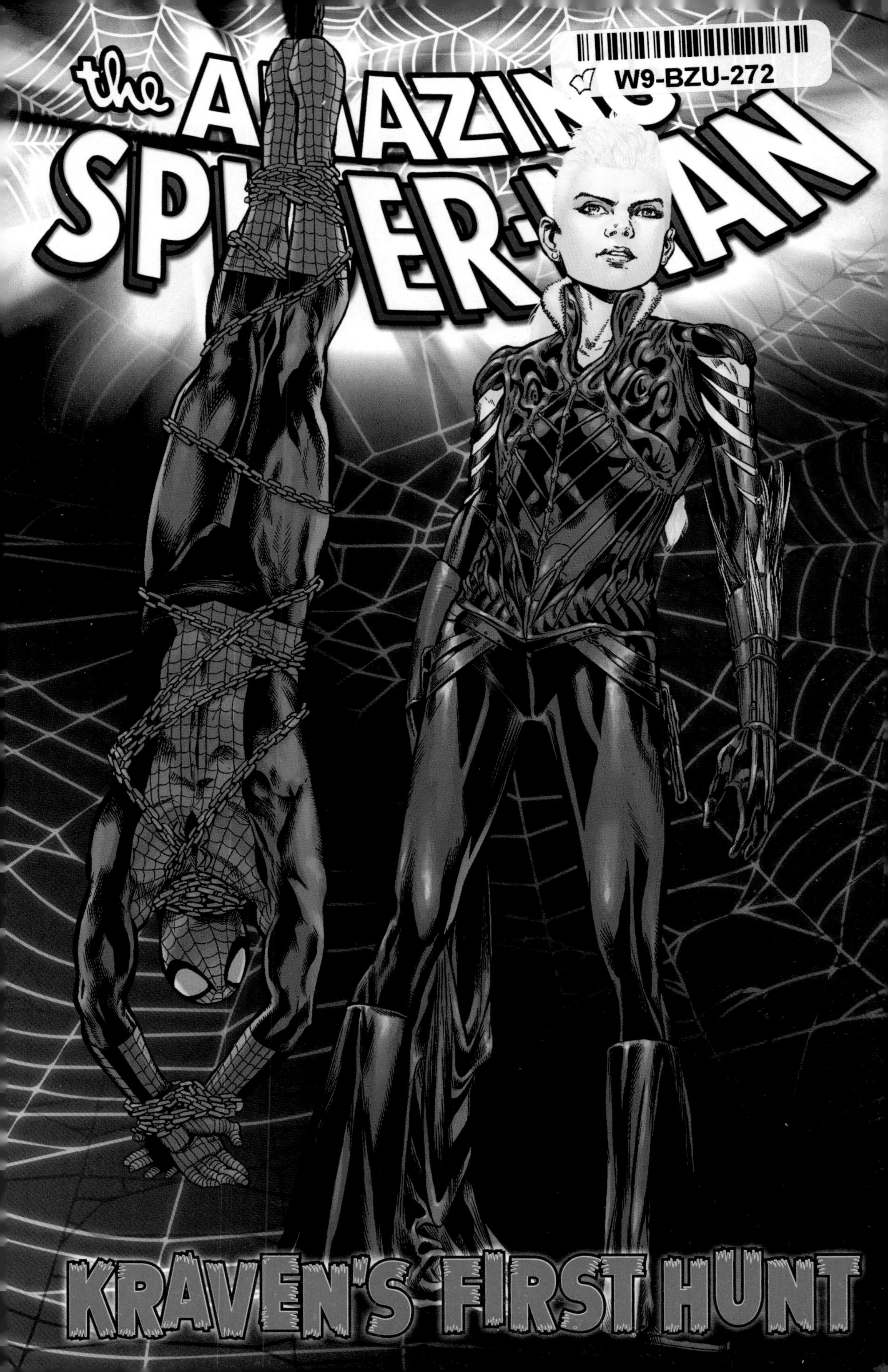
the
KRAVEN'S FIRST HUNT

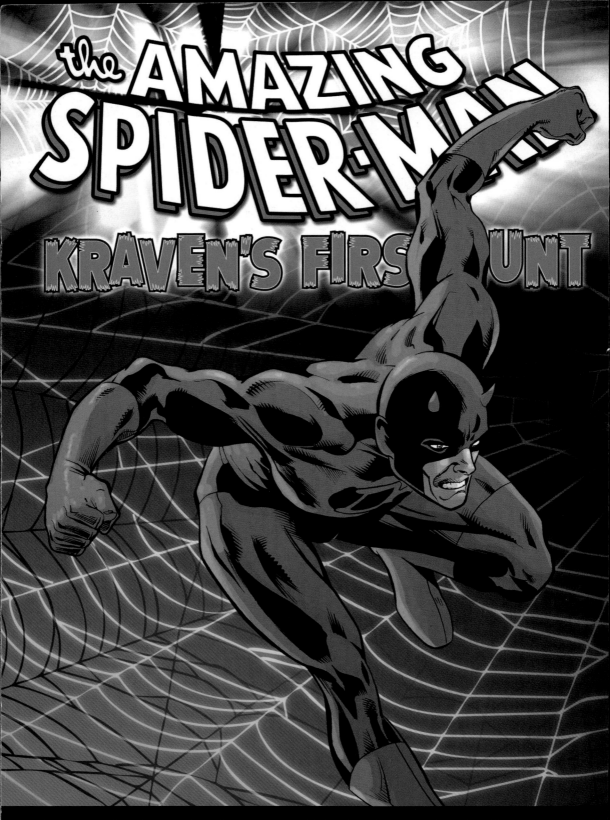

the AMAZING SPIDER-MAN

KRAVEN'S FIRST HUNT

SPIDER-MAN: KRAVEN'S FIRST HUNT. Contains material originally published in magazine form as AMAZING SPIDER-MAN #564-567 and SPIDER-MAN: BRAND NEW DAY — EXTRA! #1. Second printing 2011. ISBN# 978-0-7851-3243-1. Published by MARVEL WORLDWIDE, INC., a subsidiary of MARVEL ENTERTAINMENT, LLC. OFFICE OF PUBLICATION: 135 West 50th Street, New York, NY 10020. Copyright © 2008 Marvel Characters, Inc. All rights reserved. $14.99 per copy in the U.S. and $16.99 in Canada (GST #R127032852); Canadian Agreement #40668537. All characters featured in this issue and the distinctive names and likenesses thereof, and all related indicia are trademarks of Marvel Characters, Inc. No similarity between any of the names, characters, persons, and/or institutions in this magazine with those of any living or dead person or institution is intended, and any such similarity which may exist is purely coincidental. **Printed in the U.S.A.** ALAN FINE, EVP - Office of the President, Marvel Worldwide, Inc. and EVP & CMO Marvel Characters B.V.; DAN BUCKLEY, Publisher & President - Print, Animation & Digital Divisions; JOE QUESADA, Chief Creative Officer; JIM SOKOLOWSKI, Chief Operating Officer; DAVID BOGART, SVP of Business Affairs & Talent Management; TOM BREVOORT, SVP of Publishing; C.B. CEBULSKI, SVP of Creator & Content Development; DAVID GABRIEL, SVP of Publishing Sales & Circulation; MICHAEL PASCIULLO, SVP of Brand Planning & Communications; JIM O'KEEFE, VP of Operations & Logistics; DAN CARR, Executive Director of Publishing Technology; SUSAN CRESPI, Editorial Operations Manager; ALEX MORALES, Publishing Operations Manager; STAN LEE, Chairman Emeritus. For information regarding advertising in Marvel Comics or on Marvel.com, please contact John Dokes, SVP Integrated Sales and Marketing, at jdokes@marvel.com. For Marvel subscription inquiries, please call 800-217-9158. **Manufactured between 8/31/11 and 9/19/11 by R.R. DONNELLEY, INC., SALEM, VA, USA.**

10 9 8 7 6 5 4 3 2

AMAZING SPIDER-MAN #564

Writers: **MARC GUGGENHEIM,**
BOB GALE & DAN SLOTT
Pencils: **PAULO SIQUEIRA**
Inks: **AMILTON SANTOS & PAULO SIQUEIRA**
Colors: **ANTONIO FABELA**
Cover Art: **CHRIS BACHALO & TIM TOWNSEND**

AMAZING SPIDER-MAN #565-567

Writer: **MARC GUGGENHEIM**
Pencils (Issue #565) & Breakdowns:
PHIL JIMENEZ
Inks (Issue #565) & Finishes (Issue #567):
ANDY LANNING
Finishes (Issue #566): **MARK PENNINGTON**
Colors: **CHRIS CHUCKRY**
WITH JEROMY COX (Issue #566)
Cover Art: **PHIL JIMENEZ,**
ANDY LANNING & JEROMY COX

SPIDER-MAN: BRAND NEW DAY
– EXTRA!! #1
"BIRTHDAY BOY"

Writer: **ZEB WELLS**
Pencils: **PATRICK OLLIFFE**
Inks: **SERGE LAPOINTE**
Colors: **RAIN BEREDO**
Cover Art: **GREG LAND,**
JAY LEISTEN & FRANK D'ARMATA

Letters: **VC'S CHRIS ELIOPOULOS & CORY PETIT**
Spidey's Braintrust: **BOB GALE, MARC GUGGENHEIM,**
DAN SLOTT & ZEB WELLS
Assistant Editor: **THOMAS BRENNAN**
Editor: **STEPHEN WACKER**
Executive Editor: **TOM BREVOORT**

Collection Editor: **JENNIFER GRÜNWALD**
Assistant Editors: **ALEX STARBUCK & NELSON RIBEIRO**
Editor, Special Projects: **MARK D. BEAZLEY**
Senior Editor, Special Projects: **JEFF YOUNGQUIST**
Senior Vice President of Sales: **DAVID GABRIEL**
Book Designer: **RODOLFO MURAGUCHI**
SVP of Brand Planning & Communications: **MICHAEL PASCIULLO**

Editor in Chief: **AXEL ALONSO** • Chief Creative Officer: **JOE QUESADA**
Publisher: **DAN BUCKLEY** • Executive Producer: **ALAN FINE**

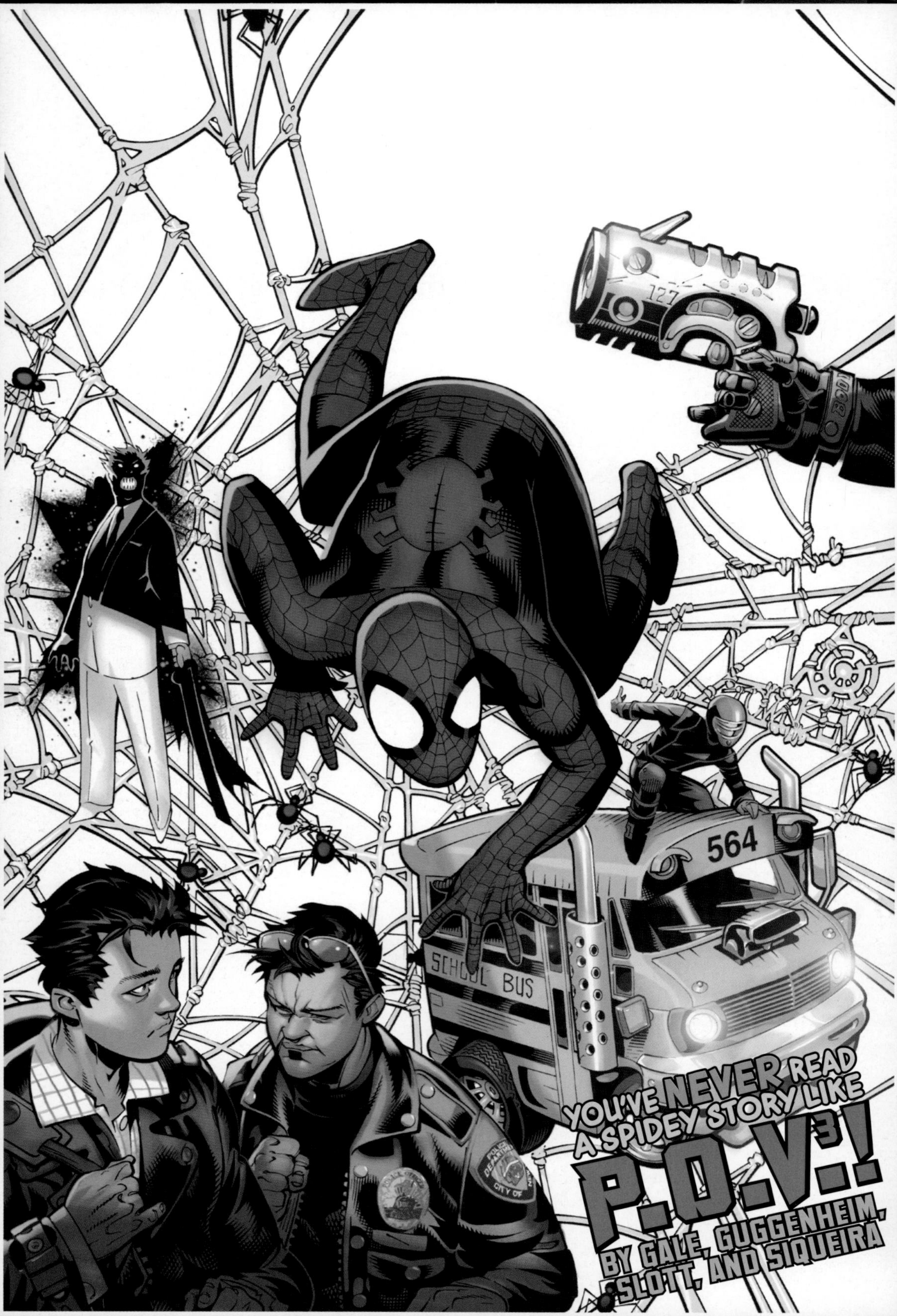
564
SCHOOL BUS
YOU'VE NEVER READ A SPIDEY STORY LIKE
P.O.V.^{3}!
BY GALE, GUGGENHEIM, SLOTT, AND SIQUEIRA

AMAZING SPIDER-MAN #564

THE OFFICIAL NEWSPAPER OF SPIDER-MAN

THE DB

ICY GLARES AT THE HOT DEBATE – CROWNE AND HOLLISTER GO TOE-TO-TOE AT HUNTER COLLEGE; CROWNE'S EMPLOYEE RECORDS AND HOLLISTER'S DAUGHTER'S DATE – LIFE TAKE CENTER STAGE! MORE ON PAGE G12

JULY 2, 2008   ·   WEDNESDAY

PERFECT STRANGERS

VISIT THE SPIDEY-BLOG!
www.marvel.com/blogs/spider-office

It's been a busy time for our man, Peter Parker. Not only has he returned to web-slinging, but he's been living back at home with Aunt May for a while. Now back on his feet, he's moved in with new friend, police officer Vin Gonzales – although they actually crossed paths months before when, as Spider-Man, Pete was involved in a high speed chase with Vin and Overdrive, a super-villain able to corrupt any form of automation to his own ends – and something of a lackey for Spidey's new nemesis, Mr. Negative…

CREDITS MOVED TO RECAP PAGE!

"ROOM" GIVEN AS PRIMARY REASON!

Written by
MARC GUGGENHEIM (Pages 1-8)
BOB GALE (Pages 9-15)
and **DAN SLOTT** (Pages 16-23)

PAULO SIQUEIRA
Pencils

**AMILTON SANTOS
& PAULO SIQUEIRA** (Pages 22-23)
Inks

ANTONIO FABELA
Colors

VC's CORIS PETITOPOLOUS
Letters

JOE SABINO
Production

TOM BRENNAN
Asst. Editor

STEPHEN WACKER
Liked "Hulk"

TOM BREVOORT
Executive Editor

JOE QUESADA
Editor In Chief

DAN BUCKLEY
Publisher

SPIDEY'S BRAINTRUST
GALE, GUGGENHEIM, SLOTT & WELLS

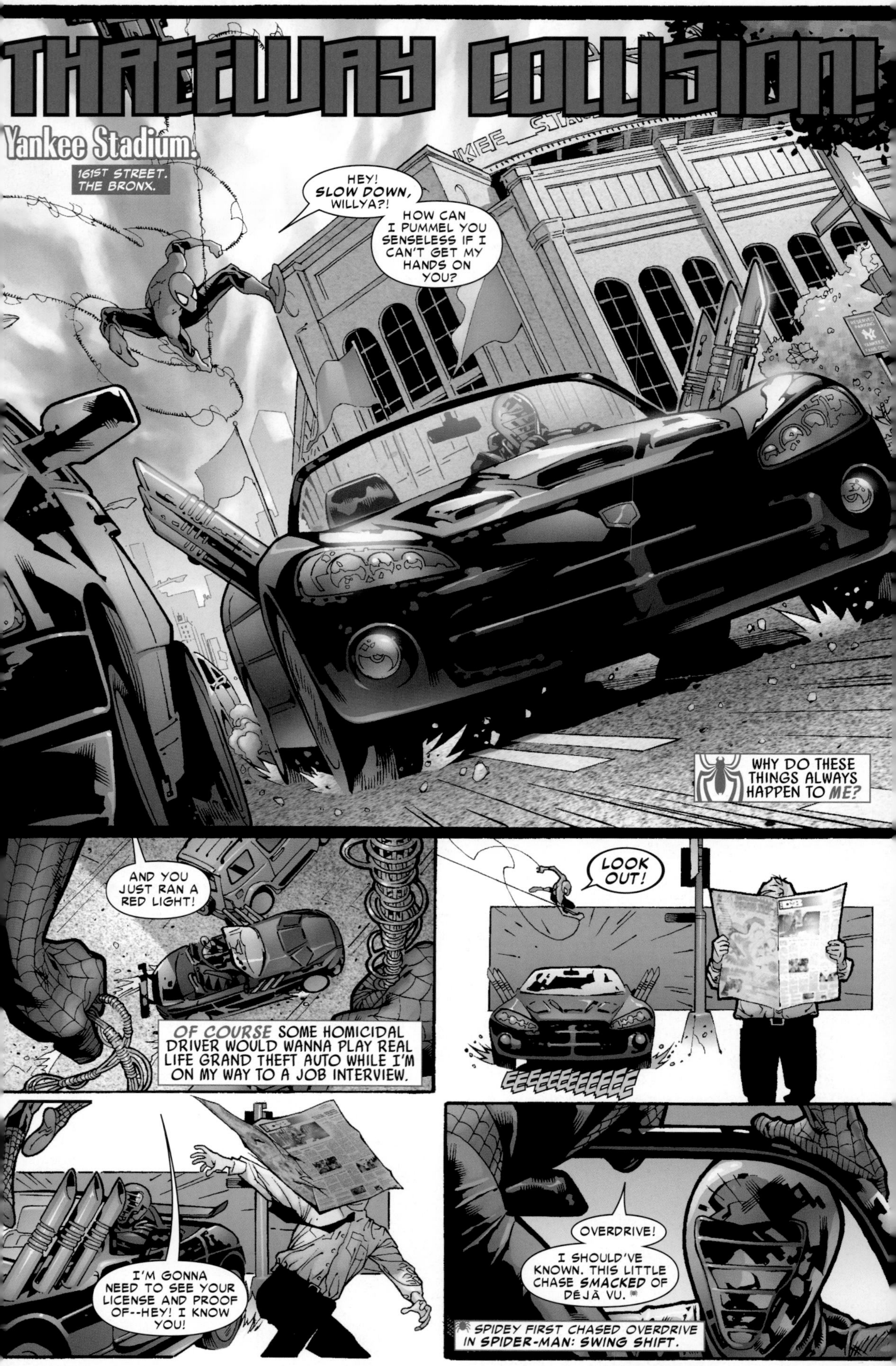
THREEWAY COLLISION!
Yankee Stadium.
161ST STREET. THE BRONX.
HEY! SLOW DOWN, WILLYA?!
HOW CAN I PUMMEL YOU SENSELESS IF I CAN'T GET MY HANDS ON YOU?
WHY DO THESE THINGS ALWAYS HAPPEN TO ME?
AND YOU JUST RAN A RED LIGHT!
OF COURSE SOME HOMICIDAL DRIVER WOULD WANNA PLAY REAL LIFE GRAND THEFT AUTO WHILE I'M ON MY WAY TO A JOB INTERVIEW.
LOOK OUT!
EEEEEEEEEEEE
I'M GONNA NEED TO SEE YOUR LICENSE AND PROOF OF--HEY! I KNOW YOU!
OVERDRIVE!
I SHOULD'VE KNOWN. THIS LITTLE CHASE SMACKED OF DÉJÀ VU.
SPIDEY FIRST CHASED OVERDRIVE IN SPIDER-MAN: SWING SHIFT.

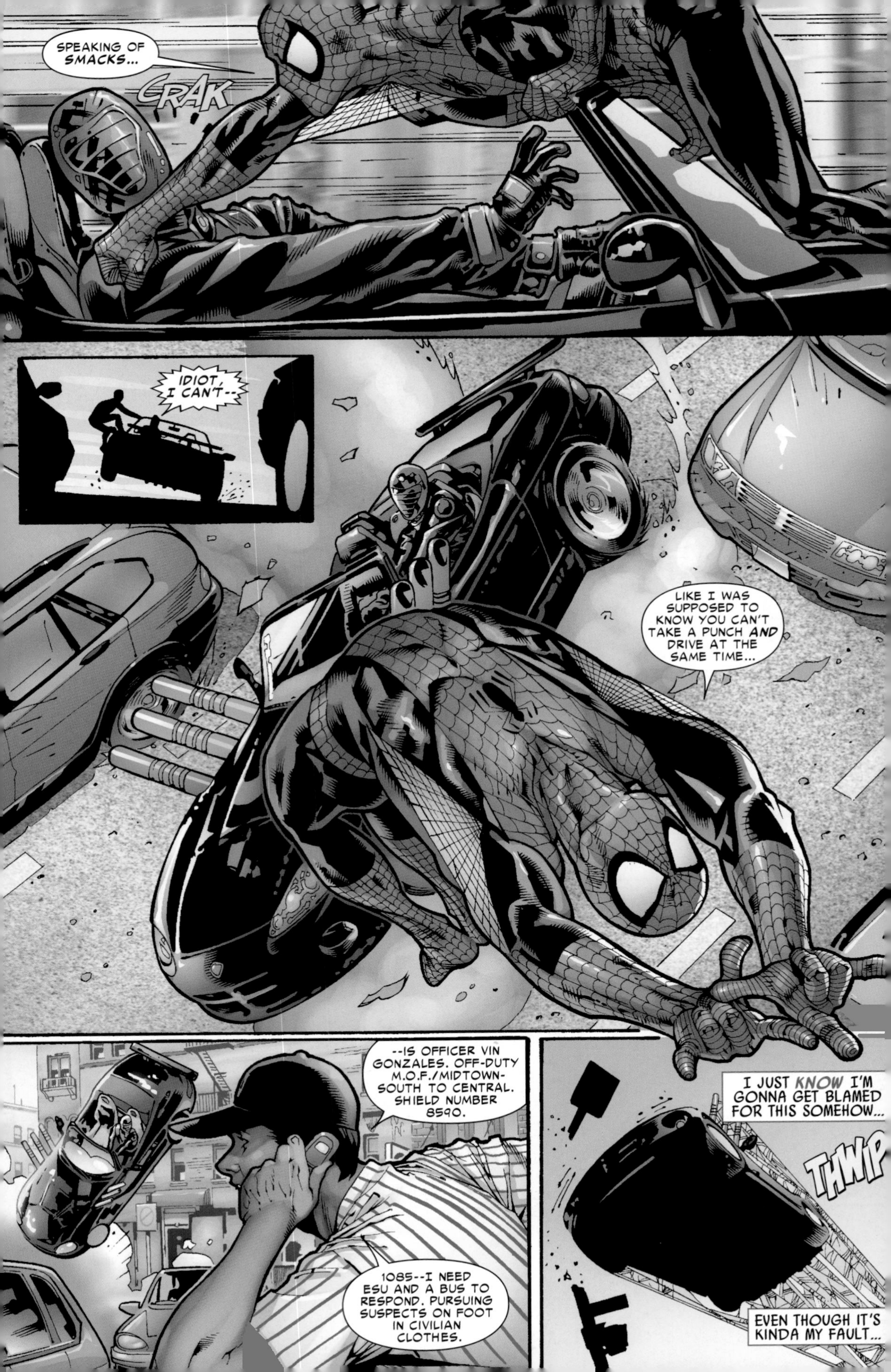
SPEAKING OF SMACKS...
CRAK
IDIOT, I CAN'T--
LIKE I WAS SUPPOSED TO KNOW YOU CAN'T TAKE A PUNCH AND DRIVE AT THE SAME TIME...
--IS OFFICER VIN GONZALES. OFF-DUTY M.O.F./MIDTOWN-SOUTH TO CENTRAL. SHIELD NUMBER 8590.
1085--I NEED ESU AND A BUS TO RESPOND. PURSUING SUSPECTS ON FOOT IN CIVILIAN CLOTHES.
I JUST KNOW I'M GONNA GET BLAMED FOR THIS SOMEHOW...
THWIP
EVEN THOUGH IT'S KINDA MY FAULT...

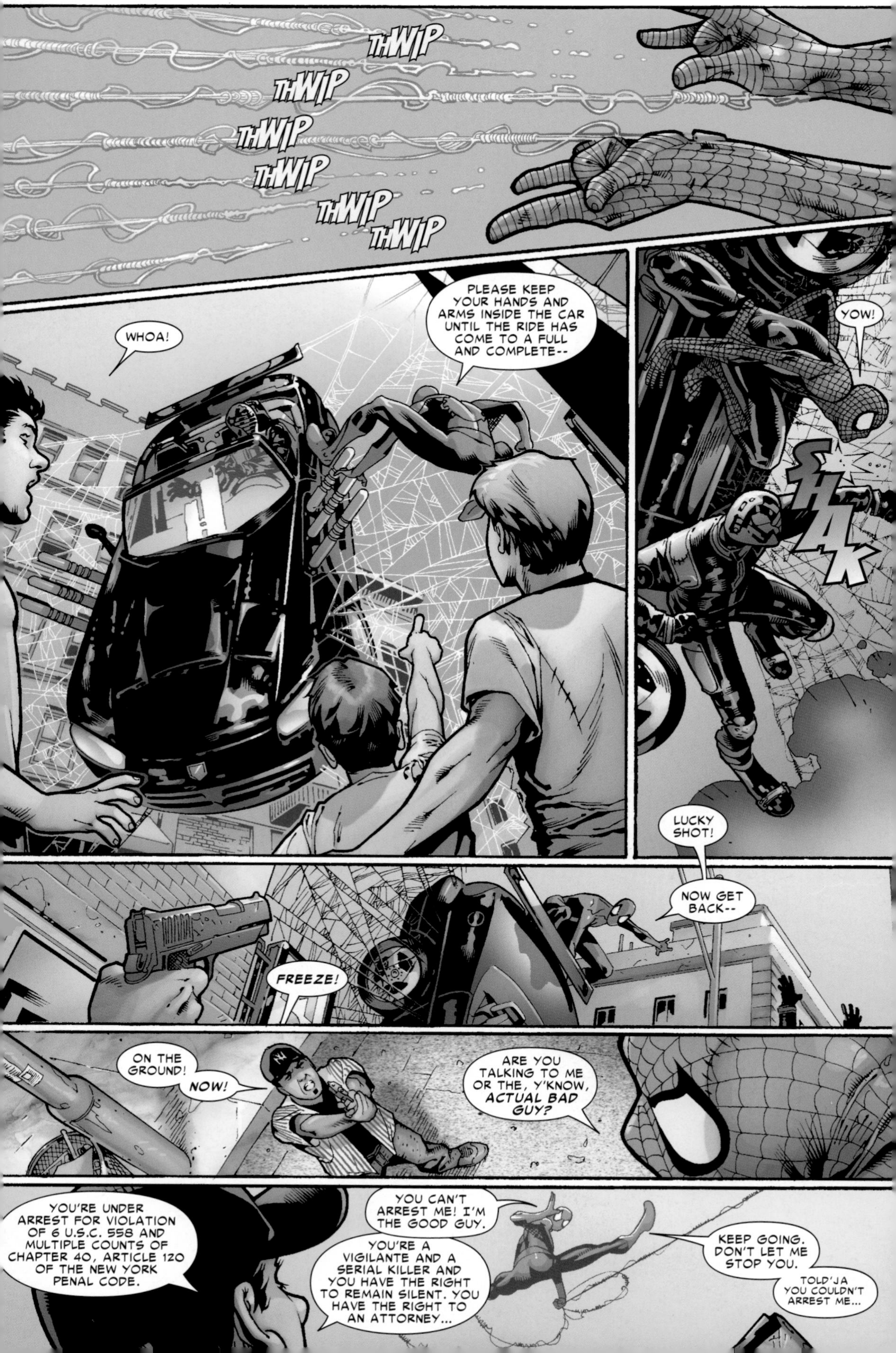

THWIP
THWIP
THWIP
THWIP
THWIP
THWIP
WHOA!
PLEASE KEEP YOUR HANDS AND ARMS INSIDE THE CAR UNTIL THE RIDE HAS COME TO A FULL AND COMPLETE--
YOW!
THAK
LUCKY SHOT!
NOW GET BACK--
FREEZE!
ON THE GROUND! NOW!
ARE YOU TALKING TO ME OR THE, Y'KNOW, ACTUAL BAD GUY?
YOU'RE UNDER ARREST FOR VIOLATION OF 6 U.S.C. 558 AND MULTIPLE COUNTS OF CHAPTER 40, ARTICLE 120 OF THE NEW YORK PENAL CODE.
YOU CAN'T ARREST ME! I'M THE GOOD GUY.
YOU'RE A VIGILANTE AND A SERIAL KILLER AND YOU HAVE THE RIGHT TO REMAIN SILENT. YOU HAVE THE RIGHT TO AN ATTORNEY...
KEEP GOING. DON'T LET ME STOP YOU.
TOLD'JA YOU COULDN'T ARREST ME...

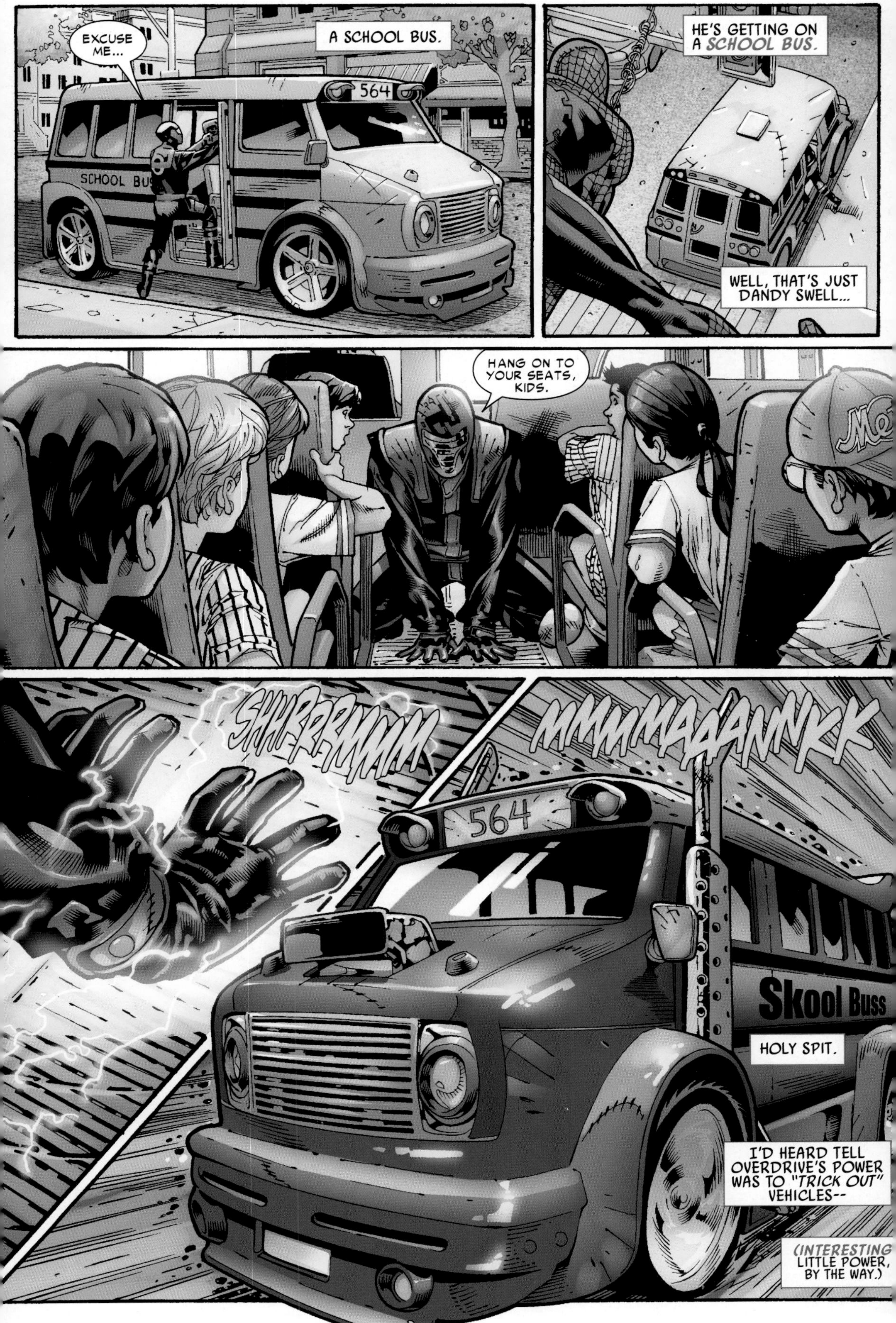
EXCUSE ME...
A SCHOOL BUS.
564
SCHOOL BUS
HE'S GETTING ON A SCHOOL BUS.
WELL, THAT'S JUST DANDY SWELL...
HANG ON TO YOUR SEATS, KIDS.
SHHRRRMMMM
MMMMAAAANNKK
564
Skool Buss
HOLY SPIT.
I'D HEARD TELL OVERDRIVE'S POWER WAS TO "TRICK OUT" VEHICLES--
(INTERESTING LITTLE POWER, BY THE WAY.)

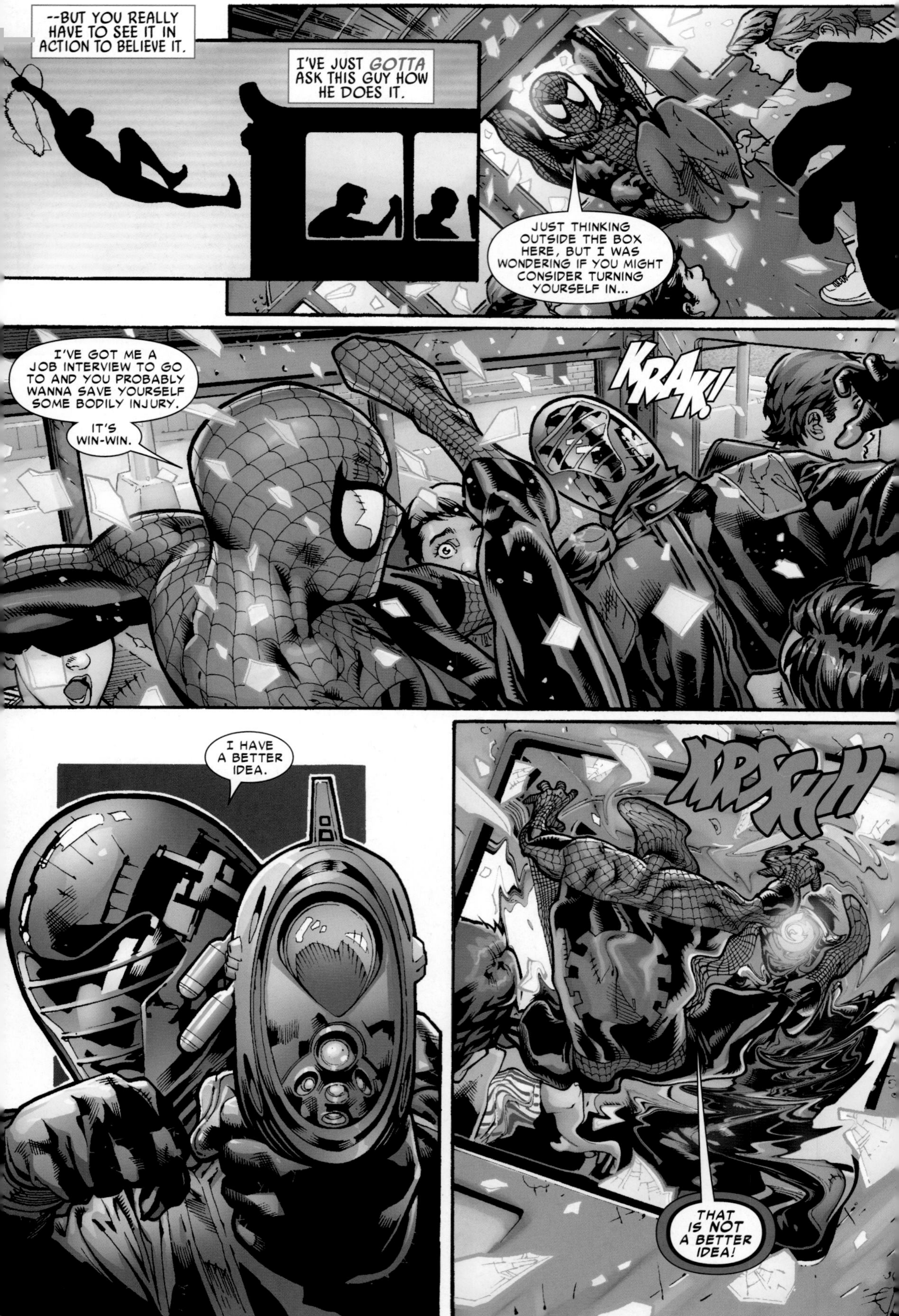
--BUT YOU REALLY HAVE TO SEE IT IN ACTION TO BELIEVE IT.
I'VE JUST GOTTA ASK THIS GUY HOW HE DOES IT.
JUST THINKING OUTSIDE THE BOX HERE, BUT I WAS WONDERING IF YOU MIGHT CONSIDER TURNING YOURSELF IN...
I'VE GOT ME A JOB INTERVIEW TO GO TO AND YOU PROBABLY WANNA SAVE YOURSELF SOME BODILY INJURY.
IT'S WIN-WIN.
KRAK!
I HAVE A BETTER IDEA.
THAT IS NOT A BETTER IDEA!

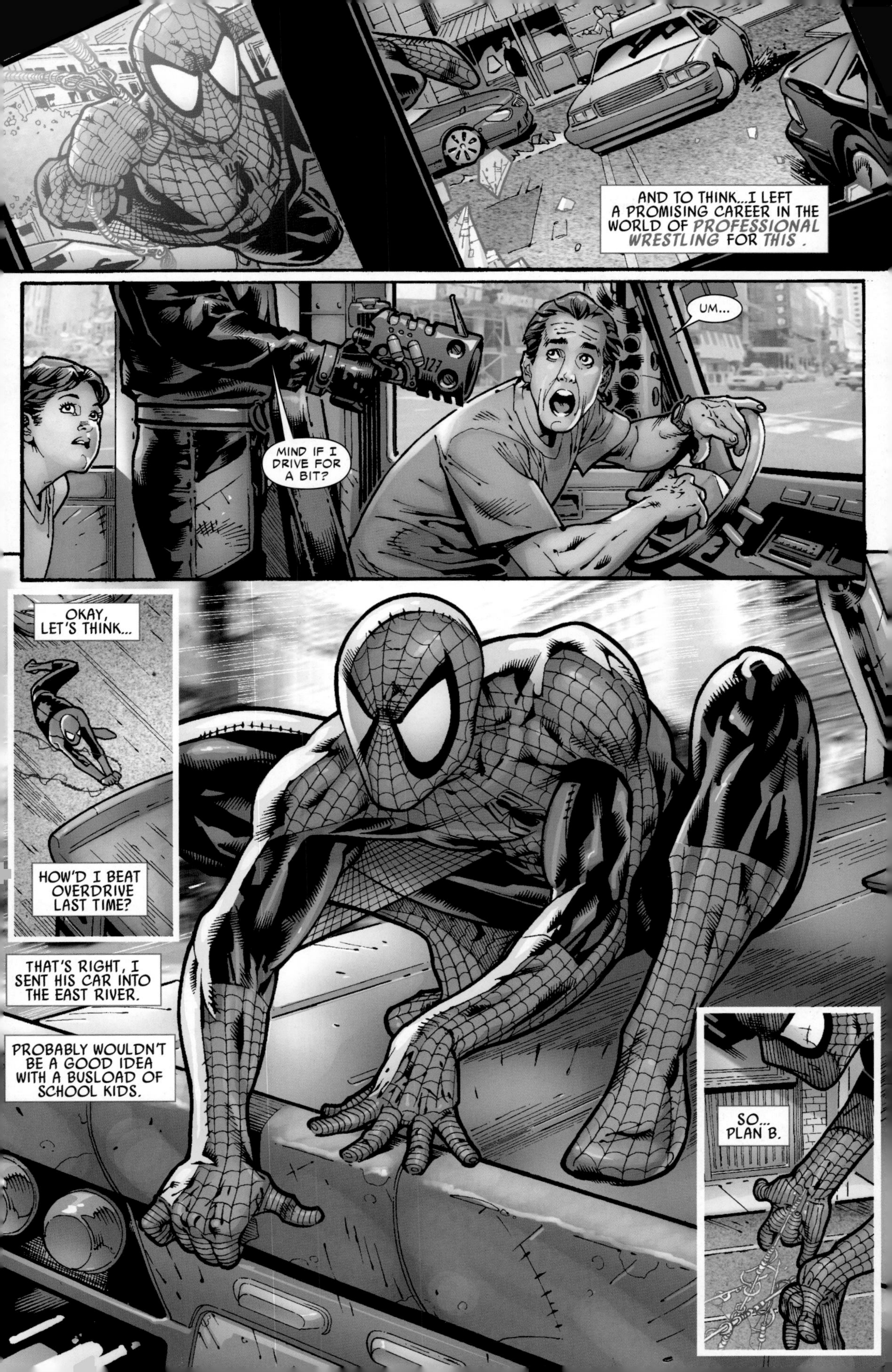
AND TO THINK...I LEFT A PROMISING CAREER IN THE WORLD OF PROFESSIONAL WRESTLING FOR THIS .
UM...
MIND IF I DRIVE FOR A BIT?
OKAY, LET'S THINK...
HOW'D I BEAT OVERDRIVE LAST TIME?
THAT'S RIGHT, I SENT HIS CAR INTO THE EAST RIVER.
PROBABLY WOULDN'T BE A GOOD IDEA WITH A BUSLOAD OF SCHOOL KIDS.
SO... PLAN B.

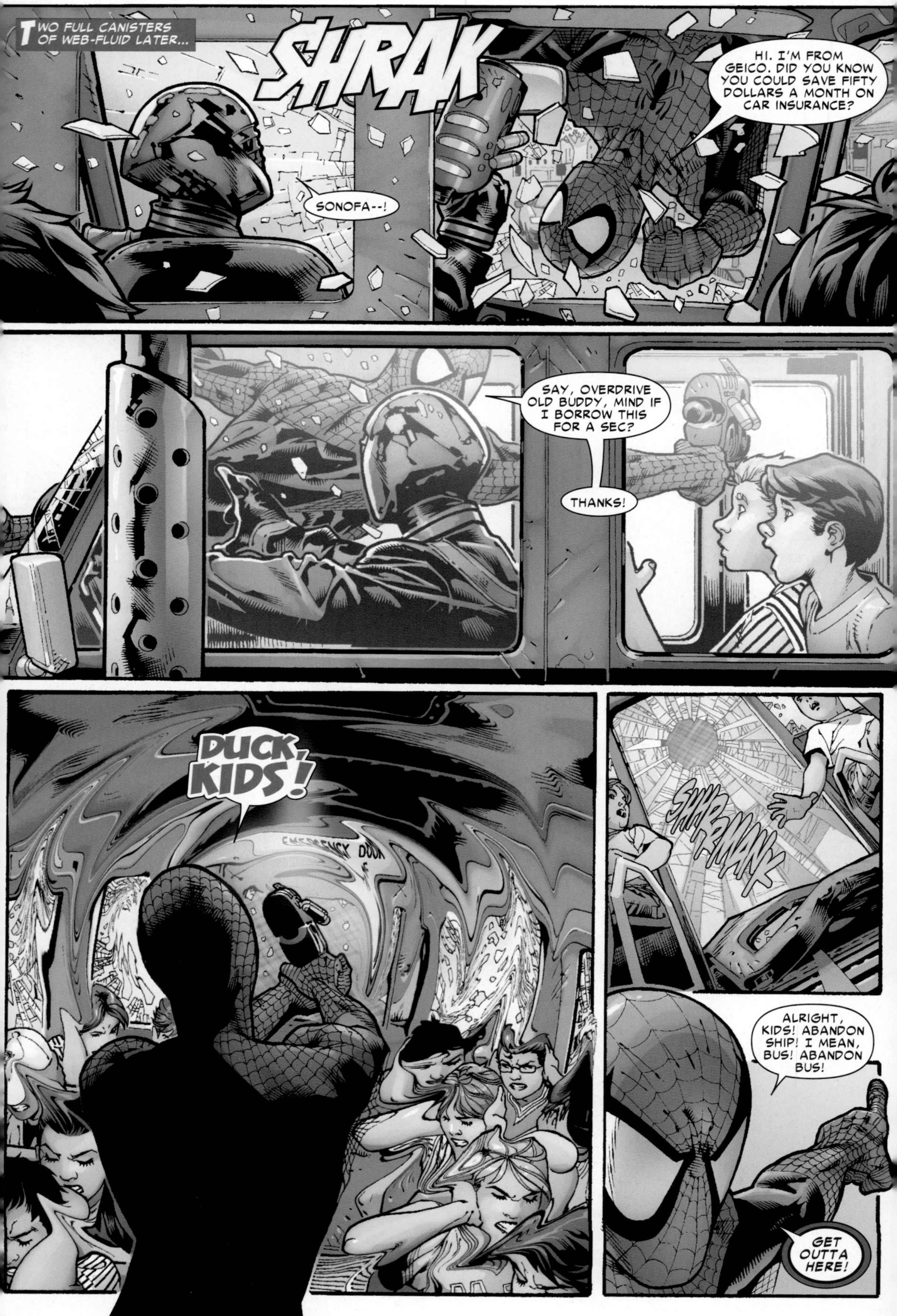
TWO FULL CANISTERS OF WEB-FLUID LATER...
SHRAK
HI. I'M FROM GEICO. DID YOU KNOW YOU COULD SAVE FIFTY DOLLARS A MONTH ON CAR INSURANCE?
SONOFA--!
SAY, OVERDRIVE OLD BUDDY, MIND IF I BORROW THIS FOR A SEC?
THANKS!
DUCK, KIDS!
EMERGENCY DOOR
ALRIGHT, KIDS! ABANDON SHIP! I MEAN, BUS! ABANDON BUS!
GET OUTTA HERE!

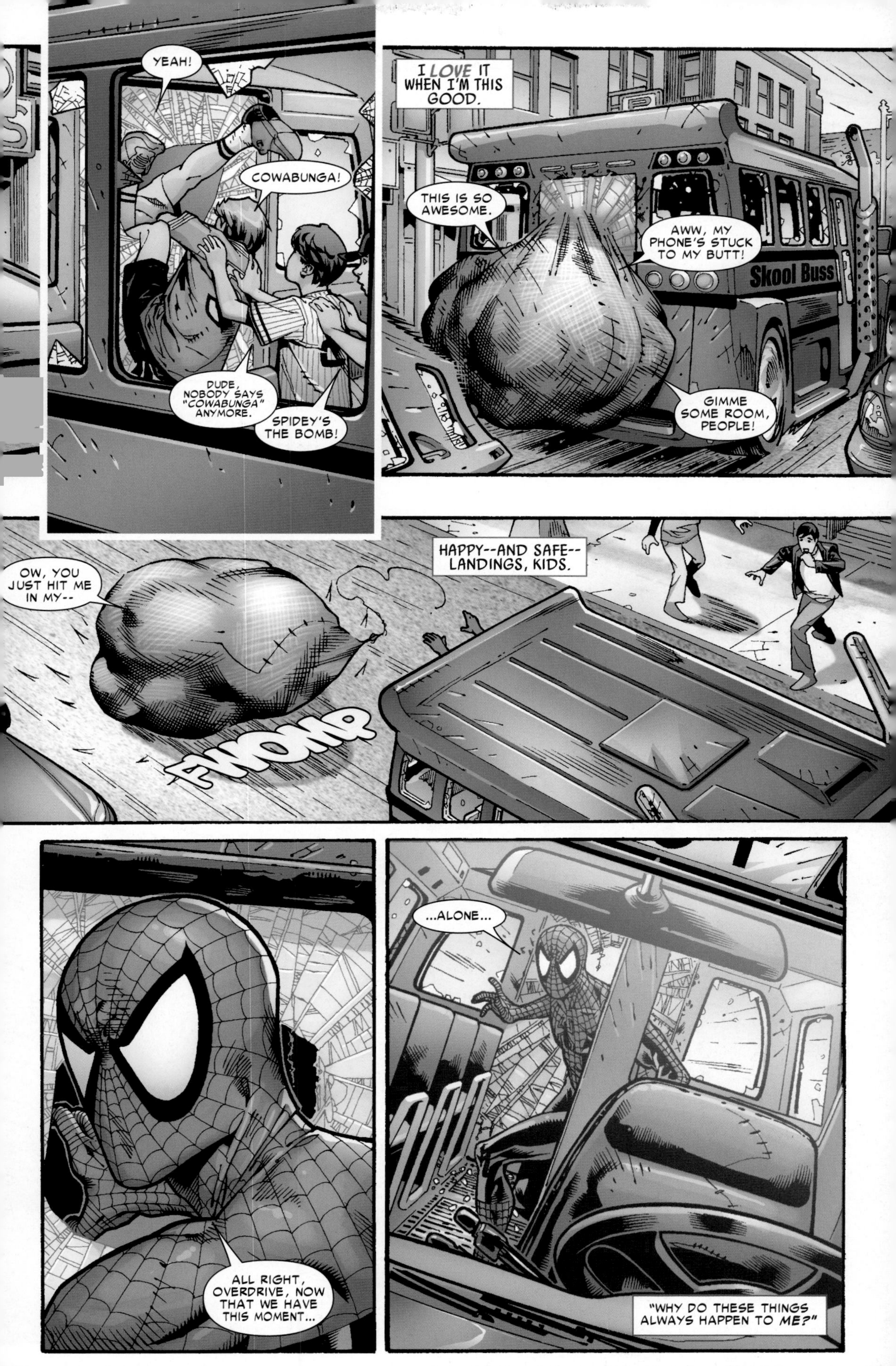
YEAH!
COWABUNGA!
DUDE, NOBODY SAYS "COWABUNGA" ANYMORE.
SPIDEY'S THE BOMB!
I LOVE IT WHEN I'M THIS GOOD.
THIS IS SO AWESOME.
AWW, MY PHONE'S STUCK TO MY BUTT!
Skool Buss
GIMME SOME ROOM, PEOPLE!
HAPPY--AND SAFE--LANDINGS, KIDS.
OW, YOU JUST HIT ME IN MY--
FWOMP
ALL RIGHT, OVERDRIVE, NOW THAT WE HAVE THIS MOMENT...
...ALONE...
"WHY DO THESE THINGS ALWAYS HAPPEN TO ME?"

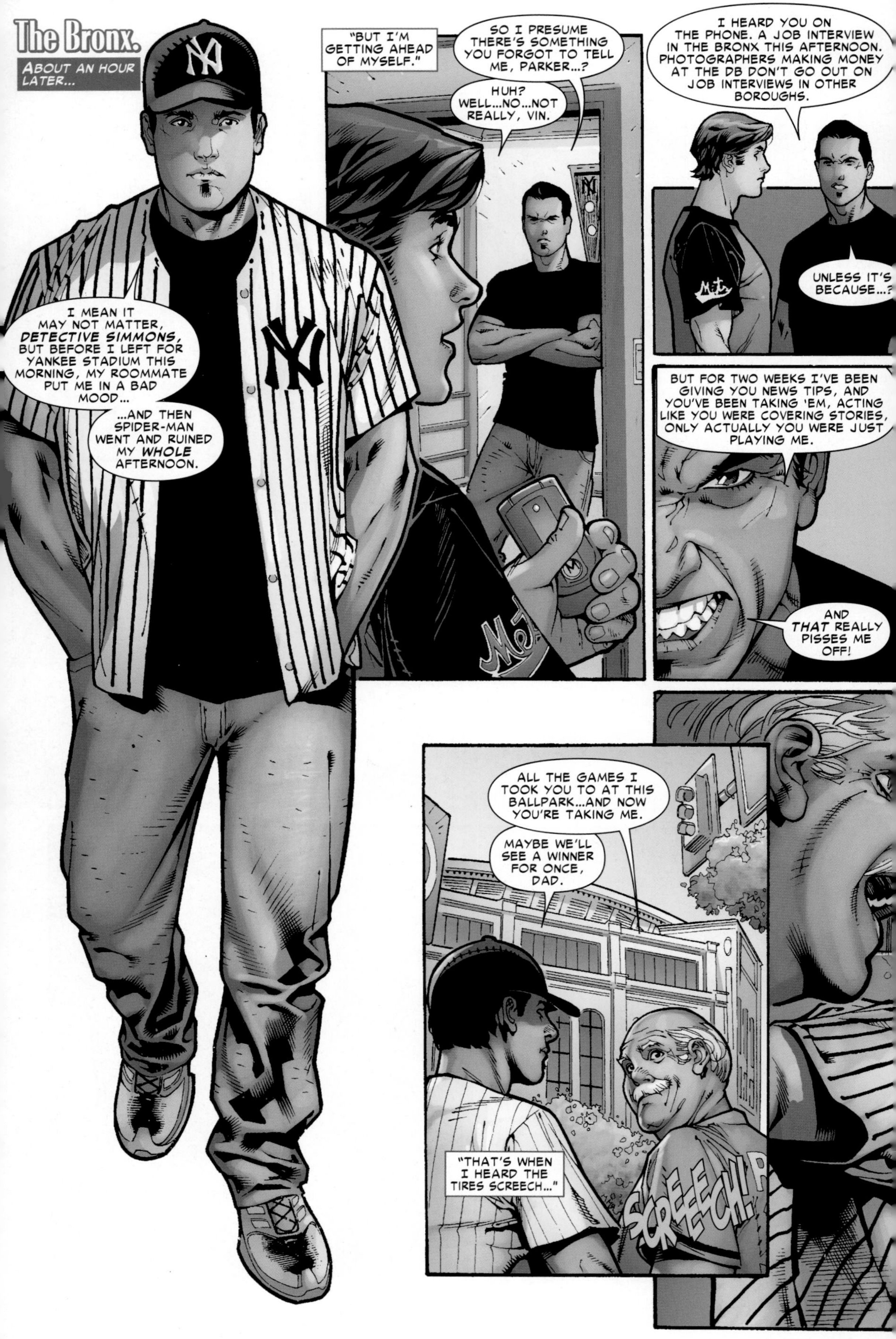
The Bronx.
ABOUT AN HOUR LATER...
I MEAN IT MAY NOT MATTER, DETECTIVE SIMMONS, BUT BEFORE I LEFT FOR YANKEE STADIUM THIS MORNING, MY ROOMMATE PUT ME IN A BAD MOOD...
...AND THEN SPIDER-MAN WENT AND RUINED MY WHOLE AFTERNOON.
"BUT I'M GETTING AHEAD OF MYSELF."
SO I PRESUME THERE'S SOMETHING YOU FORGOT TO TELL ME, PARKER...?
HUH? WELL...NO...NOT REALLY, VIN.
I HEARD YOU ON THE PHONE. A JOB INTERVIEW IN THE BRONX THIS AFTERNOON. PHOTOGRAPHERS MAKING MONEY AT THE DB DON'T GO OUT ON JOB INTERVIEWS IN OTHER BOROUGHS.
UNLESS IT'S BECAUSE...?
BUT FOR TWO WEEKS I'VE BEEN GIVING YOU NEWS TIPS, AND YOU'VE BEEN TAKING 'EM, ACTING LIKE YOU WERE COVERING STORIES, ONLY ACTUALLY YOU WERE JUST PLAYING ME.
AND THAT REALLY PISSES ME OFF!
ALL THE GAMES I TOOK YOU TO AT THIS BALLPARK...AND NOW YOU'RE TAKING ME.
MAYBE WE'LL SEE A WINNER FOR ONCE, DAD.
"THAT'S WHEN I HEARD THE TIRES SCREECH..."
SCREEECH!

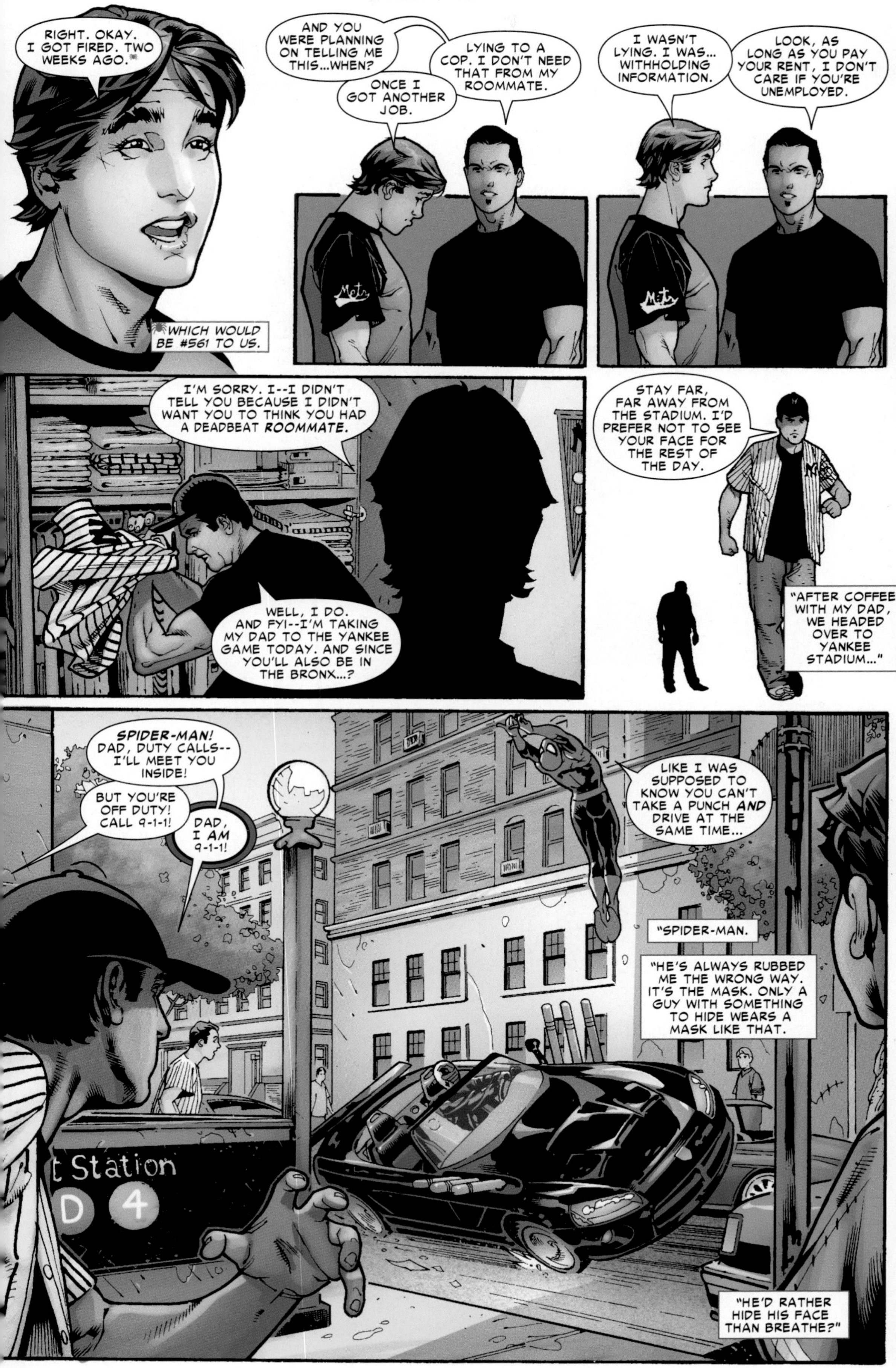
RIGHT. OKAY. I GOT FIRED. TWO WEEKS AGO.*
*WHICH WOULD BE #561 TO US.
AND YOU WERE PLANNING ON TELLING ME THIS...WHEN?
ONCE I GOT ANOTHER JOB.
LYING TO A COP. I DON'T NEED THAT FROM MY ROOMMATE.
I WASN'T LYING. I WAS... WITHHOLDING INFORMATION.
LOOK, AS LONG AS YOU PAY YOUR RENT, I DON'T CARE IF YOU'RE UNEMPLOYED.
I'M SORRY. I--I DIDN'T TELL YOU BECAUSE I DIDN'T WANT YOU TO THINK YOU HAD A DEADBEAT ROOMMATE.
WELL, I DO. AND FYI--I'M TAKING MY DAD TO THE YANKEE GAME TODAY. AND SINCE YOU'LL ALSO BE IN THE BRONX...?
STAY FAR, FAR AWAY FROM THE STADIUM. I'D PREFER NOT TO SEE YOUR FACE FOR THE REST OF THE DAY.
"AFTER COFFEE WITH MY DAD, WE HEADED OVER TO YANKEE STADIUM..."
SPIDER-MAN! DAD, DUTY CALLS-- I'LL MEET YOU INSIDE!
BUT YOU'RE OFF DUTY! CALL 9-1-1!
DAD, I AM 9-1-1!
LIKE I WAS SUPPOSED TO KNOW YOU CAN'T TAKE A PUNCH AND DRIVE AT THE SAME TIME...
"SPIDER-MAN.
"HE'S ALWAYS RUBBED ME THE WRONG WAY. IT'S THE MASK. ONLY A GUY WITH SOMETHING TO HIDE WEARS A MASK LIKE THAT.
"HE'D RATHER HIDE HIS FACE THAN BREATHE?"
t Station
D 4

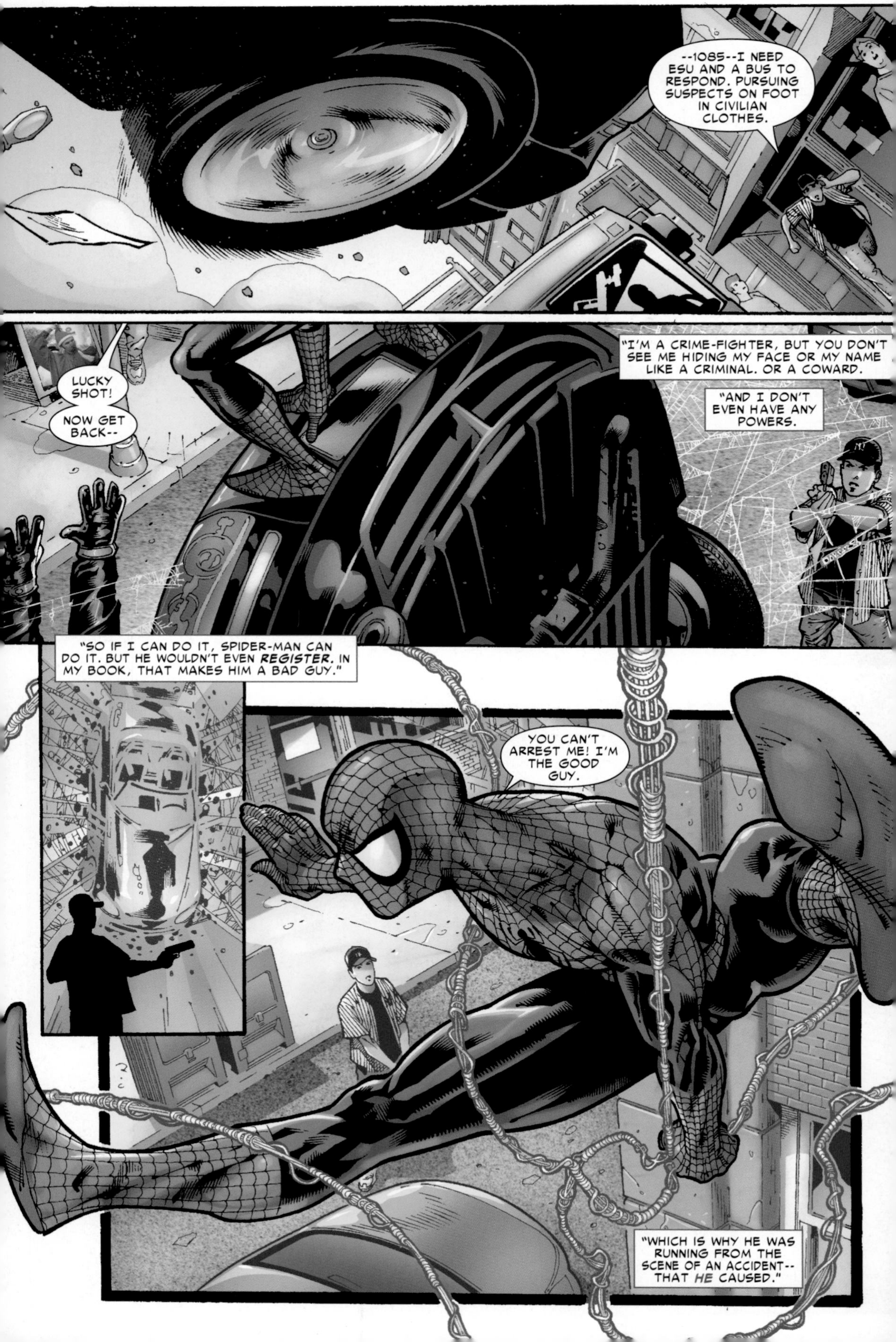
--1085--I NEED ESU AND A BUS TO RESPOND. PURSUING SUSPECTS ON FOOT IN CIVILIAN CLOTHES.
LUCKY SHOT!
NOW GET BACK--
"I'M A CRIME-FIGHTER, BUT YOU DON'T SEE ME HIDING MY FACE OR MY NAME LIKE A CRIMINAL. OR A COWARD.
"AND I DON'T EVEN HAVE ANY POWERS.
"SO IF I CAN DO IT, SPIDER-MAN CAN DO IT. BUT HE WOULDN'T EVEN *REGISTER*. IN MY BOOK, THAT MAKES HIM A BAD GUY."
YOU CAN'T ARREST ME! I'M THE GOOD GUY.
"WHICH IS WHY HE WAS RUNNING FROM THE SCENE OF AN ACCIDENT-- THAT *HE* CAUSED."

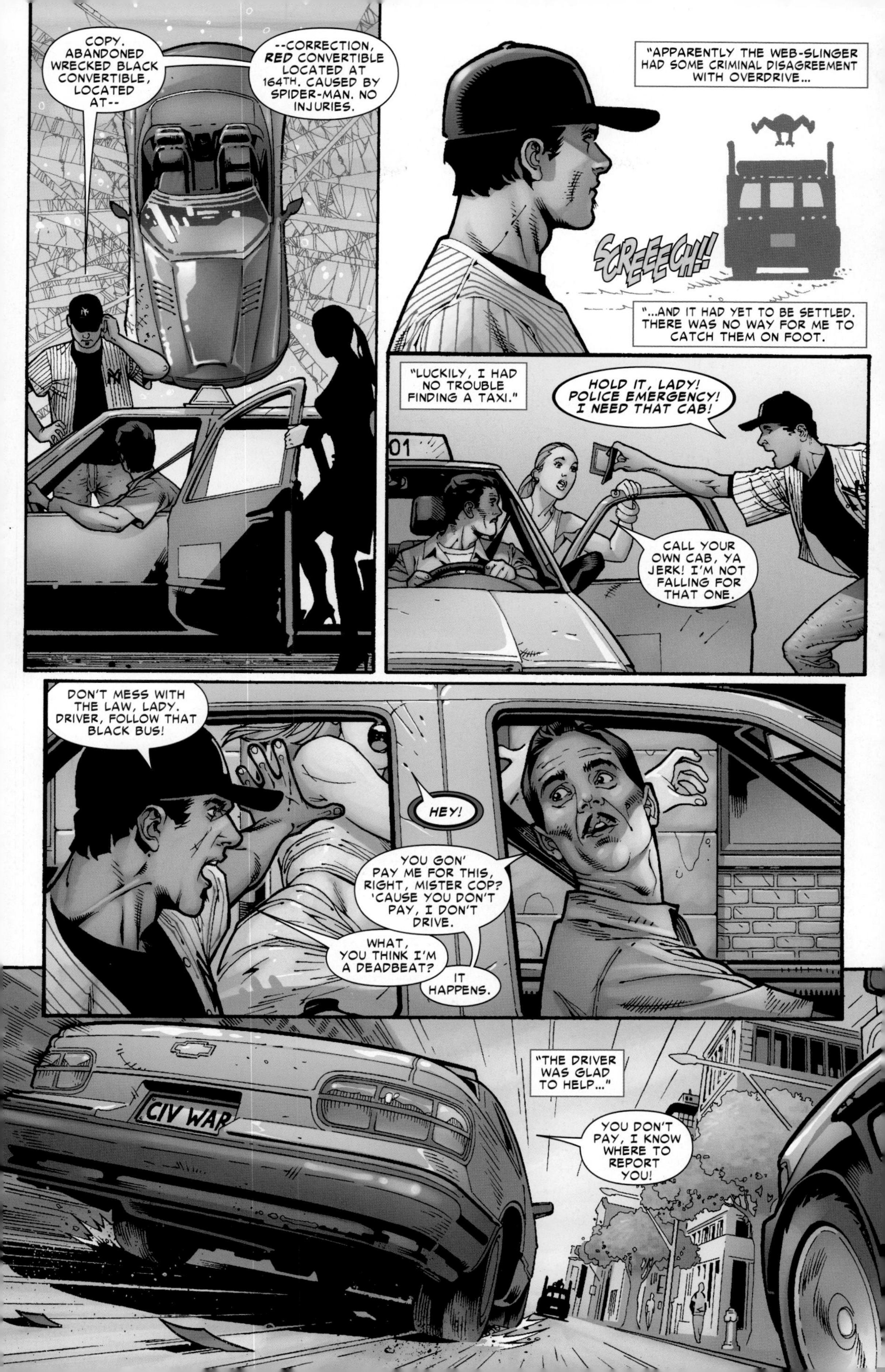
COPY. ABANDONED WRECKED BLACK CONVERTIBLE, LOCATED AT--
--CORRECTION, RED CONVERTIBLE LOCATED AT 164TH. CAUSED BY SPIDER-MAN. NO INJURIES.
"APPARENTLY THE WEB-SLINGER HAD SOME CRIMINAL DISAGREEMENT WITH OVERDRIVE...
SCREEECH!!
"...AND IT HAD YET TO BE SETTLED. THERE WAS NO WAY FOR ME TO CATCH THEM ON FOOT.
"LUCKILY, I HAD NO TROUBLE FINDING A TAXI."
HOLD IT, LADY! POLICE EMERGENCY! I NEED THAT CAB!
CALL YOUR OWN CAB, YA JERK! I'M NOT FALLING FOR THAT ONE.
DON'T MESS WITH THE LAW, LADY. DRIVER, FOLLOW THAT BLACK BUS!
HEY!
YOU GON' PAY ME FOR THIS, RIGHT, MISTER COP? 'CAUSE YOU DON'T PAY, I DON'T DRIVE.
WHAT, YOU THINK I'M A DEADBEAT?
IT HAPPENS.
CIV WAR
"THE DRIVER WAS GLAD TO HELP..."
YOU DON'T PAY, I KNOW WHERE TO REPORT YOU!

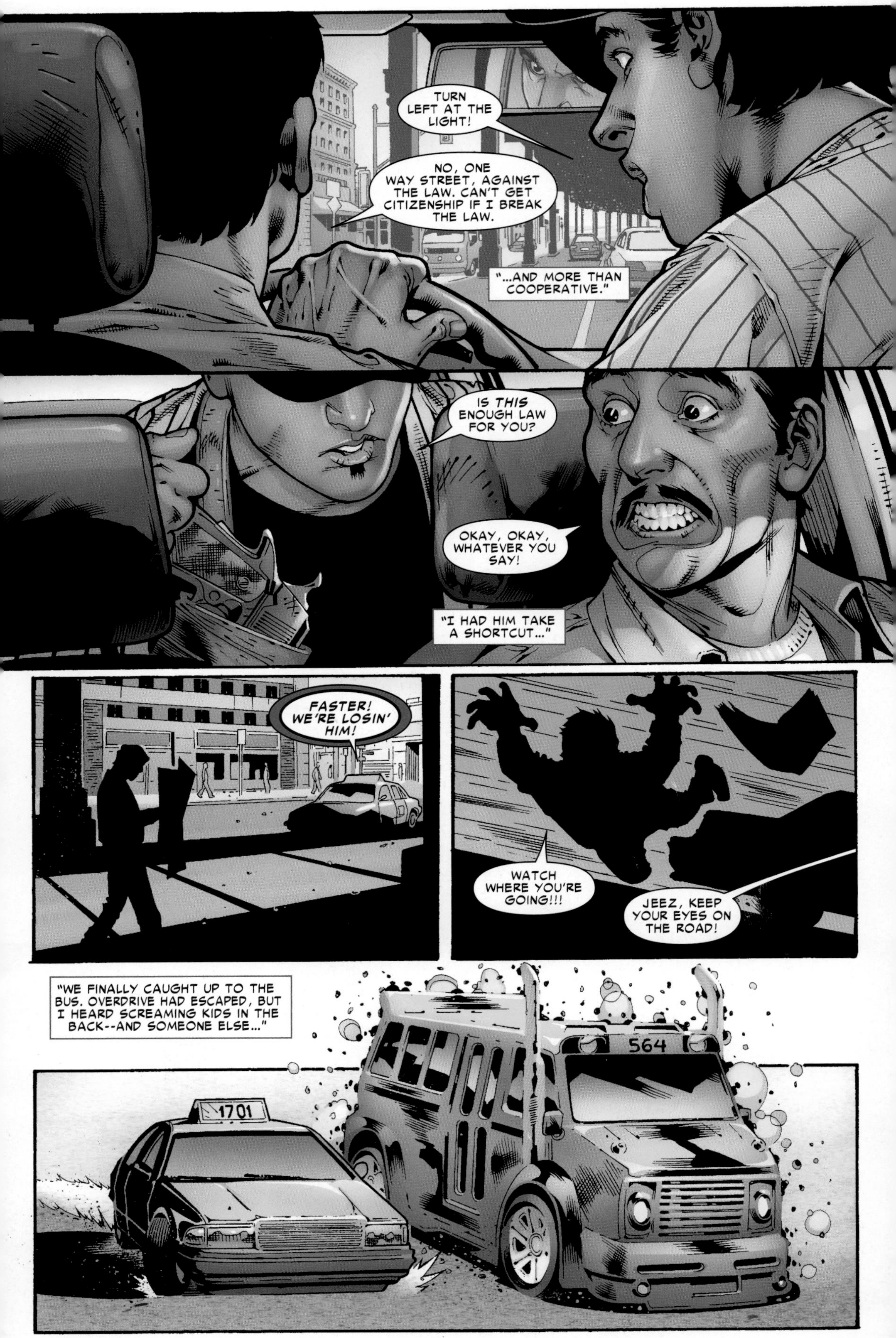
TURN LEFT AT THE LIGHT!
NO, ONE WAY STREET, AGAINST THE LAW. CAN'T GET CITIZENSHIP IF I BREAK THE LAW.
"...AND MORE THAN COOPERATIVE."
IS THIS ENOUGH LAW FOR YOU?
OKAY, OKAY, WHATEVER YOU SAY!
"I HAD HIM TAKE A SHORTCUT..."
FASTER! WE'RE LOSIN' HIM!
WATCH WHERE YOU'RE GOING!!!
JEEZ, KEEP YOUR EYES ON THE ROAD!
"WE FINALLY CAUGHT UP TO THE BUS. OVERDRIVE HAD ESCAPED, BUT I HEARD SCREAMING KIDS IN THE BACK--AND SOMEONE ELSE..."
564
1701

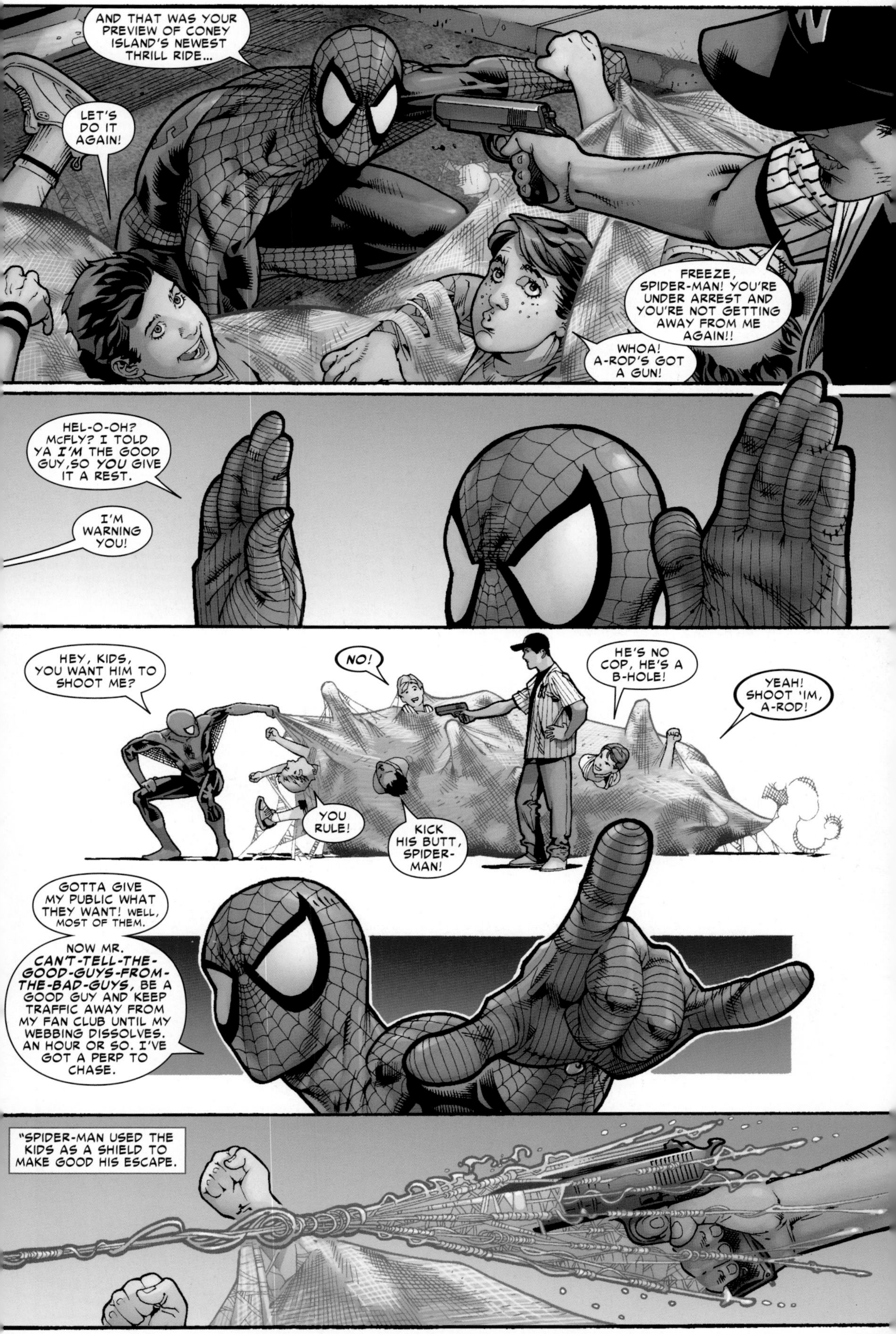
AND THAT WAS YOUR PREVIEW OF CONEY ISLAND'S NEWEST THRILL RIDE...
LET'S DO IT AGAIN!
FREEZE, SPIDER-MAN! YOU'RE UNDER ARREST AND YOU'RE NOT GETTING AWAY FROM ME AGAIN!!
WHOA! A-ROD'S GOT A GUN!
HEL-O-OH? McFLY? I TOLD YA I'M THE GOOD GUY, SO YOU GIVE IT A REST.
I'M WARNING YOU!
HEY, KIDS, YOU WANT HIM TO SHOOT ME?
NO!
HE'S NO COP, HE'S A B-HOLE!
YEAH! SHOOT 'IM, A-ROD!
YOU RULE!
KICK HIS BUTT, SPIDER-MAN!
GOTTA GIVE MY PUBLIC WHAT THEY WANT! WELL, MOST OF THEM.
NOW MR. CAN'T-TELL-THE-GOOD-GUYS-FROM-THE-BAD-GUYS, BE A GOOD GUY AND KEEP TRAFFIC AWAY FROM MY FAN CLUB UNTIL MY WEBBING DISSOLVES. AN HOUR OR SO. I'VE GOT A PERP TO CHASE.
"SPIDER-MAN USED THE KIDS AS A SHIELD TO MAKE GOOD HIS ESCAPE.

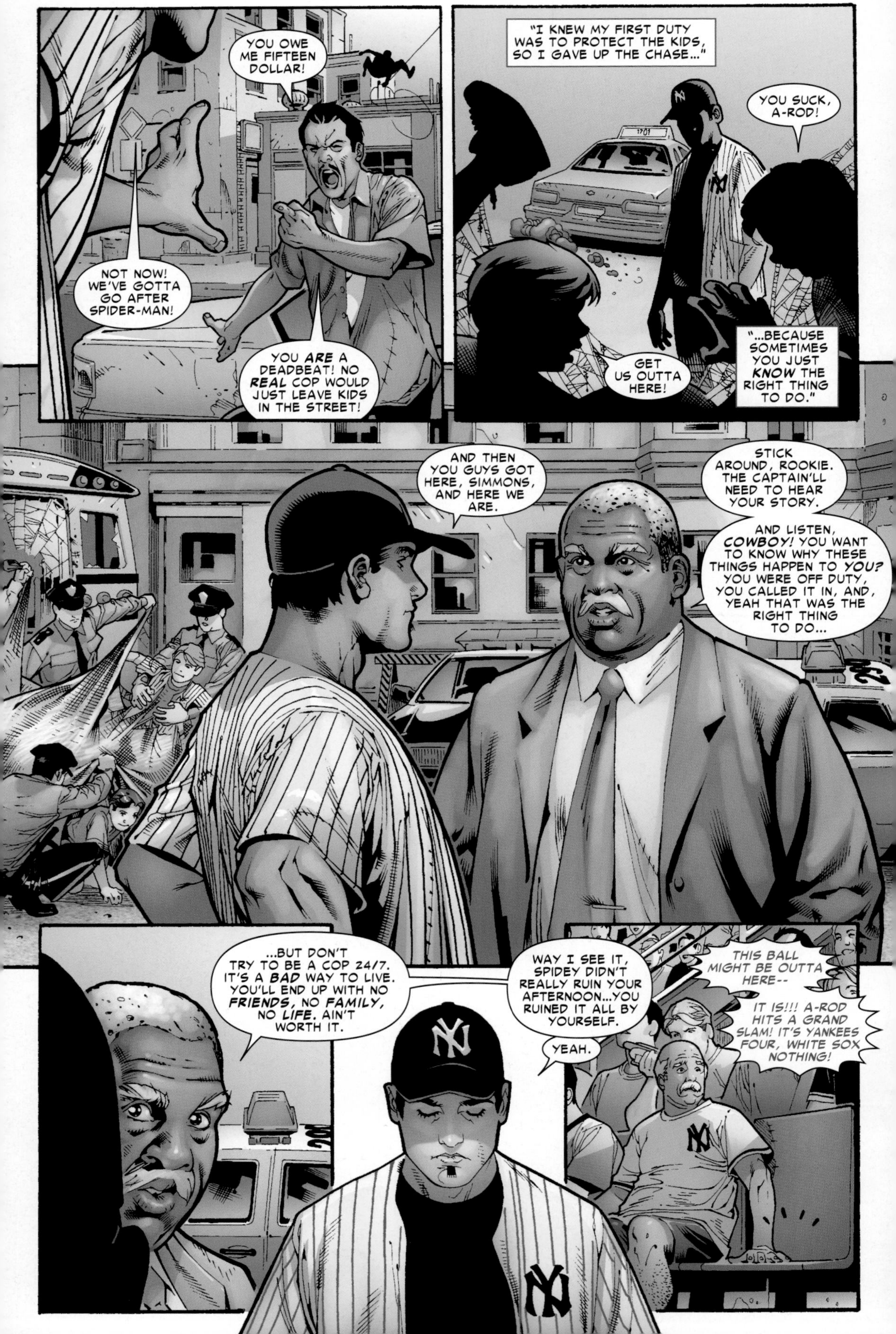
YOU OWE ME FIFTEEN DOLLAR!
NOT NOW! WE'VE GOTTA GO AFTER SPIDER-MAN!
YOU ARE A DEADBEAT! NO REAL COP WOULD JUST LEAVE KIDS IN THE STREET!
"I KNEW MY FIRST DUTY WAS TO PROTECT THE KIDS, SO I GAVE UP THE CHASE..."
YOU SUCK, A-ROD!
GET US OUTTA HERE!
"...BECAUSE SOMETIMES YOU JUST KNOW THE RIGHT THING TO DO."
AND THEN YOU GUYS GOT HERE, SIMMONS, AND HERE WE ARE.
STICK AROUND, ROOKIE. THE CAPTAIN'LL NEED TO HEAR YOUR STORY.
AND LISTEN, COWBOY! YOU WANT TO KNOW WHY THESE THINGS HAPPEN TO YOU? YOU WERE OFF DUTY, YOU CALLED IT IN, AND, YEAH THAT WAS THE RIGHT THING TO DO...
...BUT DON'T TRY TO BE A COP 24/7. IT'S A BAD WAY TO LIVE. YOU'LL END UP WITH NO FRIENDS, NO FAMILY, NO LIFE. AIN'T WORTH IT.
WAY I SEE IT, SPIDEY DIDN'T REALLY RUIN YOUR AFTERNOON...YOU RUINED IT ALL BY YOURSELF.
YEAH.
THIS BALL MIGHT BE OUTTA HERE--
IT IS!!! A-ROD HITS A GRAND SLAM! IT'S YANKEES FOUR, WHITE SOX NOTHING!

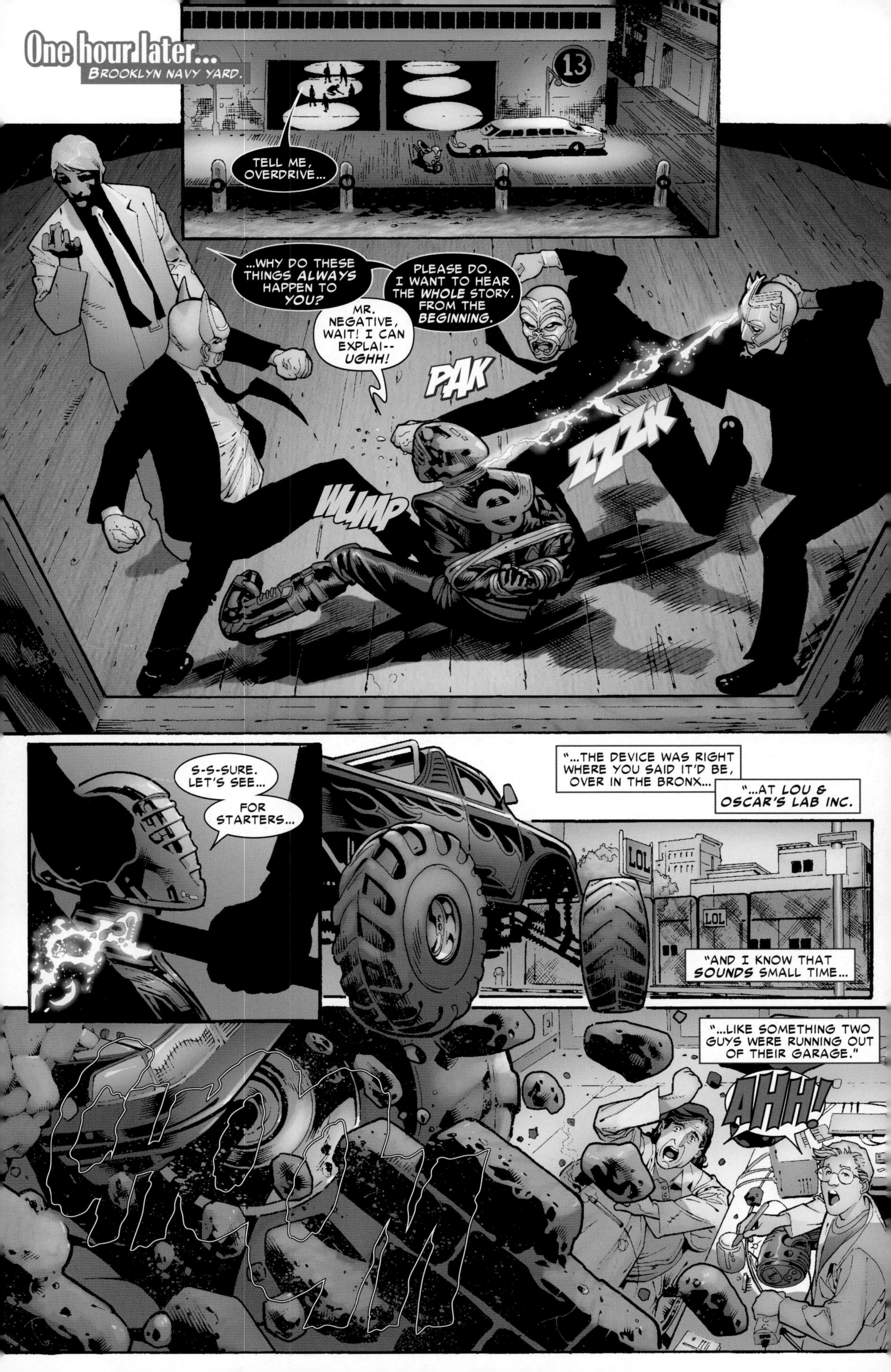

One hour later...
BROOKLYN NAVY YARD.
13
TELL ME, OVERDRIVE...
...WHY DO THESE THINGS ALWAYS HAPPEN TO YOU?
PLEASE DO. I WANT TO HEAR THE WHOLE STORY. FROM THE BEGINNING.
MR. NEGATIVE, WAIT! I CAN EXPLAI-- UGHH!
PAK
ZZZK
WUMP
S-S-SURE. LET'S SEE...
FOR STARTERS...
"...THE DEVICE WAS RIGHT WHERE YOU SAID IT'D BE, OVER IN THE BRONX...
"...AT LOU & OSCAR'S LAB INC.
LOL
"AND I KNOW THAT SOUNDS SMALL TIME...
"...LIKE SOMETHING TWO GUYS WERE RUNNING OUT OF THEIR GARAGE."
AHH!

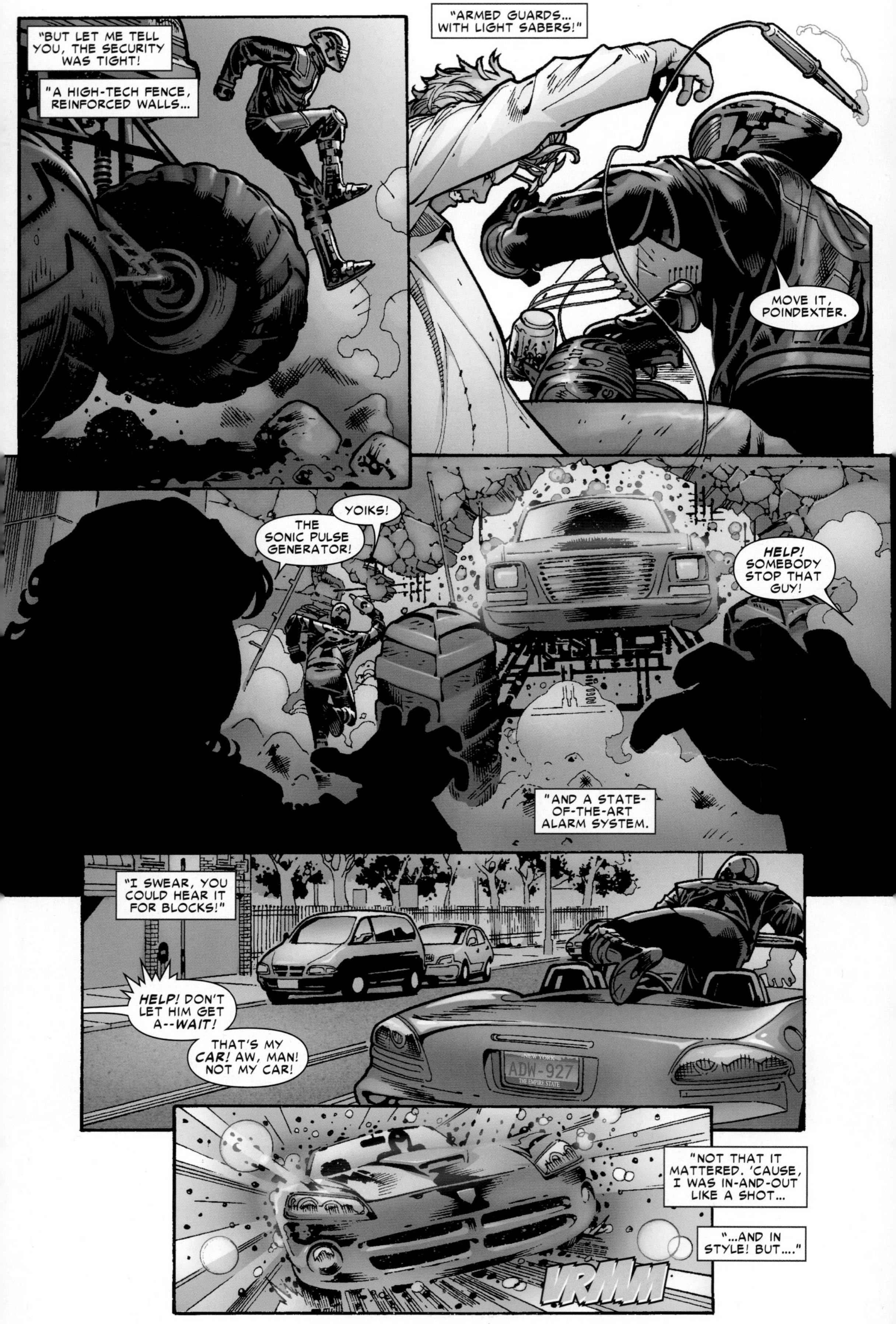
"BUT LET ME TELL YOU, THE SECURITY WAS TIGHT!
"A HIGH-TECH FENCE, REINFORCED WALLS...
"ARMED GUARDS... WITH LIGHT SABERS!"
MOVE IT, POINDEXTER.
THE SONIC PULSE GENERATOR!
YOIKS!
HELP! SOMEBODY STOP THAT GUY!
"AND A STATE-OF-THE-ART ALARM SYSTEM.
"I SWEAR, YOU COULD HEAR IT FOR BLOCKS!"
HELP! DON'T LET HIM GET A--WAIT!
THAT'S MY CAR! AW, MAN! NOT MY CAR!
NEW YORK
ADW-927
THE EMPIRE STATE
"NOT THAT IT MATTERED. 'CAUSE, I WAS IN-AND-OUT LIKE A SHOT...
"...AND IN STYLE! BUT...."
VRMM

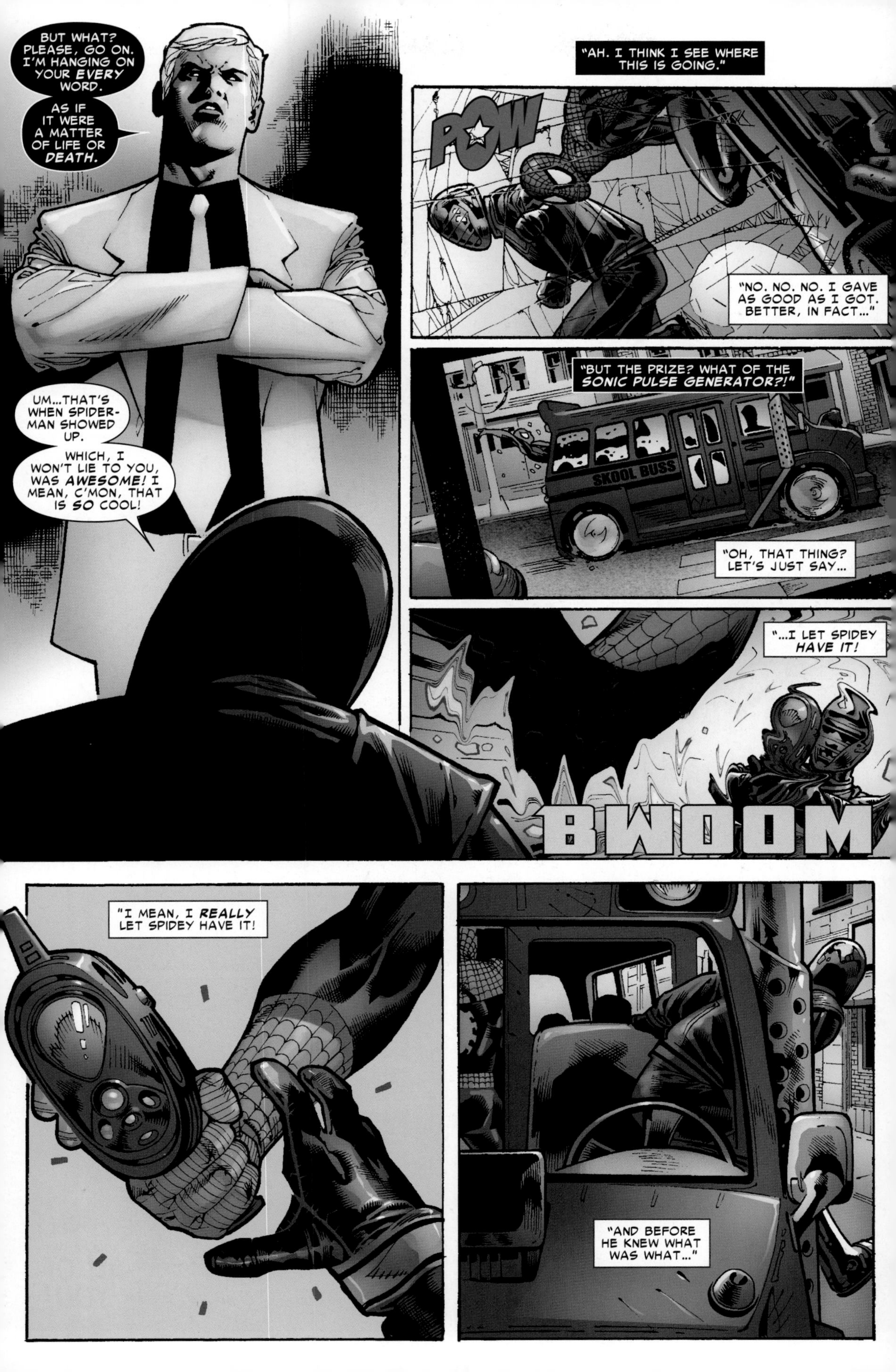
BUT WHAT? PLEASE, GO ON. I'M HANGING ON YOUR EVERY WORD.
AS IF IT WERE A MATTER OF LIFE OR DEATH.
"AH. I THINK I SEE WHERE THIS IS GOING."
POW
"NO. NO. NO. I GAVE AS GOOD AS I GOT. BETTER, IN FACT..."
UM...THAT'S WHEN SPIDER-MAN SHOWED UP.
WHICH, I WON'T LIE TO YOU, WAS AWESOME! I MEAN, C'MON, THAT IS SO COOL!
"BUT THE PRIZE? WHAT OF THE SONIC PULSE GENERATOR?!"
SKOOL BUSS
"OH, THAT THING? LET'S JUST SAY...
"...I LET SPIDEY HAVE IT!
BWOOM
"I MEAN, I REALLY LET SPIDEY HAVE IT!
"AND BEFORE HE KNEW WHAT WAS WHAT..."

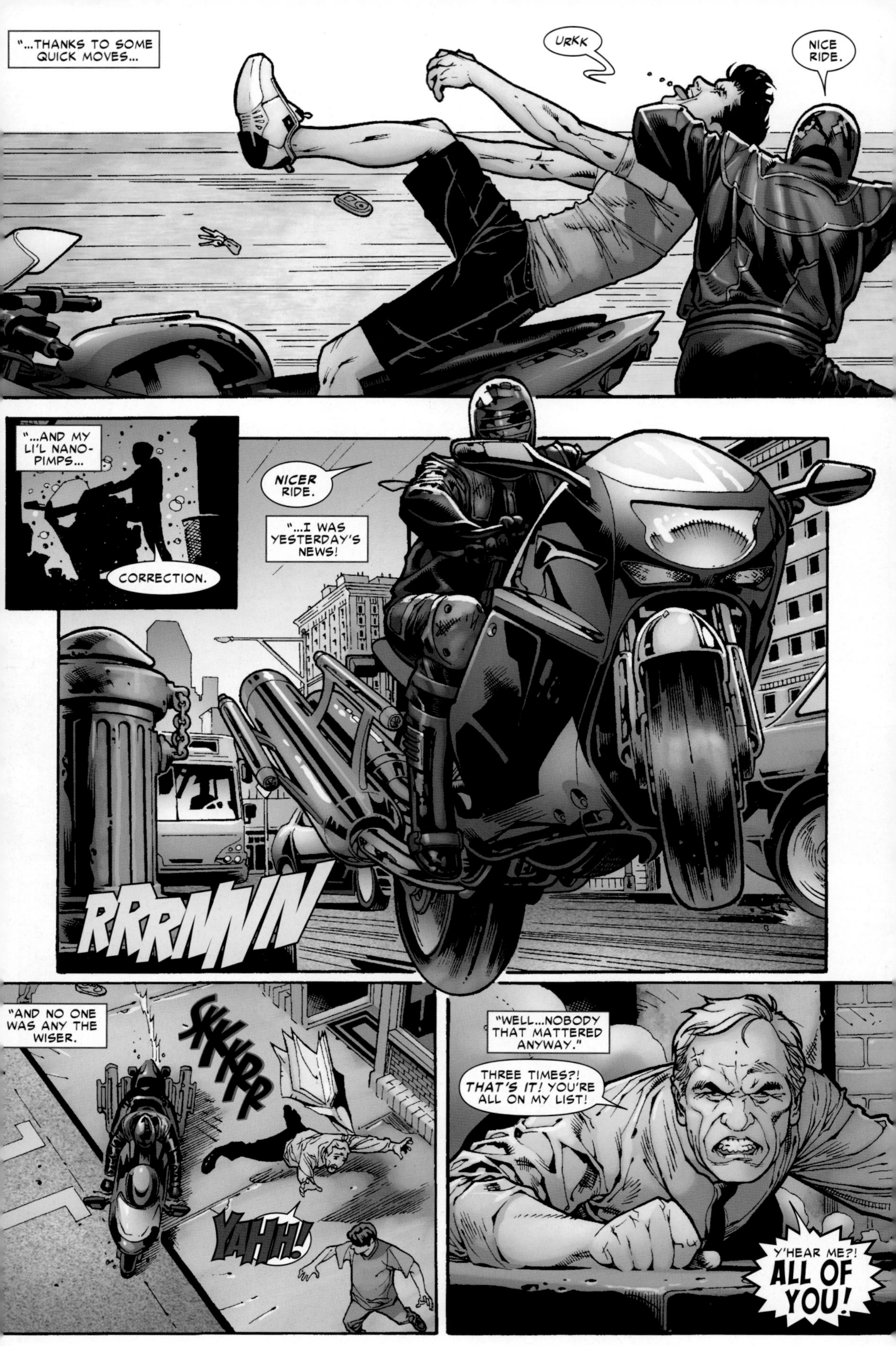
"...THANKS TO SOME QUICK MOVES...
URKK
NICE RIDE.
"...AND MY LI'L NANO-PIMPS...
CORRECTION.
NICER RIDE.
"...I WAS YESTERDAY'S NEWS!
RRRMNN
"AND NO ONE WAS ANY THE WISER.
SKKKRR
YAHH!
"WELL...NOBODY THAT MATTERED ANYWAY."
THREE TIMES?! THAT'S IT! YOU'RE ALL ON MY LIST!
Y'HEAR ME?! ALL OF YOU!

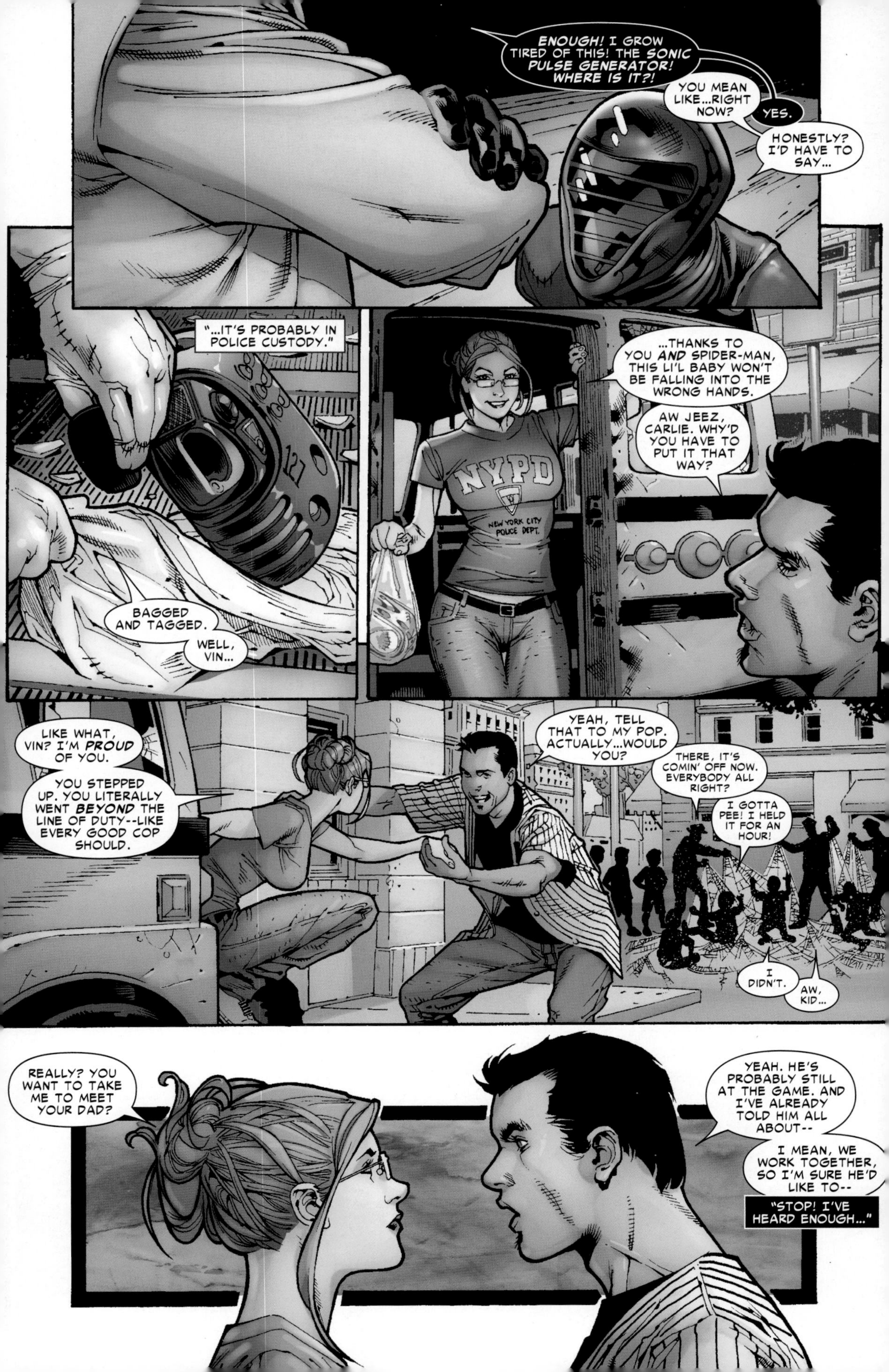
ENOUGH! I GROW TIRED OF THIS! THE SONIC PULSE GENERATOR! WHERE IS IT?!
YOU MEAN LIKE...RIGHT NOW?
YES.
HONESTLY? I'D HAVE TO SAY...
"...IT'S PROBABLY IN POLICE CUSTODY."
BAGGED AND TAGGED.
WELL, VIN...
...THANKS TO YOU AND SPIDER-MAN, THIS LI'L BABY WON'T BE FALLING INTO THE WRONG HANDS.
AW JEEZ, CARLIE. WHY'D YOU HAVE TO PUT IT THAT WAY?
NYPD
NEW YORK CITY POLICE DEPT.
LIKE WHAT, VIN? I'M PROUD OF YOU.
YOU STEPPED UP. YOU LITERALLY WENT BEYOND THE LINE OF DUTY--LIKE EVERY GOOD COP SHOULD.
YEAH, TELL THAT TO MY POP. ACTUALLY...WOULD YOU?
THERE, IT'S COMIN' OFF NOW. EVERYBODY ALL RIGHT?
I GOTTA PEE! I HELD IT FOR AN HOUR!
I DIDN'T.
AW, KID...
REALLY? YOU WANT TO TAKE ME TO MEET YOUR DAD?
YEAH. HE'S PROBABLY STILL AT THE GAME. AND I'VE ALREADY TOLD HIM ALL ABOUT--
I MEAN, WE WORK TOGETHER, SO I'M SURE HE'D LIKE TO--
"STOP! I'VE HEARD ENOUGH..."

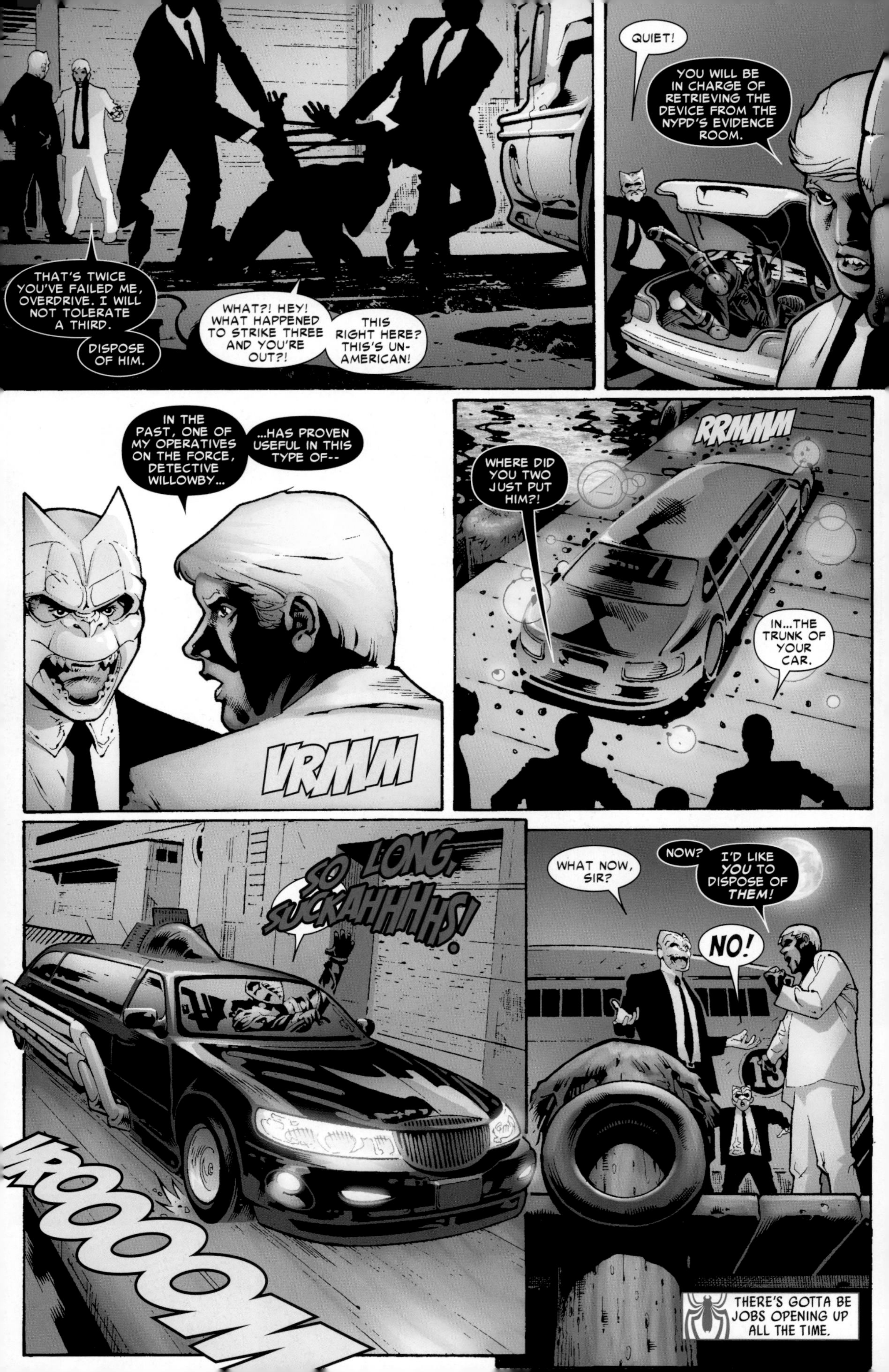
THAT'S TWICE YOU'VE FAILED ME, OVERDRIVE. I WILL NOT TOLERATE A THIRD.
DISPOSE OF HIM.
WHAT?! HEY! WHAT HAPPENED TO STRIKE THREE AND YOU'RE OUT?!
THIS RIGHT HERE? THIS'S UN-AMERICAN!
QUIET!
YOU WILL BE IN CHARGE OF RETRIEVING THE DEVICE FROM THE NYPD'S EVIDENCE ROOM.
IN THE PAST, ONE OF MY OPERATIVES ON THE FORCE, DETECTIVE WILLOWBY...
...HAS PROVEN USEFUL IN THIS TYPE OF--
VRMM
RRMMM
WHERE DID YOU TWO JUST PUT HIM?!
IN...THE TRUNK OF YOUR CAR.
SO LONG, SUCKAHHHHS!
VROOOOOM
WHAT NOW, SIR?
NOW?
I'D LIKE *YOU* TO DISPOSE OF *THEM*!
NO!
THERE'S GOTTA BE JOBS OPENING UP ALL THE TIME.

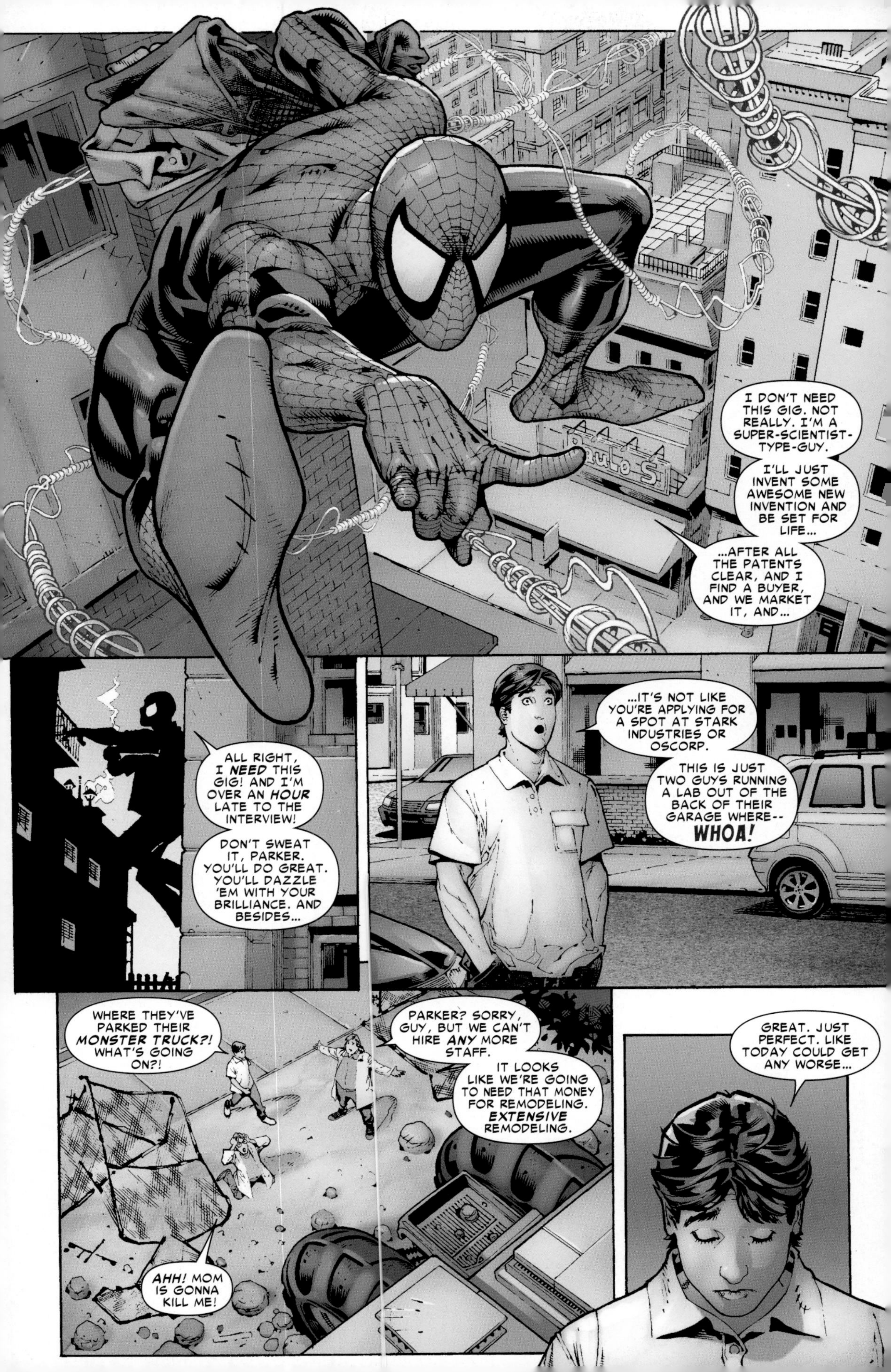
I DON'T NEED THIS GIG. NOT REALLY. I'M A SUPER-SCIENTIST-TYPE-GUY.
I'LL JUST INVENT SOME AWESOME NEW INVENTION AND BE SET FOR LIFE...
...AFTER ALL THE PATENTS CLEAR, AND I FIND A BUYER, AND WE MARKET IT, AND...
ALL RIGHT, I NEED THIS GIG! AND I'M OVER AN HOUR LATE TO THE INTERVIEW!
DON'T SWEAT IT, PARKER. YOU'LL DO GREAT. YOU'LL DAZZLE 'EM WITH YOUR BRILLIANCE. AND BESIDES...
...IT'S NOT LIKE YOU'RE APPLYING FOR A SPOT AT STARK INDUSTRIES OR OSCORP.
THIS IS JUST TWO GUYS RUNNING A LAB OUT OF THE BACK OF THEIR GARAGE WHERE-- WHOA!
WHERE THEY'VE PARKED THEIR MONSTER TRUCK?! WHAT'S GOING ON?!
PARKER? SORRY, GUY, BUT WE CAN'T HIRE ANY MORE STAFF.
IT LOOKS LIKE WE'RE GOING TO NEED THAT MONEY FOR REMODELING. EXTENSIVE REMODELING.
AHH! MOM IS GONNA KILL ME!
GREAT. JUST PERFECT. LIKE TODAY COULD GET ANY WORSE...

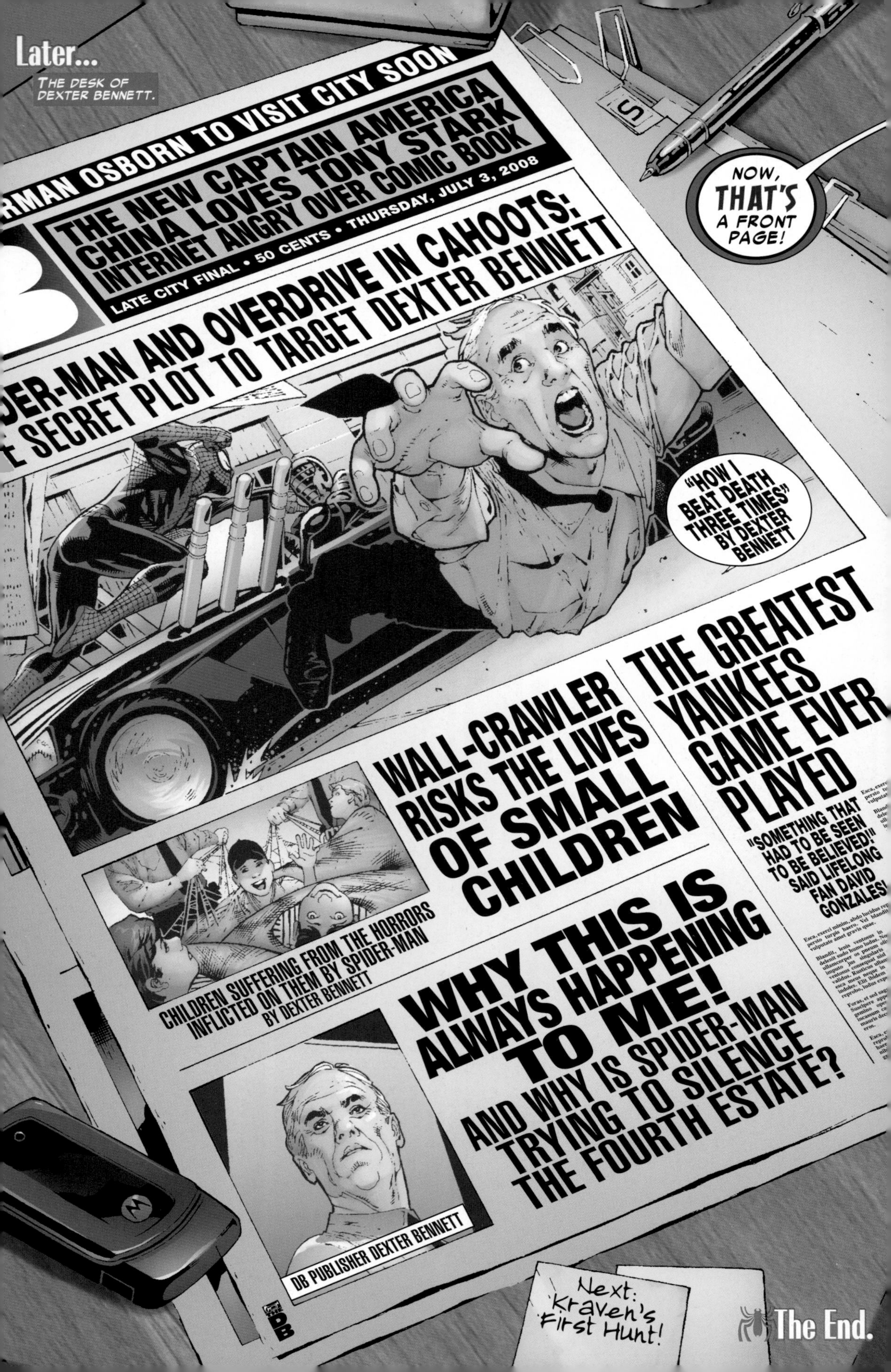
Later...
THE DESK OF DEXTER BENNETT.
RMAN OSBORN TO VISIT CITY SOON
THE NEW CAPTAIN AMERICA
CHINA LOVES TONY STARK
INTERNET ANGRY OVER COMIC BOOK
LATE CITY FINAL • 50 CENTS • THURSDAY, JULY 3, 2008
DER-MAN AND OVERDRIVE IN CAHOOTS:
E SECRET PLOT TO TARGET DEXTER BENNETT
NOW, THAT'S A FRONT PAGE!
"HOW I BEAT DEATH THREE TIMES" BY DEXTER BENNETT
WALL-CRAWLER RISKS THE LIVES OF SMALL CHILDREN
CHILDREN SUFFERING FROM THE HORRORS INFLICTED ON THEM BY SPIDER-MAN BY DEXTER BENNETT
THE GREATEST YANKEES GAME EVER PLAYED
"SOMETHING THAT HAD TO BE SEEN TO BE BELIEVED!" SAID LIFELONG FAN DAVID GONZALES!
WHY THIS IS ALWAYS HAPPENING TO ME!
AND WHY IS SPIDER-MAN TRYING TO SILENCE THE FOURTH ESTATE?
DB PUBLISHER DEXTER BENNETT
THE DB
Next: Kraven's First Hunt!
The End.

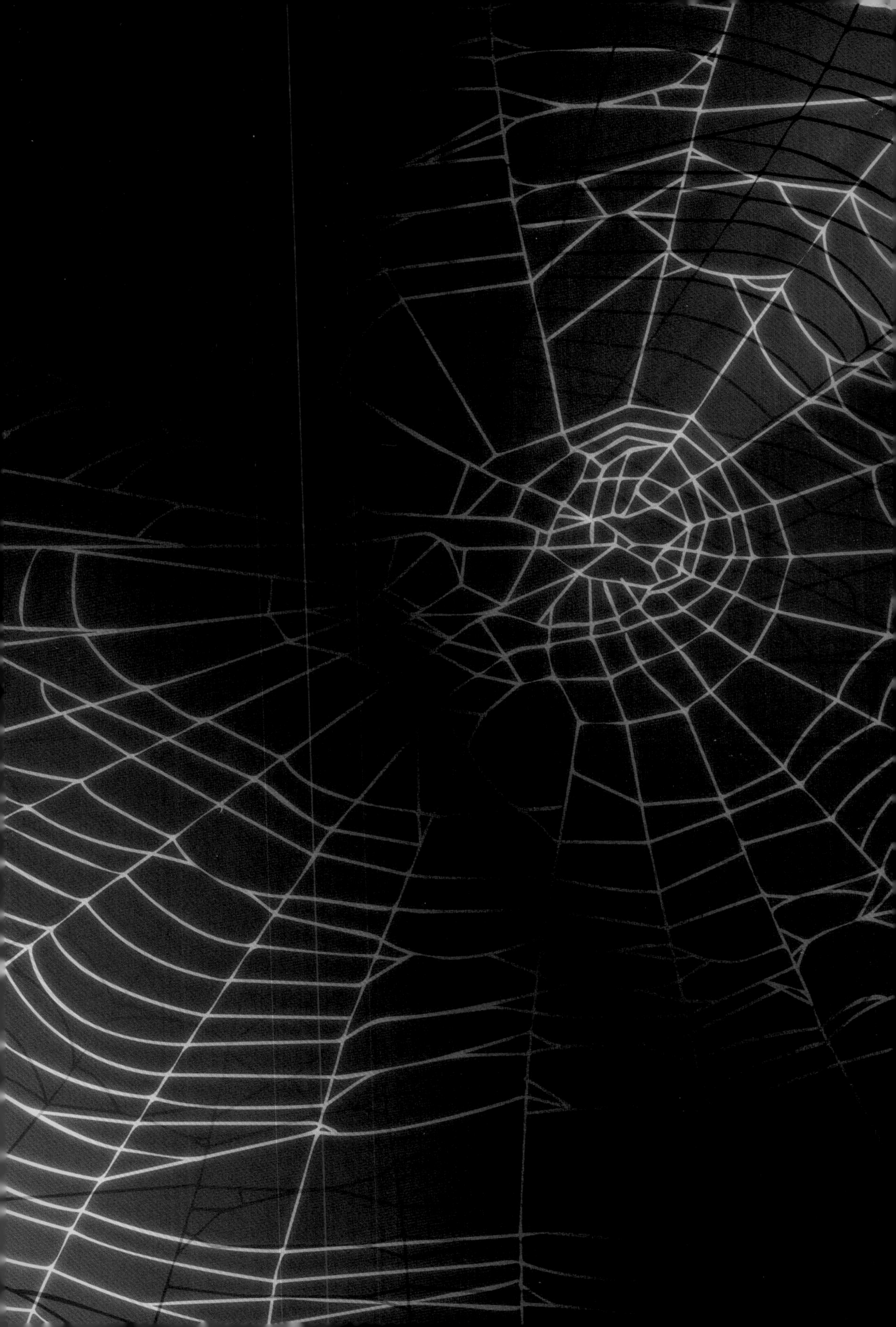

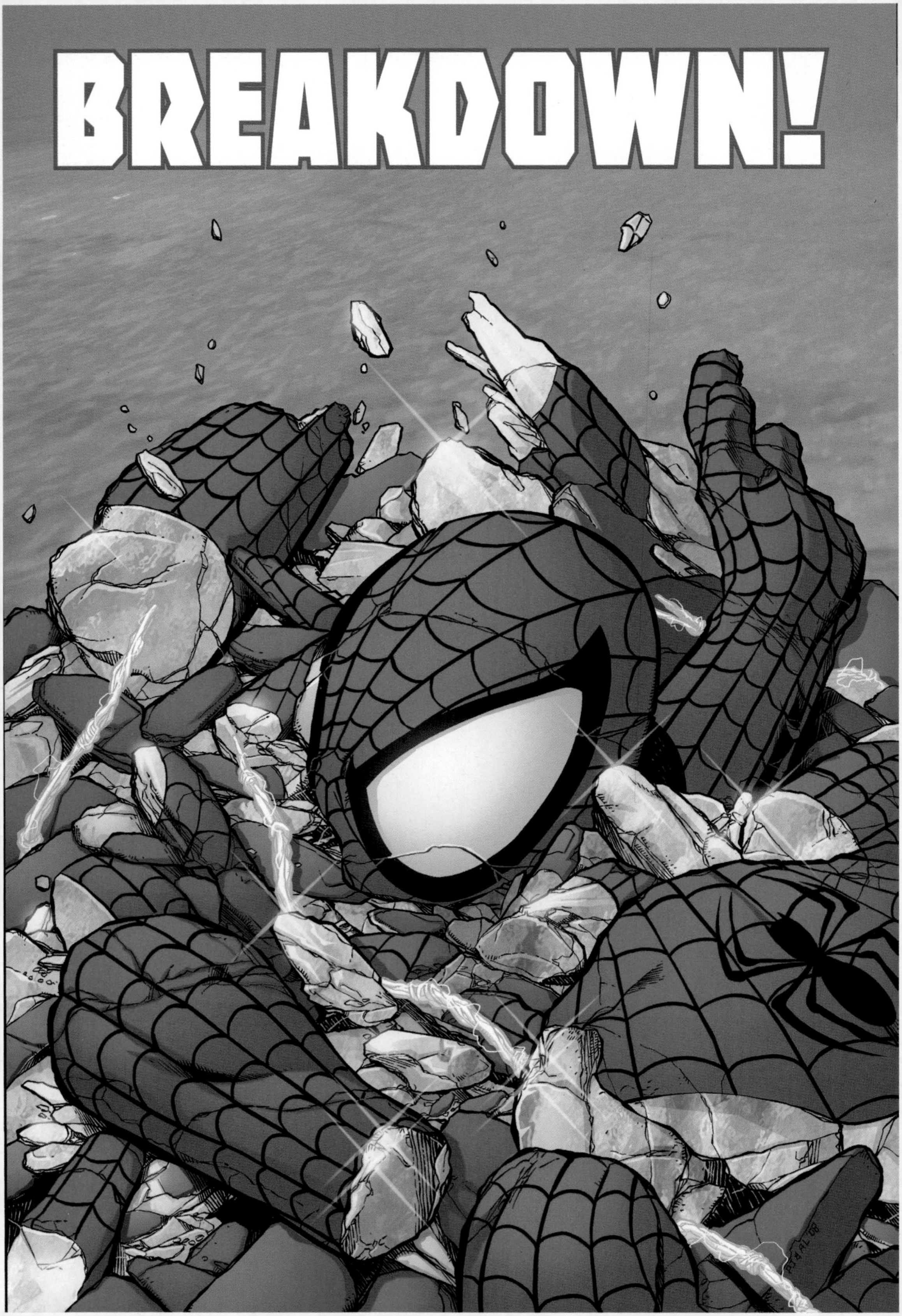
BREAKDOWN!

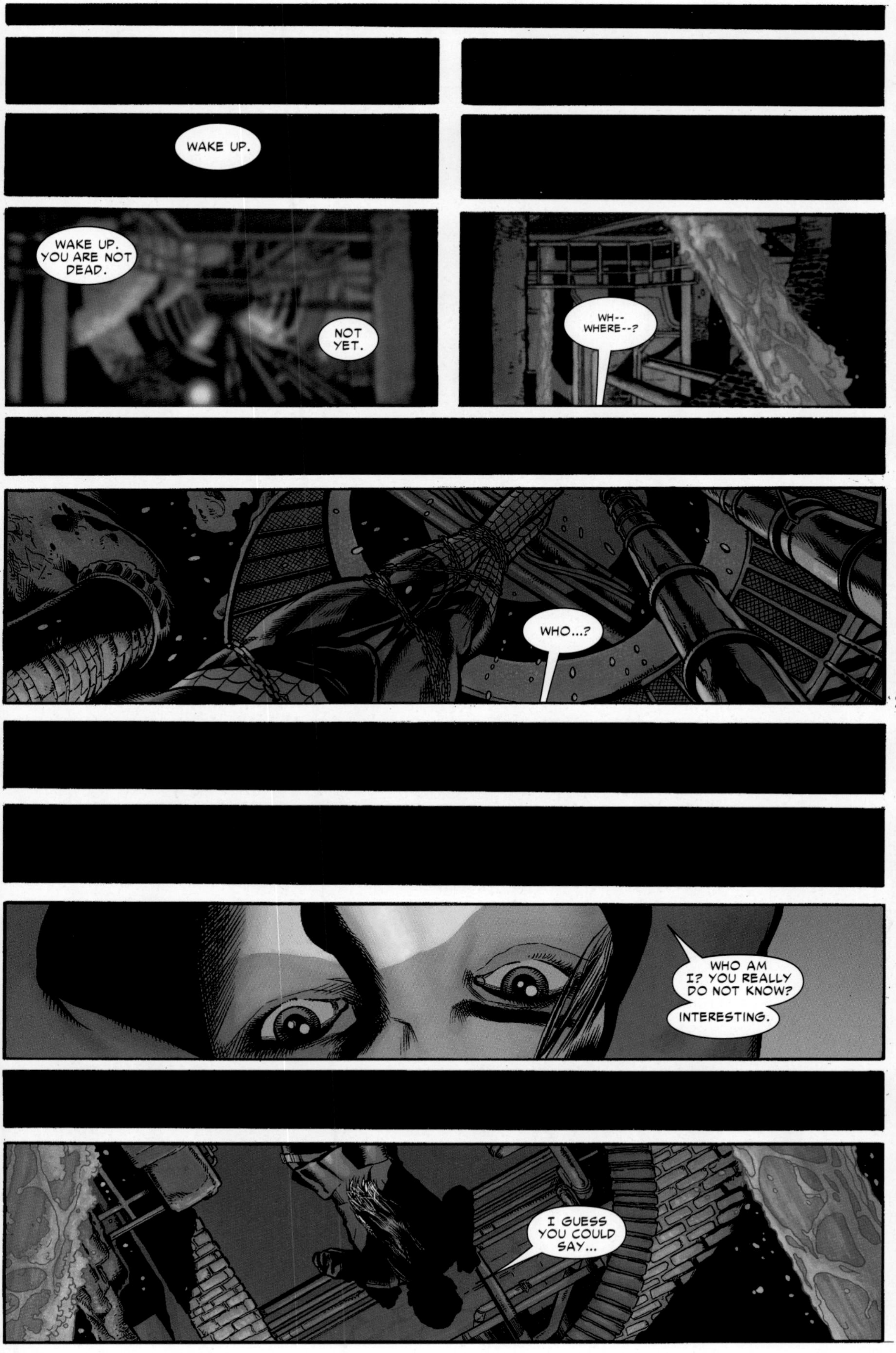
WAKE UP.
WAKE UP. YOU ARE NOT DEAD.
NOT YET.
WH-- WHERE--?
WHO...?
WHO AM I? YOU REALLY DO NOT KNOW?
INTERESTING.
I GUESS YOU COULD SAY...

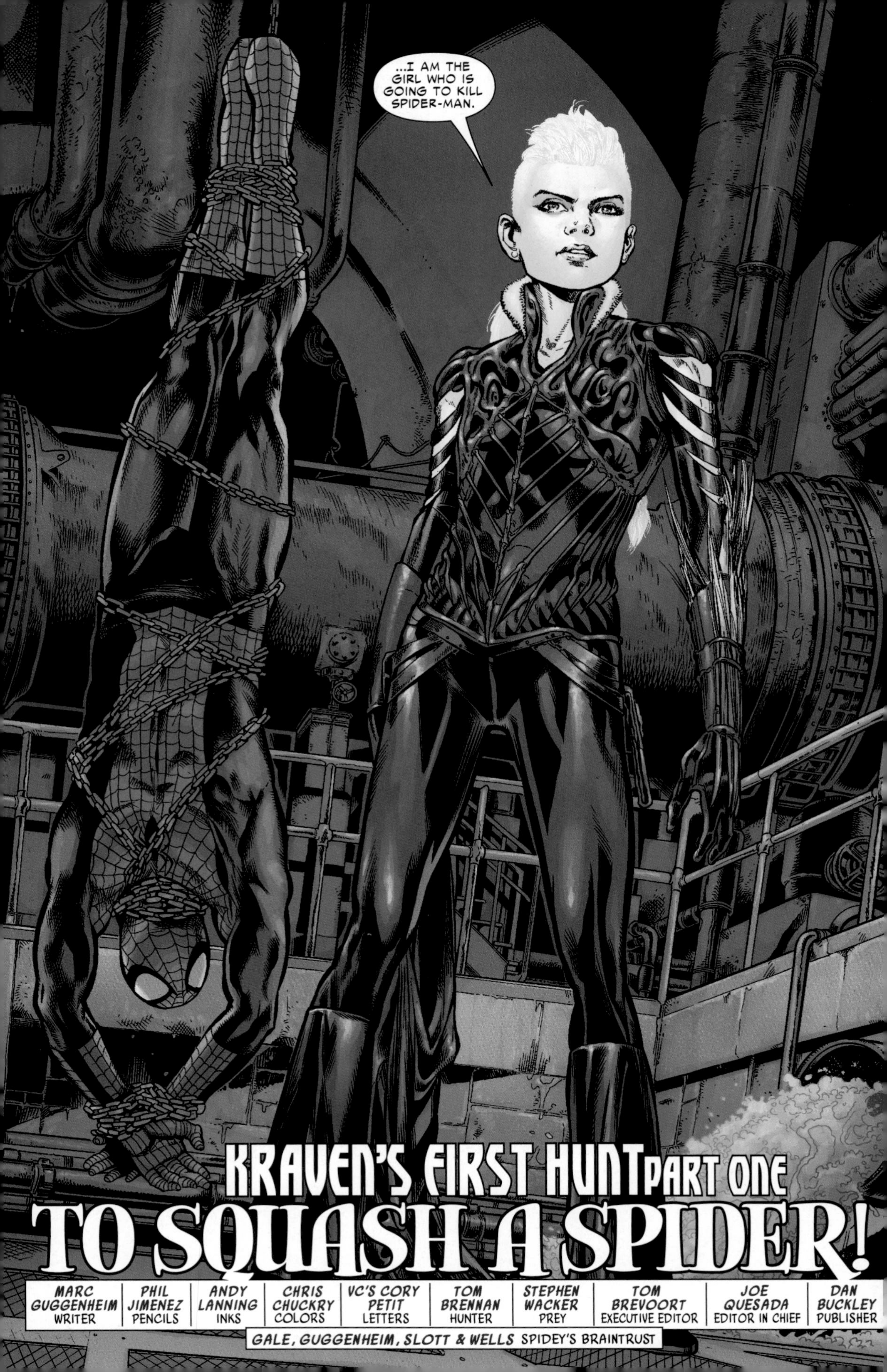
...I AM THE GIRL WHO IS GOING TO KILL SPIDER-MAN.
KRAVEN'S FIRST HUNT PART ONE
TO SQUASH A SPIDER!
MARC GUGGENHEIM WRITER
PHIL JIMENEZ PENCILS
ANDY LANNING INKS
CHRIS CHUCKRY COLORS
VC'S CORY PETIT LETTERS
TOM BRENNAN HUNTER
STEPHEN WACKER PREY
TOM BREVOORT EXECUTIVE EDITOR
JOE QUESADA EDITOR IN CHIEF
DAN BUCKLEY PUBLISHER
GALE, GUGGENHEIM, SLOTT & WELLS SPIDEY'S BRAINTRUST

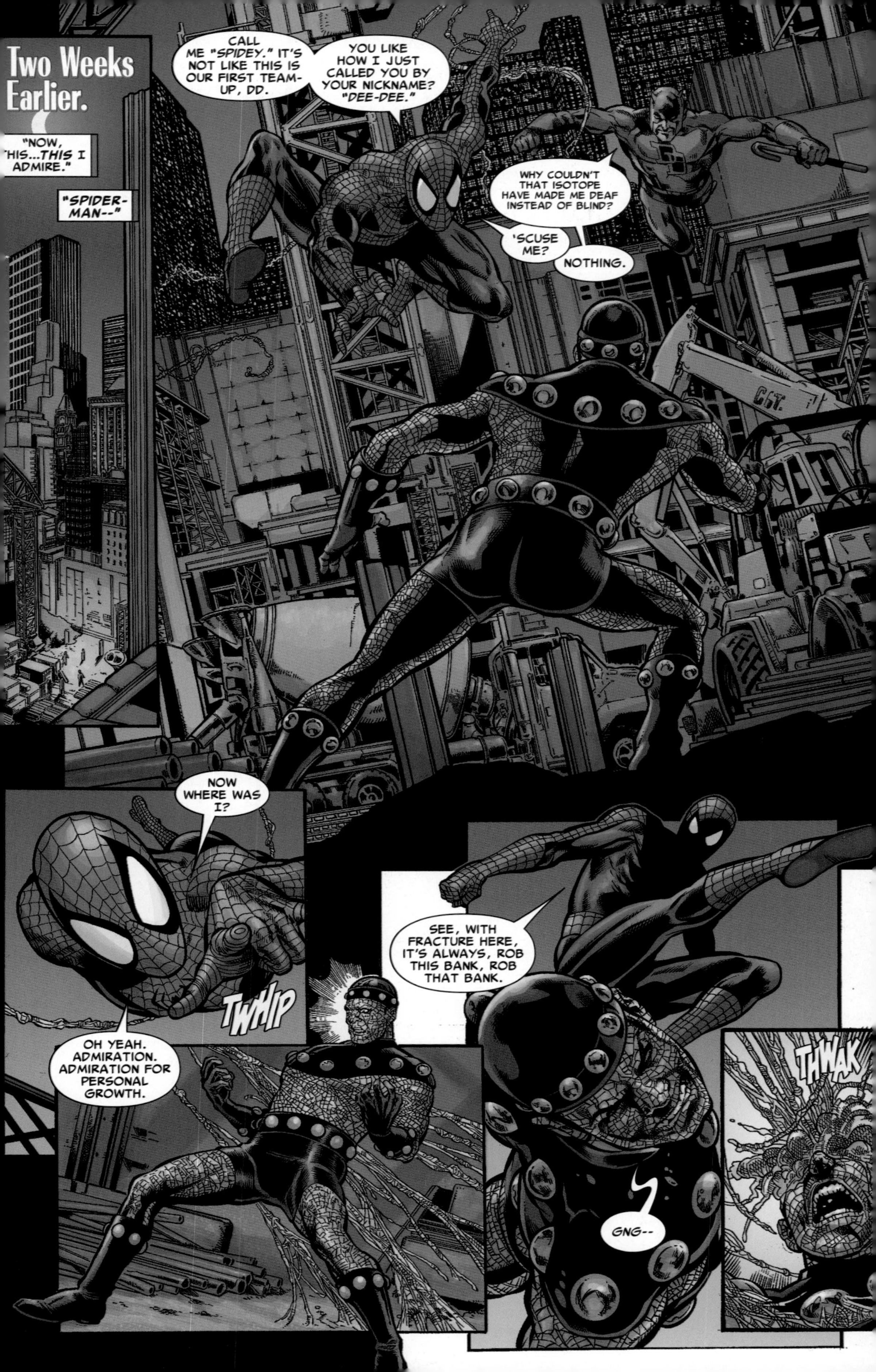

Two Weeks Earlier.
"NOW, THIS...THIS I ADMIRE."
"SPIDER-MAN--"
CALL ME "SPIDEY." IT'S NOT LIKE THIS IS OUR FIRST TEAM-UP, DD.
YOU LIKE HOW I JUST CALLED YOU BY YOUR NICKNAME? "DEE-DEE."
WHY COULDN'T THAT ISOTOPE HAVE MADE ME DEAF INSTEAD OF BLIND?
'SCUSE ME?
NOTHING.
NOW WHERE WAS I?
TWHIP
OH YEAH. ADMIRATION. ADMIRATION FOR PERSONAL GROWTH.
SEE, WITH FRACTURE HERE, IT'S ALWAYS, ROB THIS BANK, ROB THAT BANK.
GNG--
THWAK

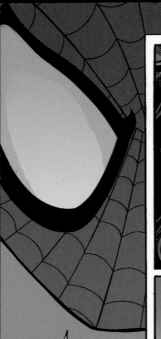

KRRK

YOU EVER STOP TALKING?

SHAK

WHICH IS KINDA POINTLESS WHEN YOU CONSIDER (A) HIS POWER TO BREAK THINGS BY TOUCHING THEM ISN'T REALLY COMPATIBLE WITH BANK ROBBERIES.

WHICH MIGHT EXPLAIN (B) WHY I ALWAYS CATCH HIM WHEN HE TRIES.

BUT THIS? AN INSURANCE SCAM? DEMOLISHING A CONSTRUCTION SITE TO COLLECT ON THE DAMAGE?

THAT'S INITIATIVE! THAT'S THINKING OUTSIDE THE BOX!

EXACTLY WHAT I WAS THINKING. IS TELEPATHY ONE OF YOUR POWERS, TOO?

DID YOU JUST MAKE A JOKE?!

YOU DID! YOU MADE A FUNNY. YOU MADE AN ACTUAL FUNNY. YOU REALLY DO HAVE A SENSE OF HUMOR!

LUKE CAGE OWES ME TEN BUCKS!

"PATIENCE," YOU THINK.

IT'S YOUR ONLY THOUGHT.

"PATIENCE."

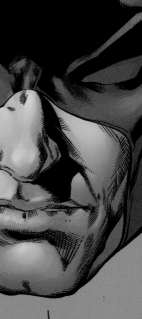

SPIDER-MAN--

DIDN'T I TELL YOU TO CALL ME "SPIDEY"?

SPIDEY--

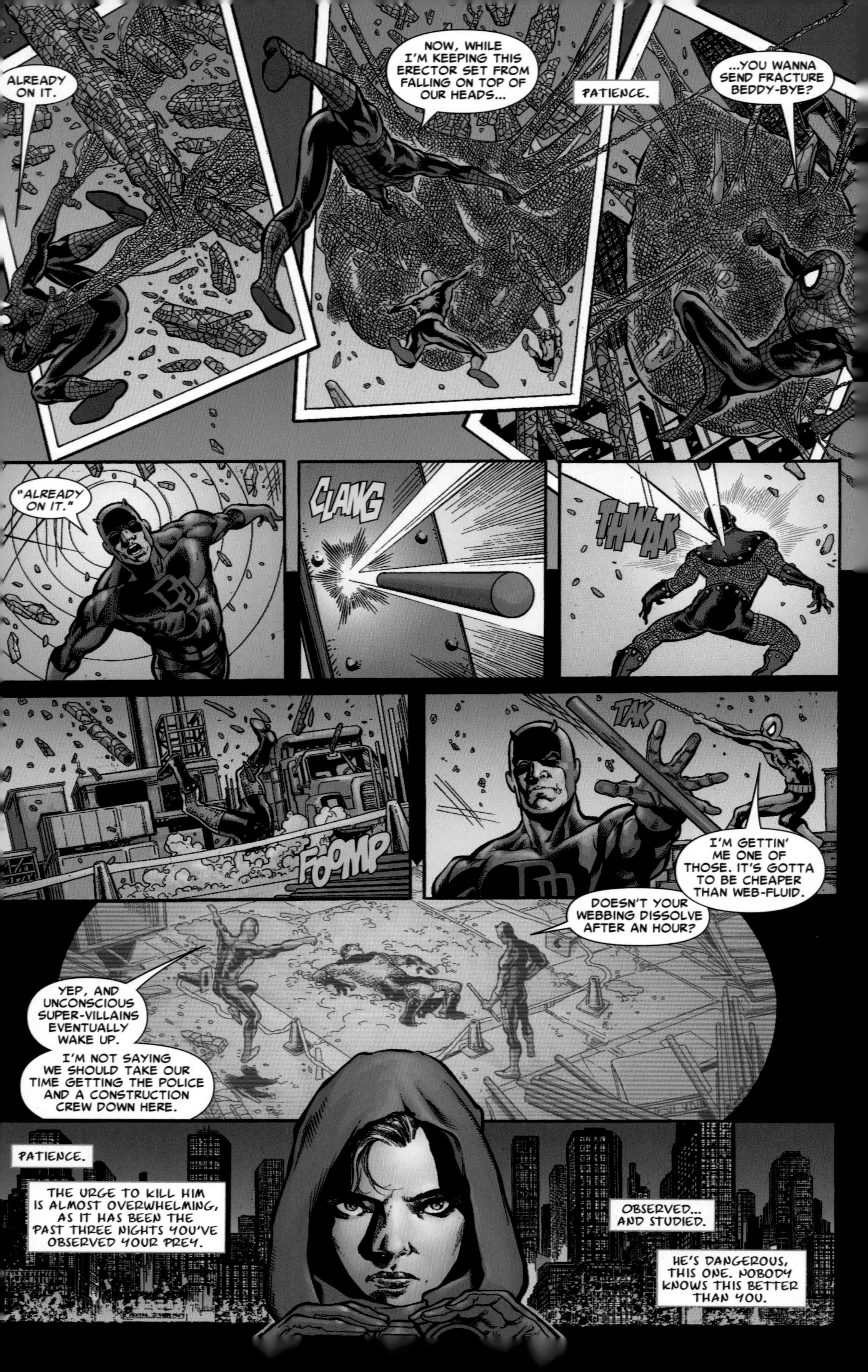
ALREADY ON IT.
NOW, WHILE I'M KEEPING THIS ERECTOR SET FROM FALLING ON TOP OF OUR HEADS...
PATIENCE.
...YOU WANNA SEND FRACTURE BEDDY-BYE?
"ALREADY ON IT."
CLANG
THWAK
FOOMP
TAK
I'M GETTIN' ME ONE OF THOSE. IT'S GOTTA TO BE CHEAPER THAN WEB-FLUID.
DOESN'T YOUR WEBBING DISSOLVE AFTER AN HOUR?
YEP, AND UNCONSCIOUS SUPER-VILLAINS EVENTUALLY WAKE UP.
I'M NOT SAYING WE SHOULD TAKE OUR TIME GETTING THE POLICE AND A CONSTRUCTION CREW DOWN HERE.
PATIENCE.
THE URGE TO KILL HIM IS ALMOST OVERWHELMING, AS IT HAS BEEN THE PAST THREE NIGHTS YOU'VE OBSERVED YOUR PREY.
OBSERVED... AND STUDIED.
HE'S DANGEROUS, THIS ONE. NOBODY KNOWS THIS BETTER THAN YOU.

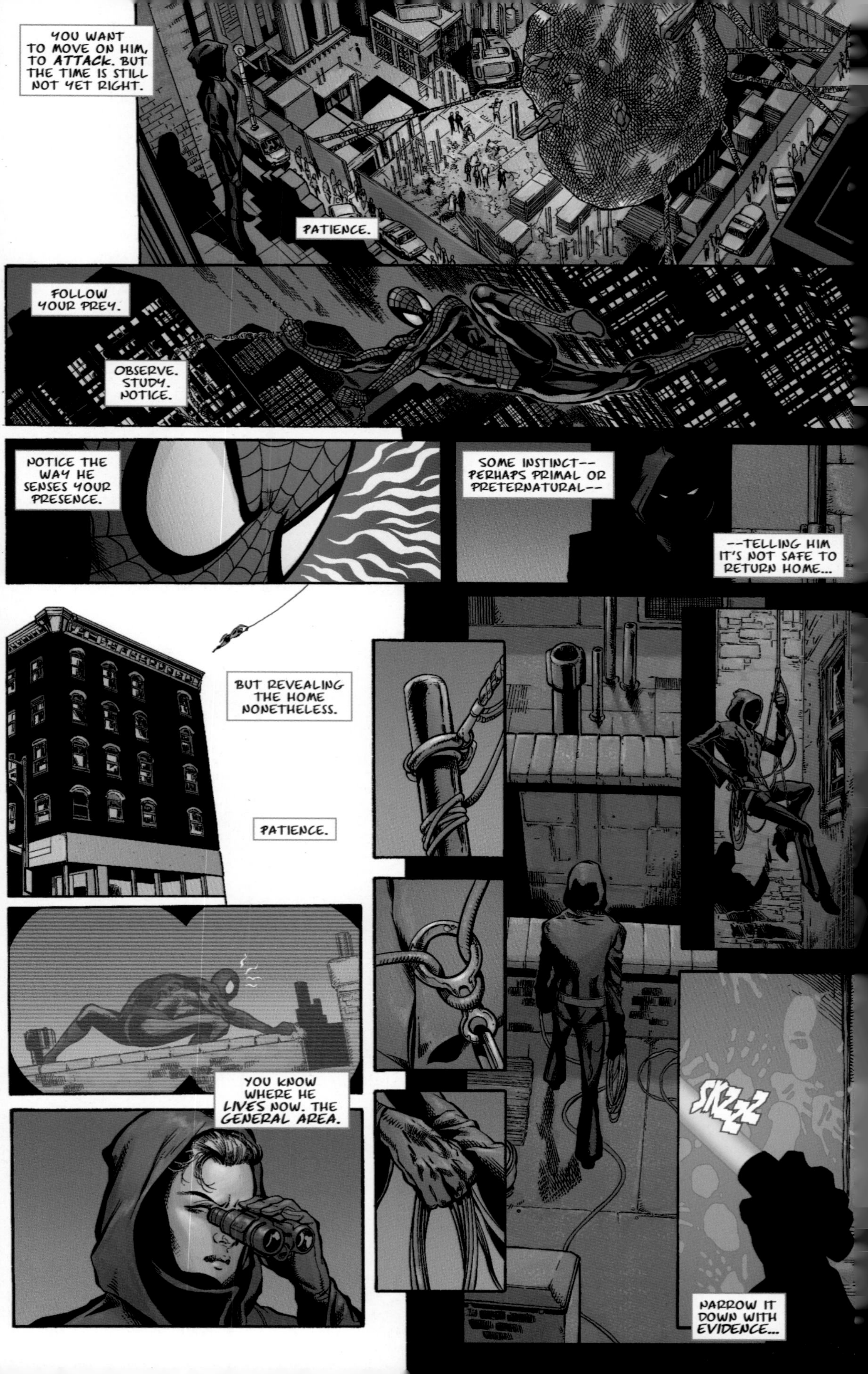
YOU WANT TO MOVE ON HIM, TO ATTACK. BUT THE TIME IS STILL NOT YET RIGHT.
PATIENCE.
FOLLOW YOUR PREY.
OBSERVE. STUDY. NOTICE.
NOTICE THE WAY HE SENSES YOUR PRESENCE.
SOME INSTINCT-- PERHAPS PRIMAL OR PRETERNATURAL--
--TELLING HIM IT'S NOT SAFE TO RETURN HOME...
BUT REVEALING THE HOME NONETHELESS.
PATIENCE.
YOU KNOW WHERE HE LIVES NOW. THE GENERAL AREA.
SKZZZ
NARROW IT DOWN WITH EVIDENCE...

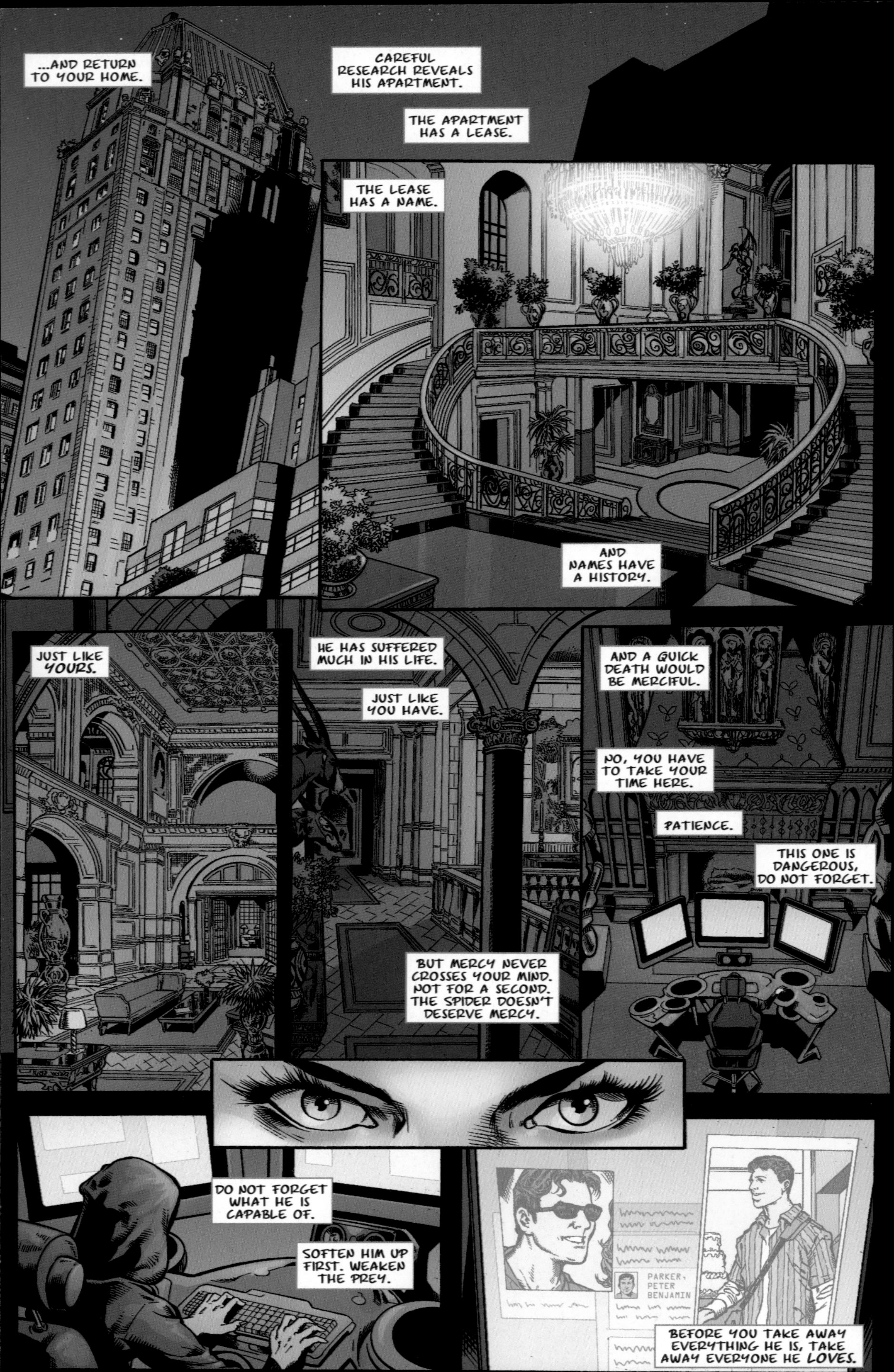
...AND RETURN TO YOUR HOME.
CAREFUL RESEARCH REVEALS HIS APARTMENT.
THE APARTMENT HAS A LEASE.
THE LEASE HAS A NAME.
AND NAMES HAVE A HISTORY.
JUST LIKE YOURS.
HE HAS SUFFERED MUCH IN HIS LIFE.
JUST LIKE YOU HAVE.
BUT MERCY NEVER CROSSES YOUR MIND. NOT FOR A SECOND. THE SPIDER DOESN'T DESERVE MERCY.
AND A QUICK DEATH WOULD BE MERCIFUL.
NO, YOU HAVE TO TAKE YOUR TIME HERE.
PATIENCE.
THIS ONE IS DANGEROUS, DO NOT FORGET.
DO NOT FORGET WHAT HE IS CAPABLE OF.
SOFTEN HIM UP FIRST. WEAKEN THE PREY.
PARKER, PETER BENJAMIN
BEFORE YOU TAKE AWAY EVERYTHING HE IS, TAKE AWAY EVERYONE HE LOVES.

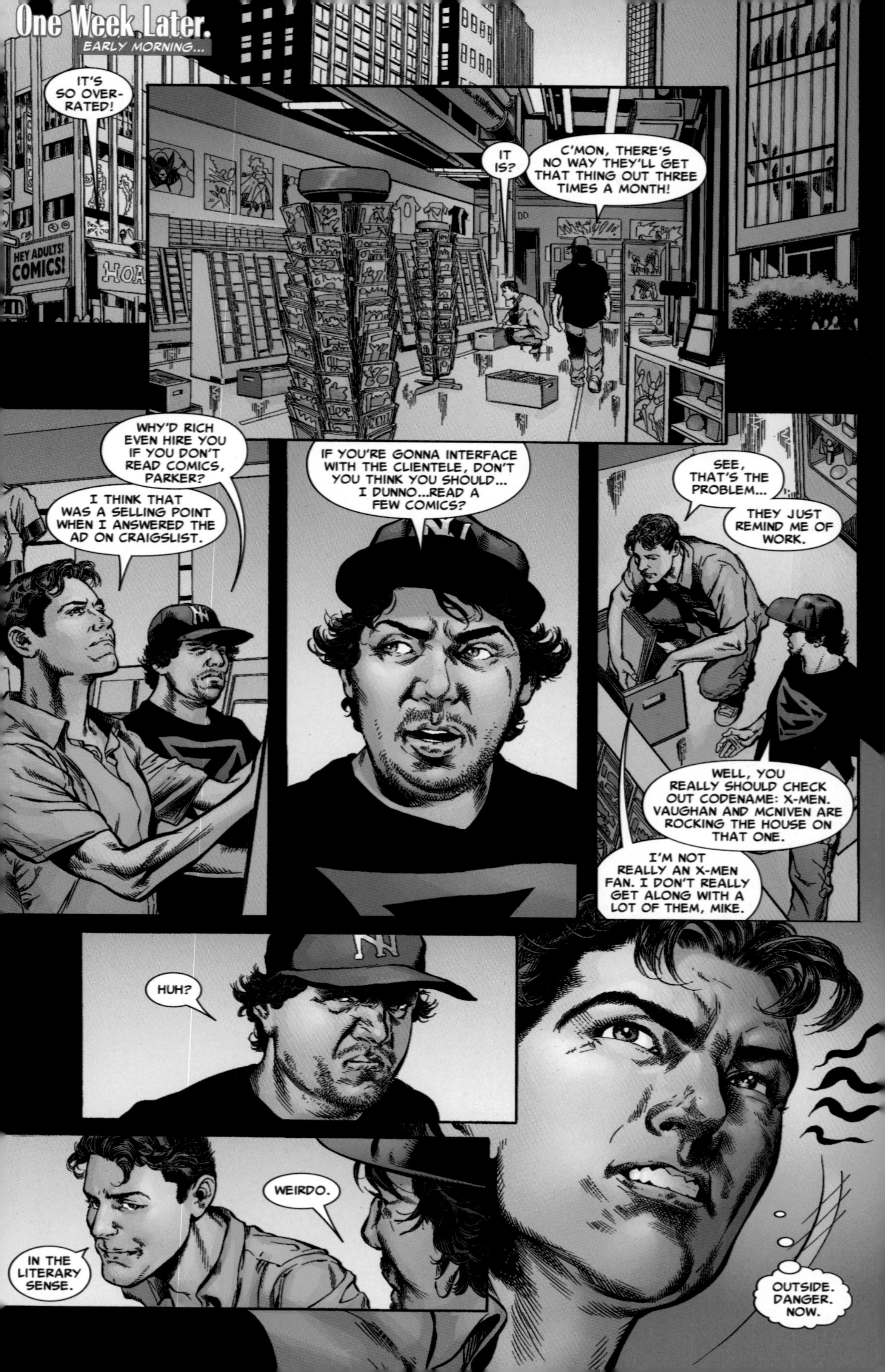
One Week Later.
EARLY MORNING...
IT'S SO OVER-RATED!
IT IS?
C'MON, THERE'S NO WAY THEY'LL GET THAT THING OUT THREE TIMES A MONTH!
HEY ADULTS! COMICS!
WHY'D RICH EVEN HIRE YOU IF YOU DON'T READ COMICS, PARKER?
I THINK THAT WAS A SELLING POINT WHEN I ANSWERED THE AD ON CRAIGSLIST.
IF YOU'RE GONNA INTERFACE WITH THE CLIENTELE, DON'T YOU THINK YOU SHOULD... I DUNNO...READ A FEW COMICS?
SEE, THAT'S THE PROBLEM...
THEY JUST REMIND ME OF WORK.
WELL, YOU REALLY SHOULD CHECK OUT CODENAME: X-MEN. VAUGHAN AND MCNIVEN ARE ROCKING THE HOUSE ON THAT ONE.
I'M NOT REALLY AN X-MEN FAN. I DON'T REALLY GET ALONG WITH A LOT OF THEM, MIKE.
HUH?
WEIRDO.
IN THE LITERARY SENSE.
OUTSIDE. DANGER. NOW.

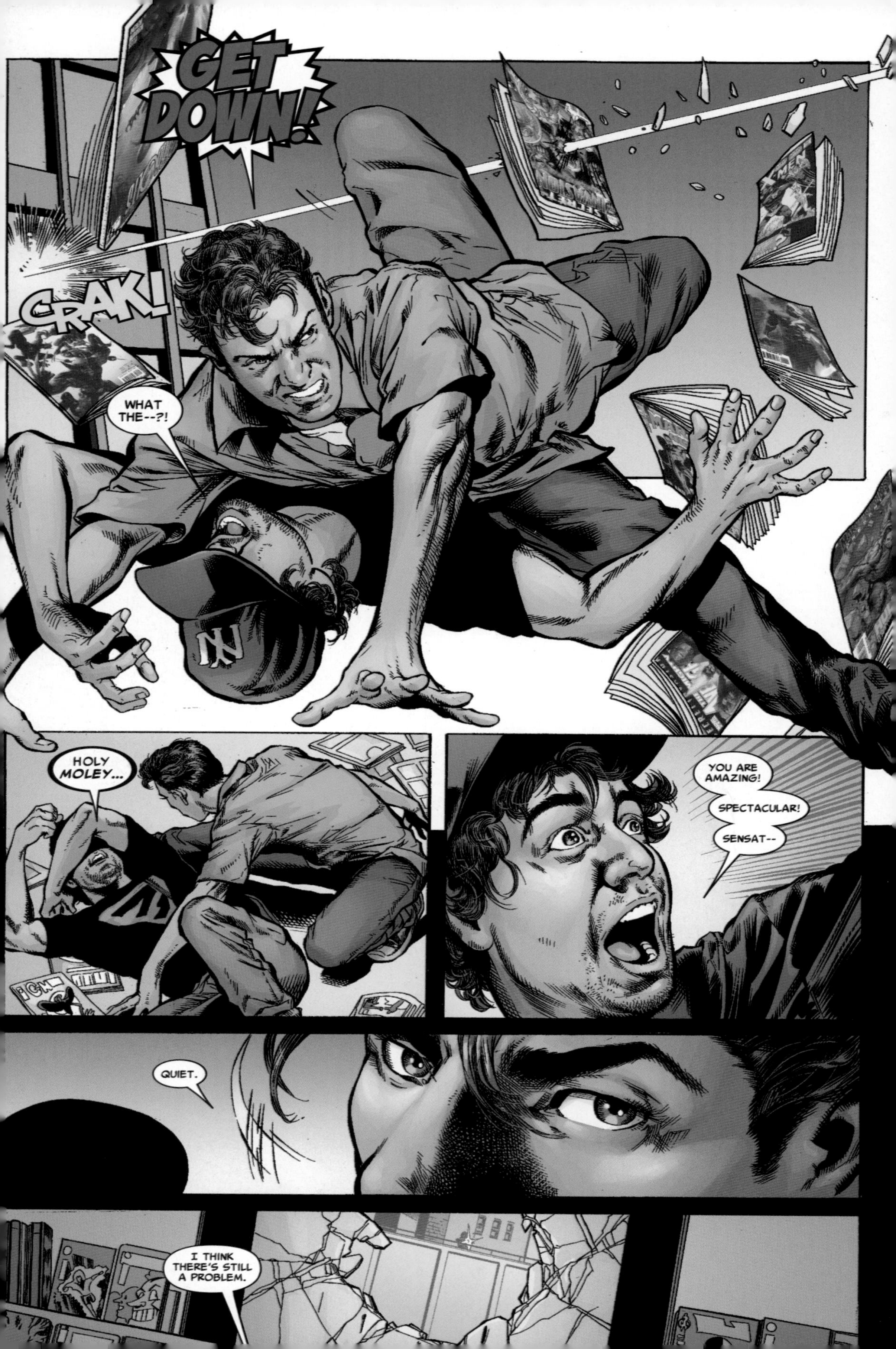
GET DOWN!
CRAK!
WHAT THE--?!
HOLY MOLEY...
YOU ARE AMAZING!
SPECTACULAR!
SENSAT--
QUIET.
I THINK THERE'S STILL A PROBLEM.

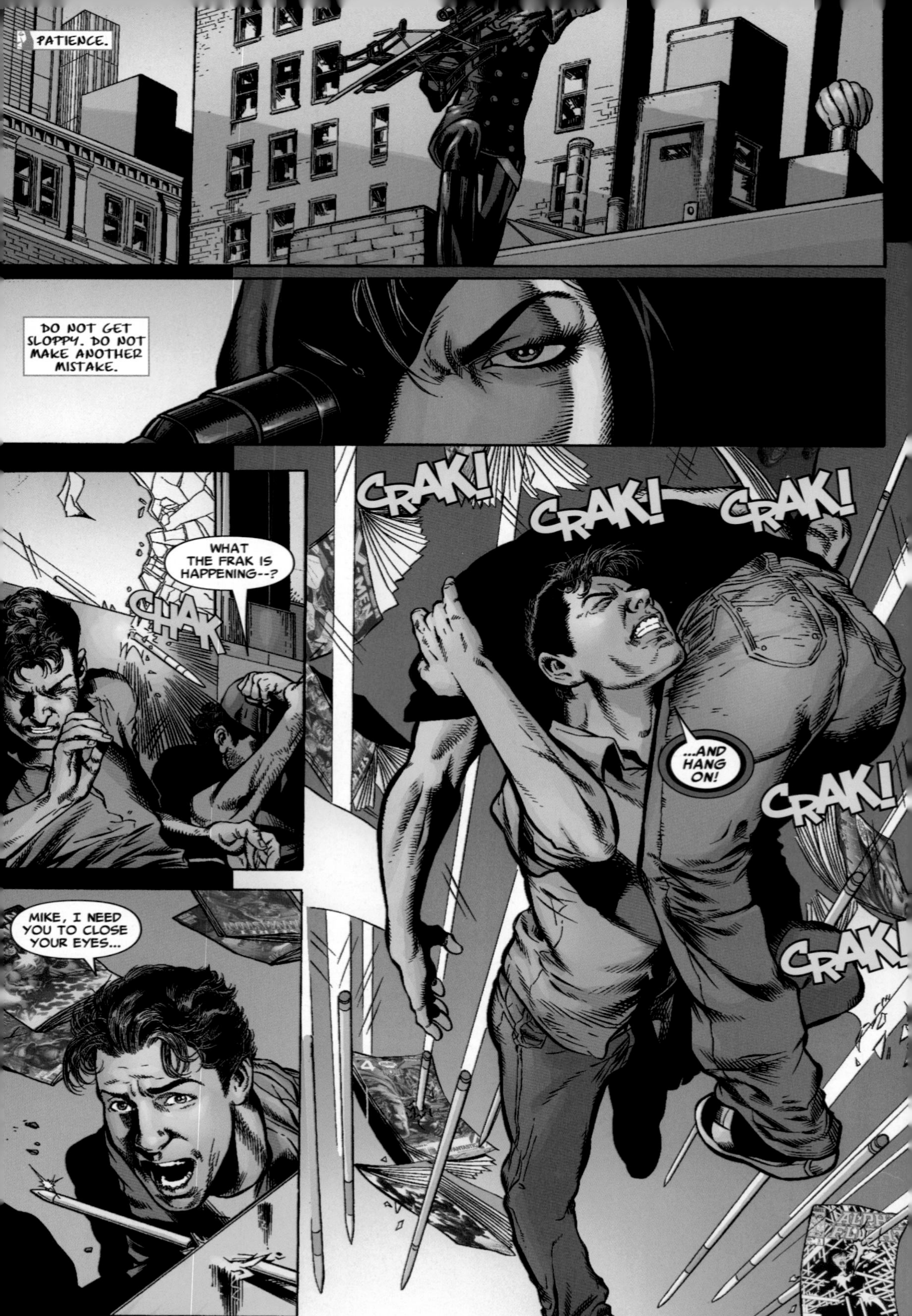
PATIENCE.
DO NOT GET SLOPPY. DO NOT MAKE ANOTHER MISTAKE.
WHAT THE FRAK IS HAPPENING--?
CHAK
CRAK!
CRAK!
CRAK!
MIKE, I NEED YOU TO CLOSE YOUR EYES...
...AND HANG ON!
CRAK!
CRAK!

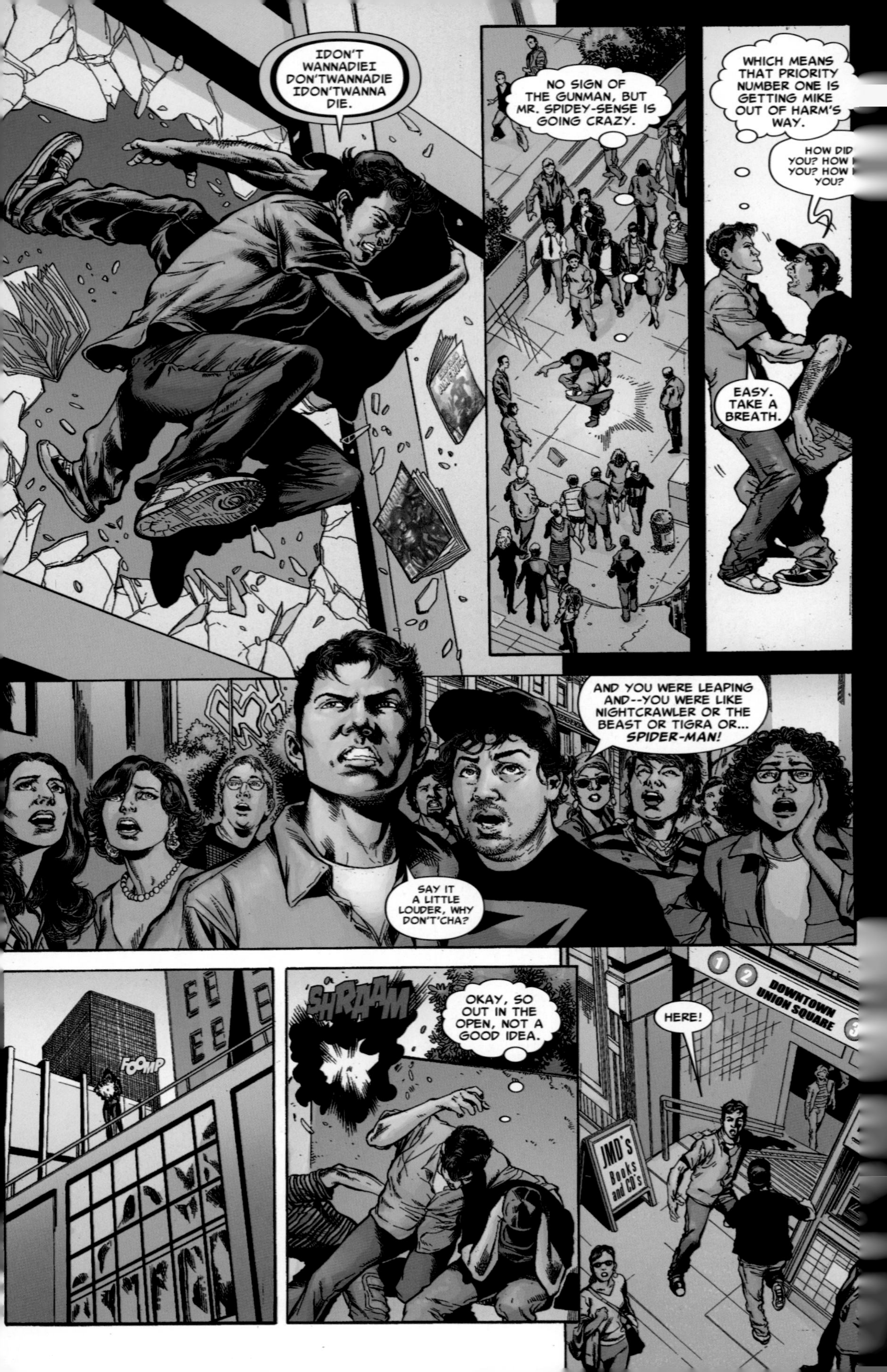
IDON'T WANNADIEI DON'TWANNADIE IDON'TWANNA DIE.
NO SIGN OF THE GUNMAN, BUT MR. SPIDEY-SENSE IS GOING CRAZY.
WHICH MEANS THAT PRIORITY NUMBER ONE IS GETTING MIKE OUT OF HARM'S WAY.
HOW DID YOU? HOW YOU? HOW YOU?
EASY. TAKE A BREATH.
AND YOU WERE LEAPING AND--YOU WERE LIKE NIGHTCRAWLER OR THE BEAST OR TIGRA OR... SPIDER-MAN!
SAY IT A LITTLE LOUDER, WHY DON'T'CHA?
FOOMP
SHRAAAM
OKAY, SO OUT IN THE OPEN, NOT A GOOD IDEA.
1 2 DOWNTOWN UNION SQUARE 3
HERE!
JMD's Books and CD's

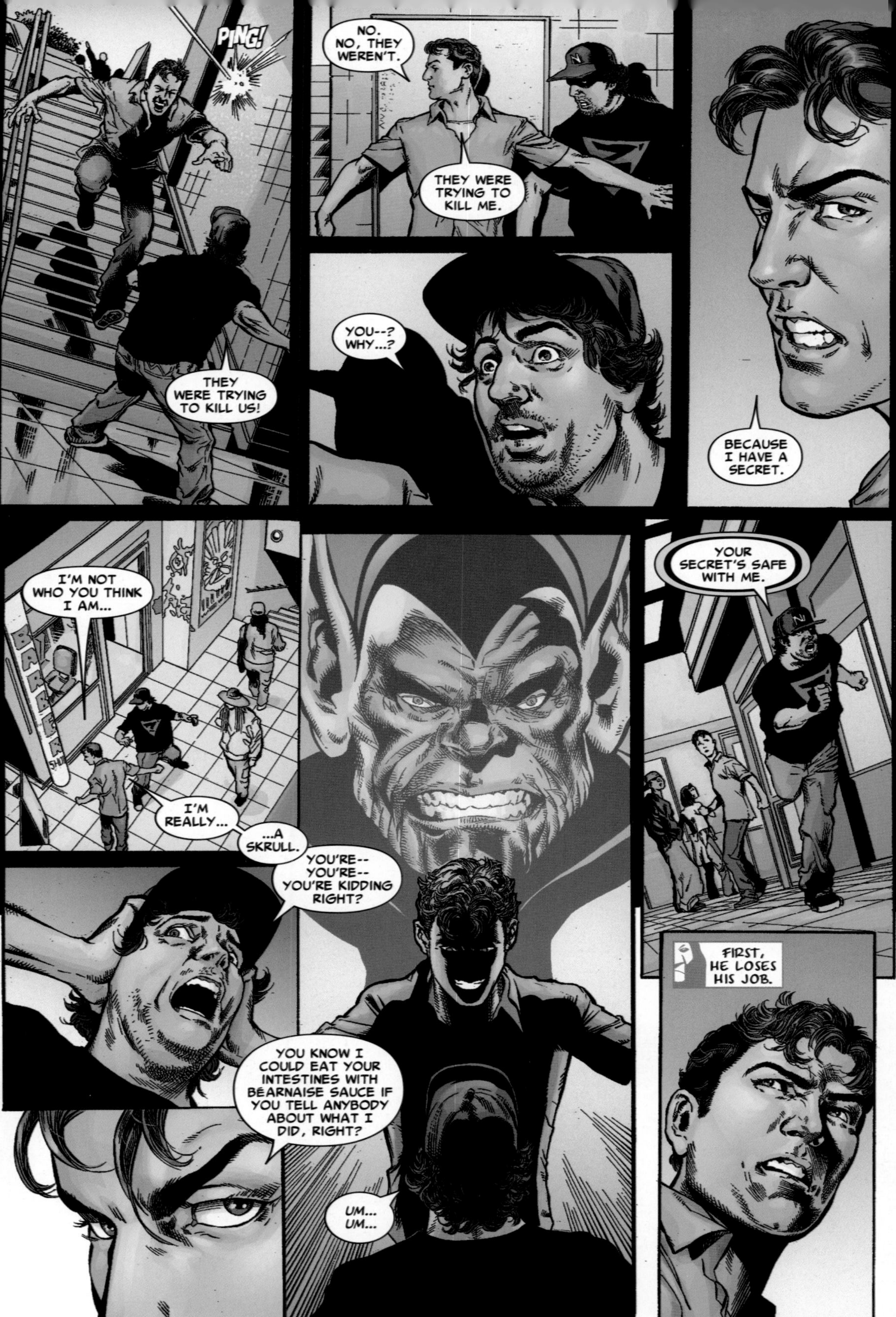
PING!
THEY WERE TRYING TO KILL US!
NO. NO, THEY WEREN'T.
THEY WERE TRYING TO KILL ME.
YOU--? WHY...?
BECAUSE I HAVE A SECRET.
I'M NOT WHO YOU THINK I AM...
I'M REALLY...
...A SKRULL.
YOU'RE-- YOU'RE-- YOU'RE KIDDING RIGHT?
YOU KNOW I COULD EAT YOUR INTESTINES WITH BÉARNAISE SAUCE IF YOU TELL ANYBODY ABOUT WHAT I DID, RIGHT?
UM... UM...
YOUR SECRET'S SAFE WITH ME.
FIRST, HE LOSES HIS JOB.

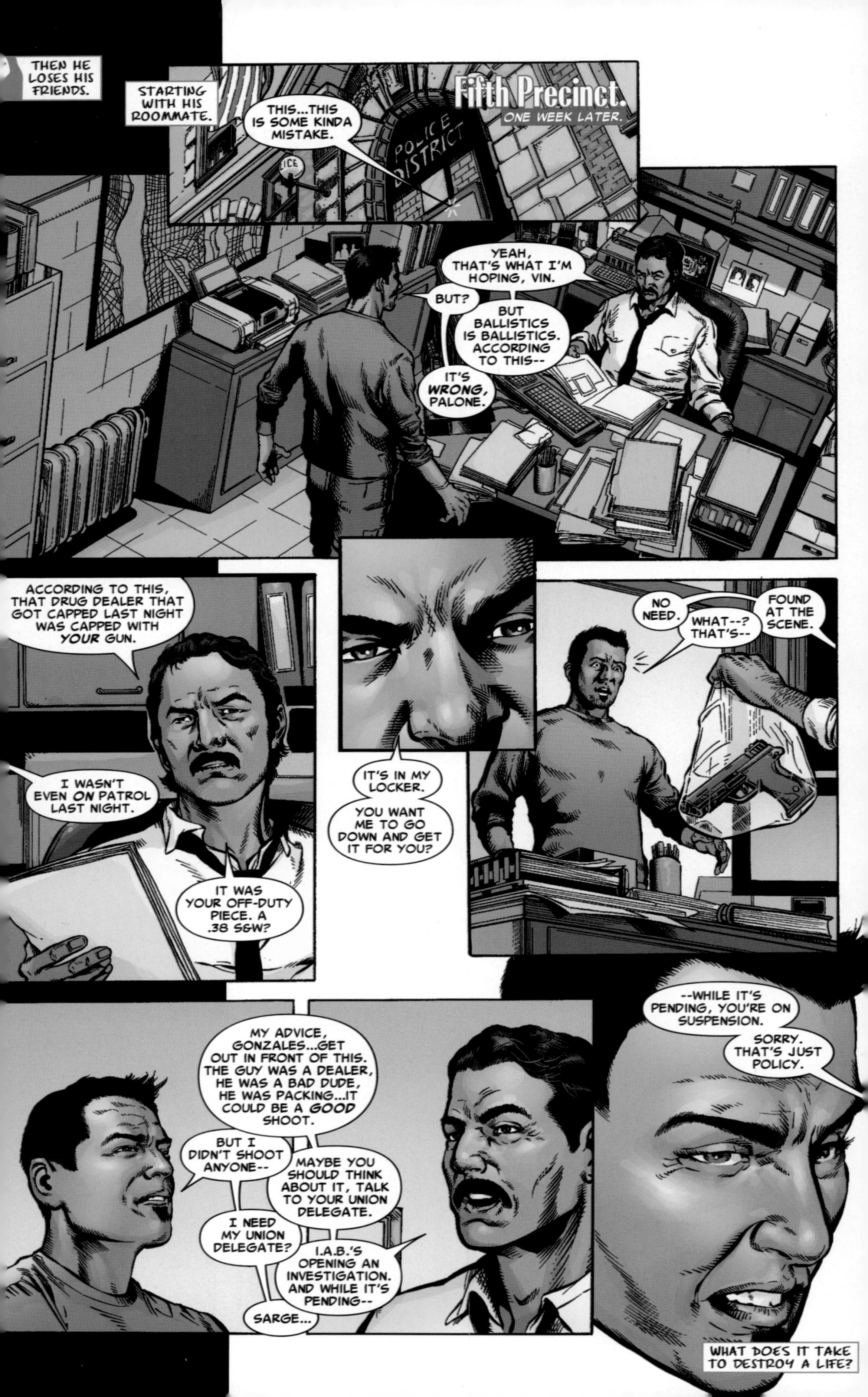
THEN HE LOSES HIS FRIENDS.
STARTING WITH HIS ROOMMATE.
Fifth Precinct.
ONE WEEK LATER.
POLICE DISTRICT
THIS...THIS IS SOME KINDA MISTAKE.
YEAH, THAT'S WHAT I'M HOPING, VIN.
BUT?
BUT BALLISTICS IS BALLISTICS. ACCORDING TO THIS--
IT'S WRONG, PALONE.
ACCORDING TO THIS, THAT DRUG DEALER THAT GOT CAPPED LAST NIGHT WAS CAPPED WITH YOUR GUN.
I WASN'T EVEN ON PATROL LAST NIGHT.
IT WAS YOUR OFF-DUTY PIECE. A .38 S&W?
IT'S IN MY LOCKER.
YOU WANT ME TO GO DOWN AND GET IT FOR YOU?
NO NEED.
FOUND AT THE SCENE.
WHAT--? THAT'S--
MY ADVICE, GONZALES...GET OUT IN FRONT OF THIS. THE GUY WAS A DEALER, HE WAS A BAD DUDE, HE WAS PACKING...IT COULD BE A GOOD SHOOT.
BUT I DIDN'T SHOOT ANYONE--
MAYBE YOU SHOULD THINK ABOUT IT, TALK TO YOUR UNION DELEGATE.
I NEED MY UNION DELEGATE?
I.A.B.'S OPENING AN INVESTIGATION. AND WHILE IT'S PENDING--
SARGE...
--WHILE IT'S PENDING, YOU'RE ON SUSPENSION.
SORRY. THAT'S JUST POLICY.
WHAT DOES IT TAKE TO DESTROY A LIFE?

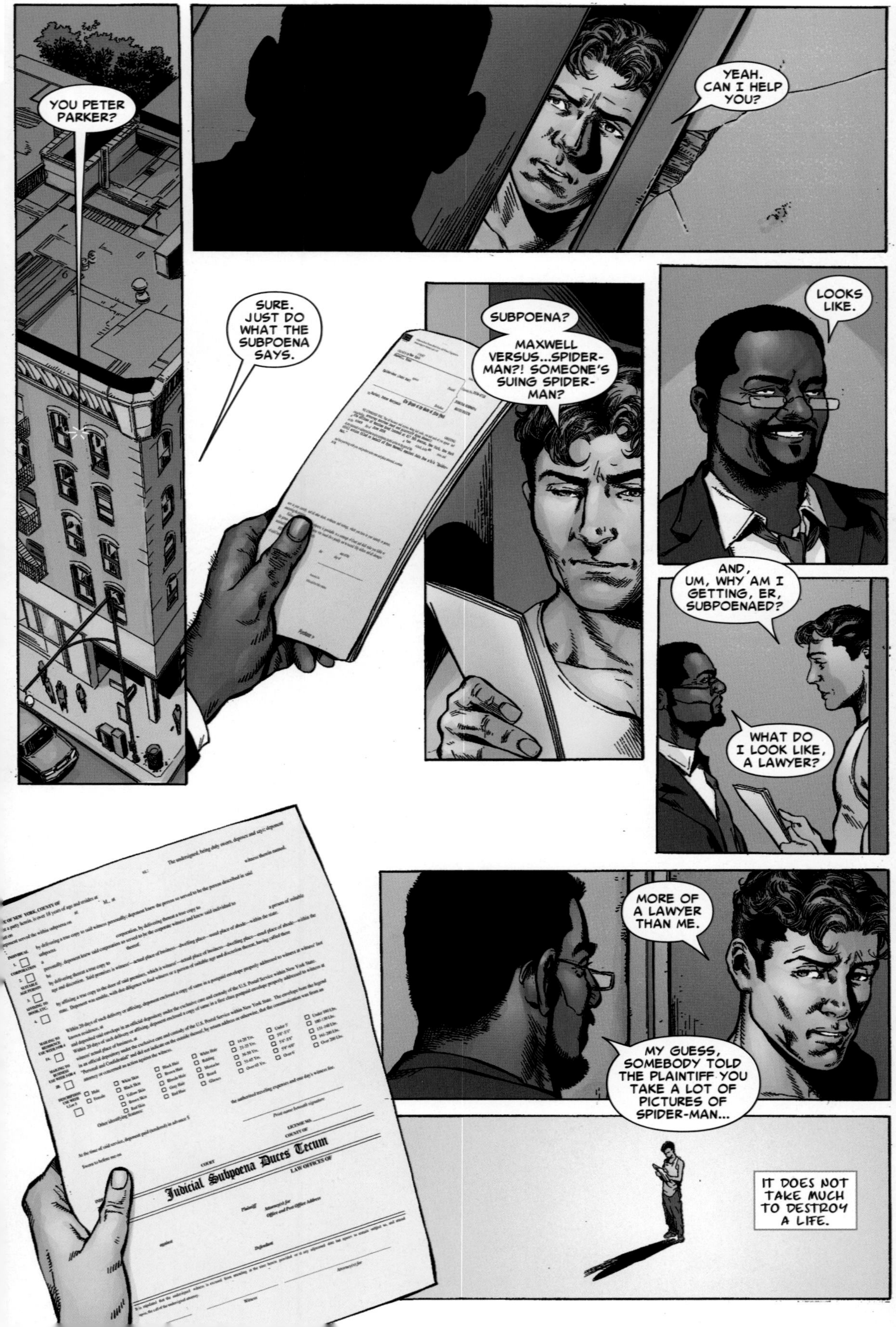
YOU PETER PARKER?
YEAH. CAN I HELP YOU?
SURE. JUST DO WHAT THE SUBPOENA SAYS.
SUBPOENA?
MAXWELL VERSUS...SPIDER-MAN?! SOMEONE'S SUING SPIDER-MAN?
LOOKS LIKE.
AND, UM, WHY AM I GETTING, ER, SUBPOENAED?
WHAT DO I LOOK LIKE, A LAWYER?
MORE OF A LAWYER THAN ME.
MY GUESS, SOMEBODY TOLD THE PLAINTIFF YOU TAKE A LOT OF PICTURES OF SPIDER-MAN...
Judicial Subpoena Duces Tecum
IT DOES NOT TAKE MUCH TO DESTROY A LIFE.

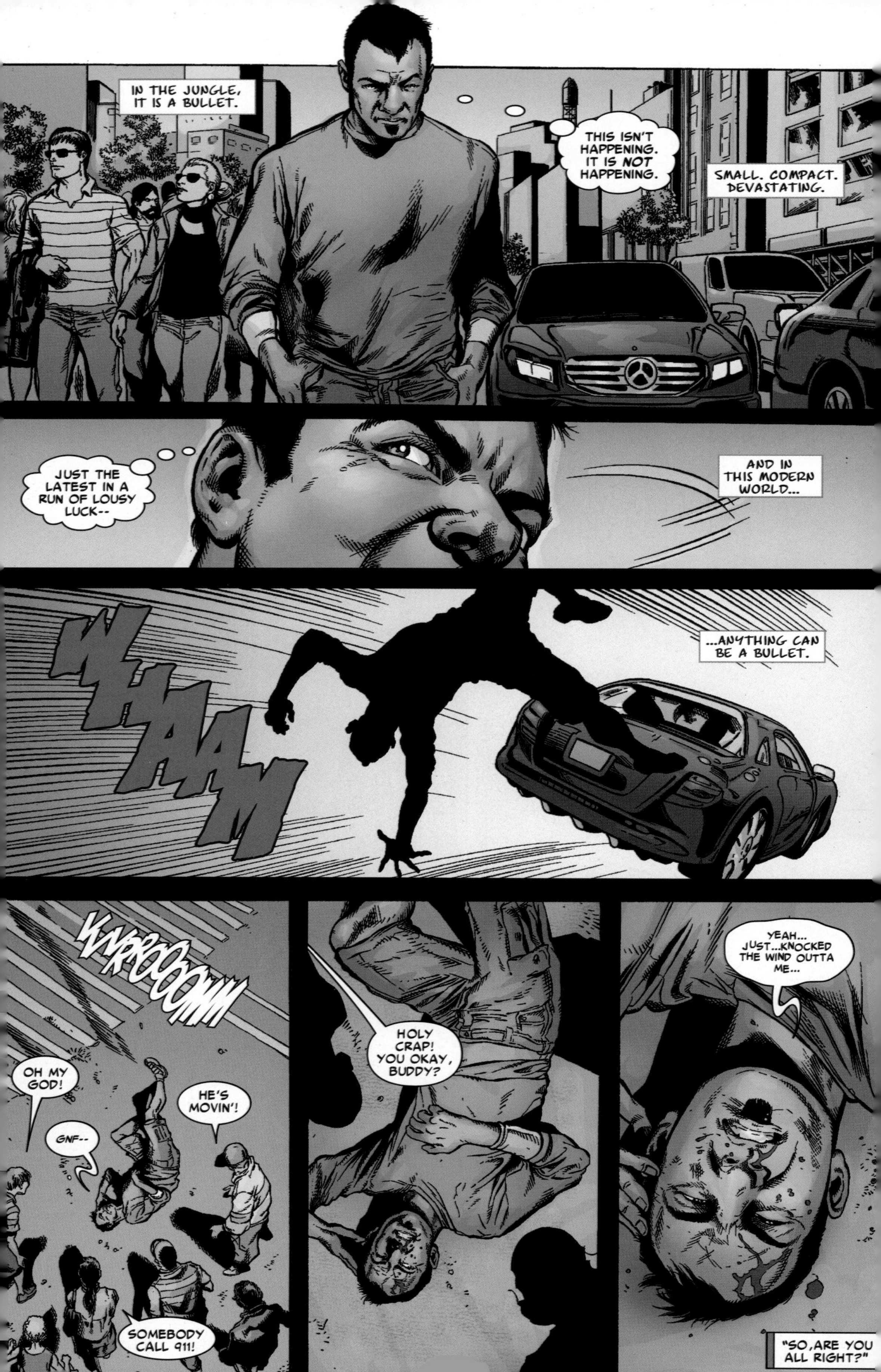
IN THE JUNGLE, IT IS A BULLET.
THIS ISN'T HAPPENING. IT IS NOT HAPPENING.
SMALL. COMPACT. DEVASTATING.
JUST THE LATEST IN A RUN OF LOUSY LUCK--
AND IN THIS MODERN WORLD...
WHAAM
...ANYTHING CAN BE A BULLET.
KWROOOOMM
OH MY GOD!
HE'S MOVIN'!
GNF--
SOMEBODY CALL 911!
HOLY CRAP! YOU OKAY, BUDDY?
YEAH... JUST...KNOCKED THE WIND OUTTA ME...
"SO, ARE YOU ALL RIGHT?"

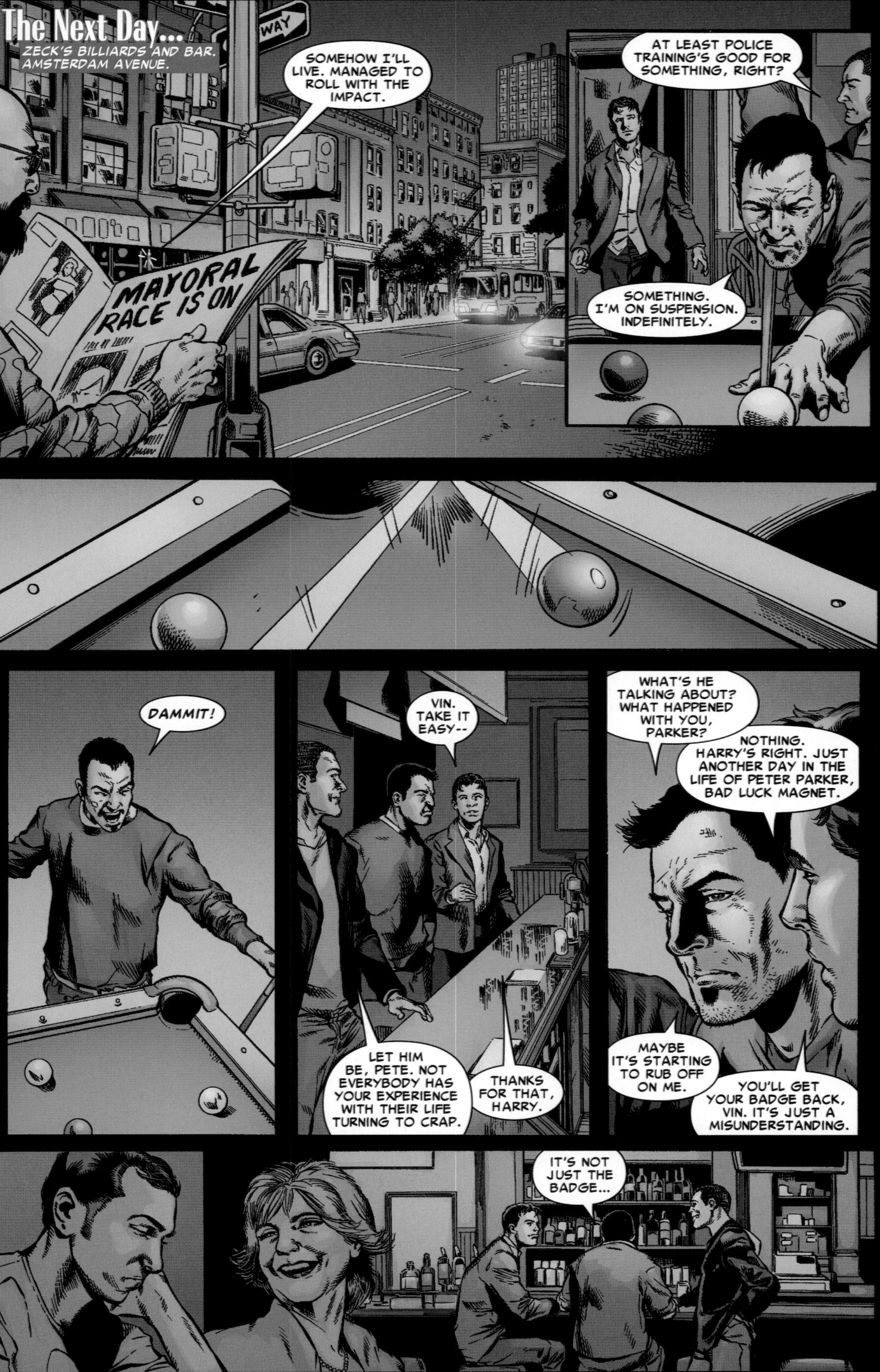
The Next Day...
ZECK'S BILLIARDS AND BAR. AMSTERDAM AVENUE.
WAY
SOMEHOW I'LL LIVE. MANAGED TO ROLL WITH THE IMPACT.
MAYORAL RACE IS ON
AT LEAST POLICE TRAINING'S GOOD FOR SOMETHING, RIGHT?
SOMETHING. I'M ON SUSPENSION. INDEFINITELY.
DAMMIT!
VIN. TAKE IT EASY--
LET HIM BE, PETE. NOT EVERYBODY HAS YOUR EXPERIENCE WITH THEIR LIFE TURNING TO CRAP.
THANKS FOR THAT, HARRY.
WHAT'S HE TALKING ABOUT? WHAT HAPPENED WITH YOU, PARKER?
NOTHING. HARRY'S RIGHT. JUST ANOTHER DAY IN THE LIFE OF PETER PARKER, BAD LUCK MAGNET.
MAYBE IT'S STARTING TO RUB OFF ON ME.
YOU'LL GET YOUR BADGE BACK, VIN. IT'S JUST A MISUNDERSTANDING.
IT'S NOT JUST THE BADGE...

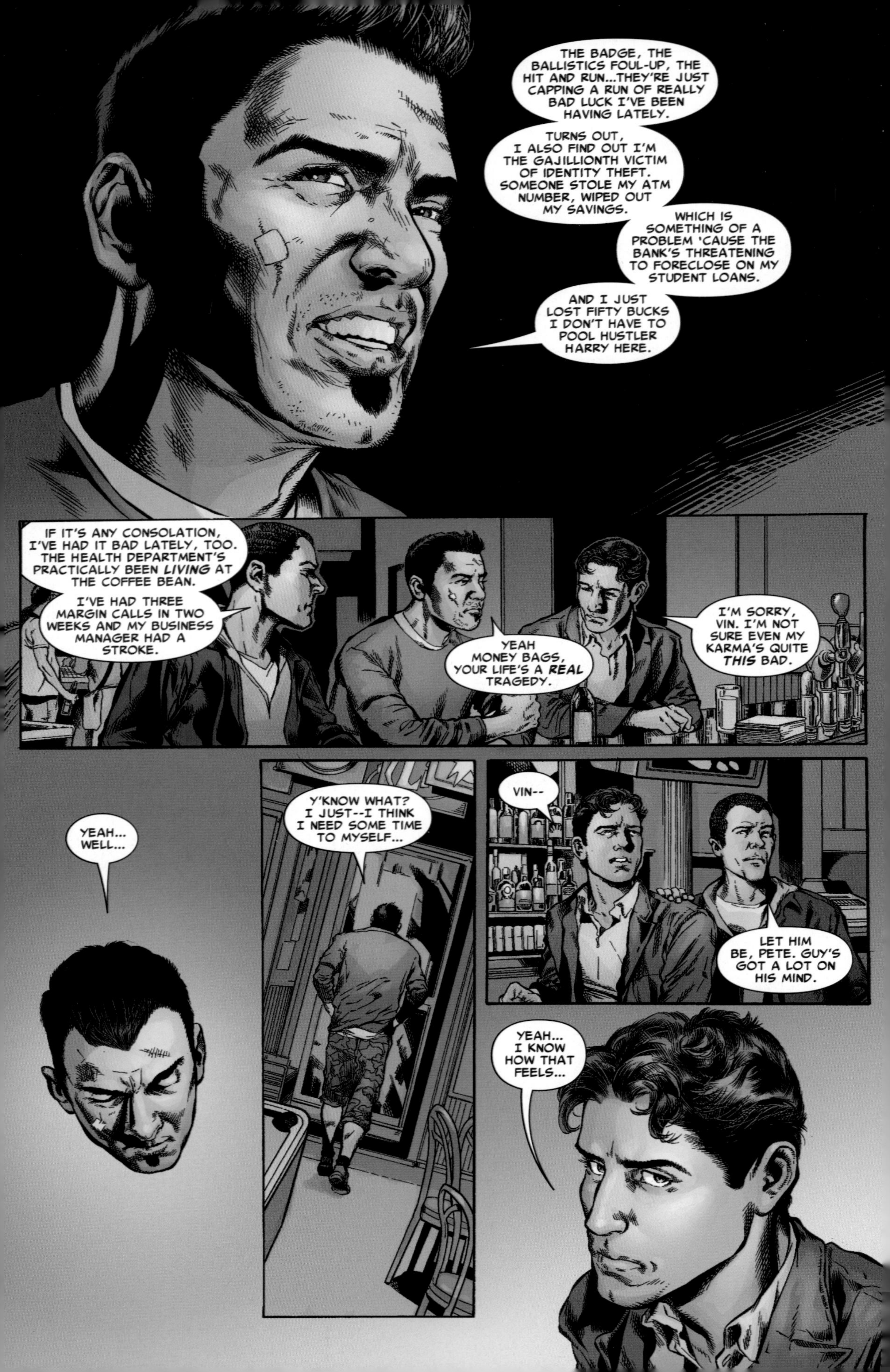
THE BADGE, THE BALLISTICS FOUL-UP, THE HIT AND RUN...THEY'RE JUST CAPPING A RUN OF REALLY BAD LUCK I'VE BEEN HAVING LATELY.
TURNS OUT, I ALSO FIND OUT I'M THE GAJILLIONTH VICTIM OF IDENTITY THEFT. SOMEONE STOLE MY ATM NUMBER, WIPED OUT MY SAVINGS.
WHICH IS SOMETHING OF A PROBLEM 'CAUSE THE BANK'S THREATENING TO FORECLOSE ON MY STUDENT LOANS.
AND I JUST LOST FIFTY BUCKS I DON'T HAVE TO POOL HUSTLER HARRY HERE.
IF IT'S ANY CONSOLATION, I'VE HAD IT BAD LATELY, TOO. THE HEALTH DEPARTMENT'S PRACTICALLY BEEN LIVING AT THE COFFEE BEAN.
I'VE HAD THREE MARGIN CALLS IN TWO WEEKS AND MY BUSINESS MANAGER HAD A STROKE.
YEAH MONEY BAGS, YOUR LIFE'S A REAL TRAGEDY.
I'M SORRY, VIN. I'M NOT SURE EVEN MY KARMA'S QUITE THIS BAD.
YEAH... WELL...
Y'KNOW WHAT? I JUST--I THINK I NEED SOME TIME TO MYSELF...
VIN--
LET HIM BE, PETE. GUY'S GOT A LOT ON HIS MIND.
YEAH... I KNOW HOW THAT FEELS...

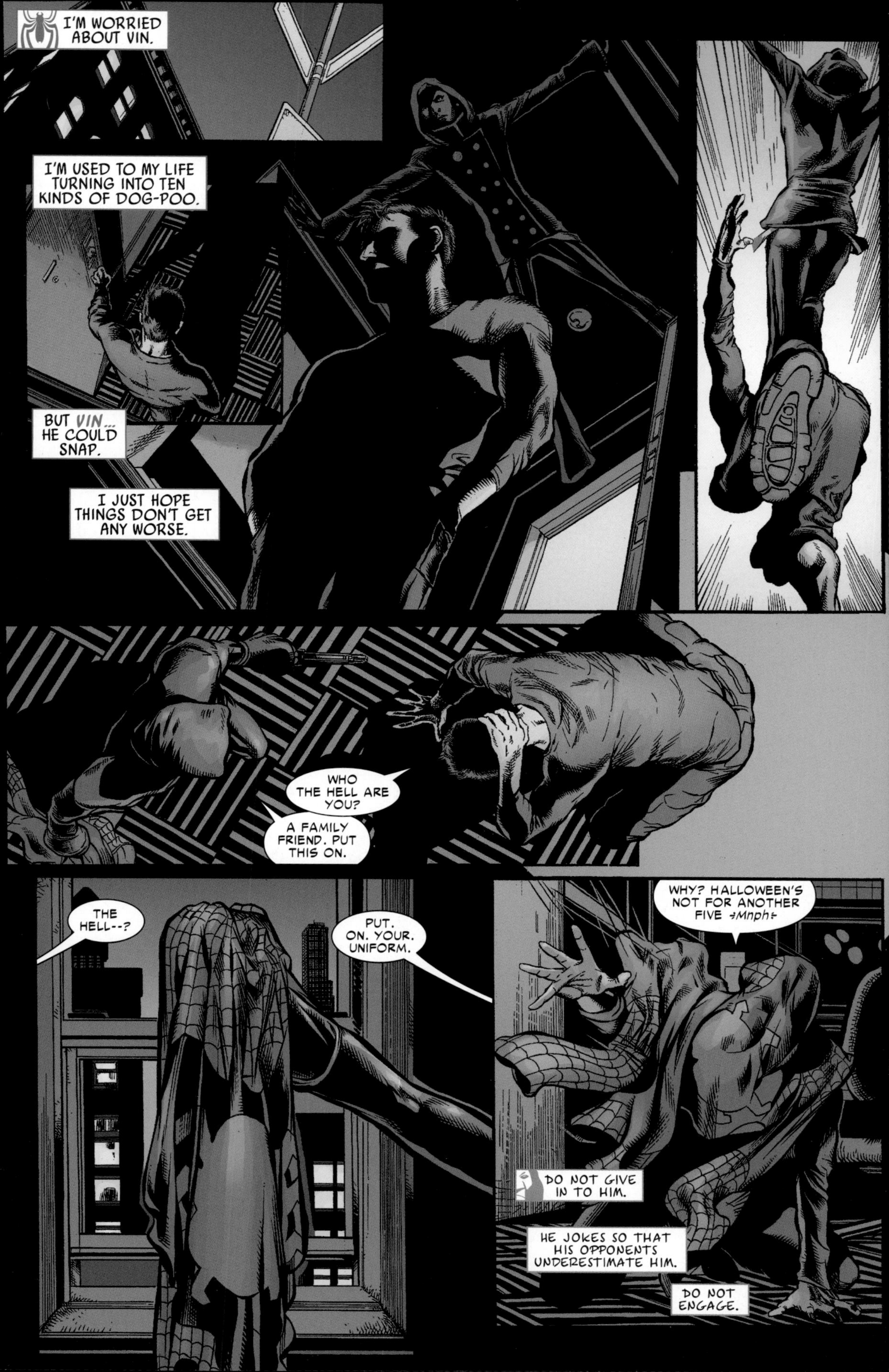
I'M WORRIED ABOUT VIN.
I'M USED TO MY LIFE TURNING INTO TEN KINDS OF DOG-POO.
BUT VIN... HE COULD SNAP.
I JUST HOPE THINGS DON'T GET ANY WORSE.
WHO THE HELL ARE YOU?
A FAMILY FRIEND. PUT THIS ON.
THE HELL--?
PUT. ON. YOUR. UNIFORM.
WHY? HALLOWEEN'S NOT FOR ANOTHER FIVE -Mnph-
DO NOT GIVE IN TO HIM.
HE JOKES SO THAT HIS OPPONENTS UNDERESTIMATE HIM.
DO NOT ENGAGE.

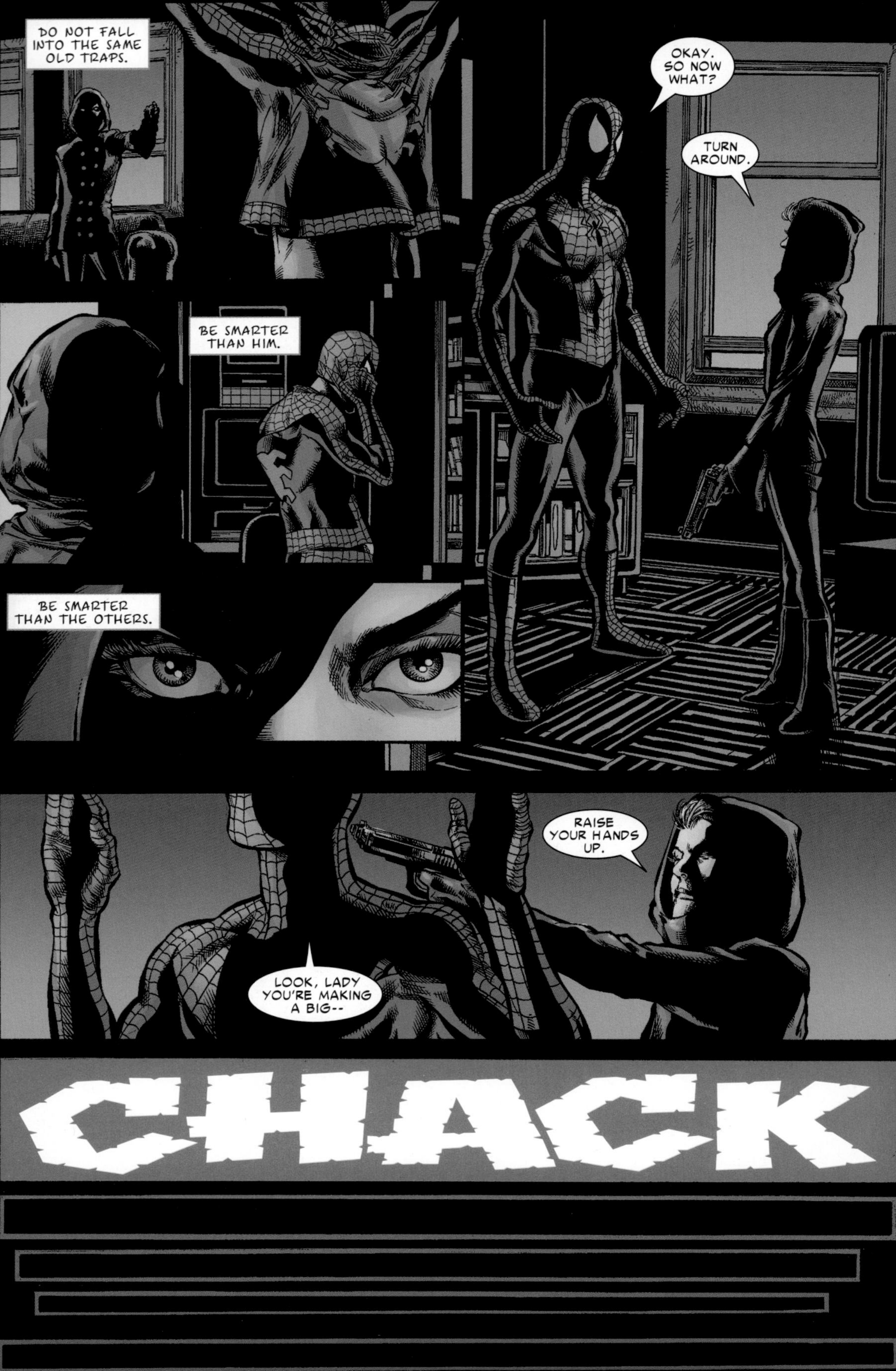

DO NOT FALL INTO THE SAME OLD TRAPS.
BE SMARTER THAN HIM.
BE SMARTER THAN THE OTHERS.
OKAY. SO NOW WHAT?
TURN AROUND.
RAISE YOUR HANDS UP.
LOOK, LADY YOU'RE MAKING A BIG--
CHACK

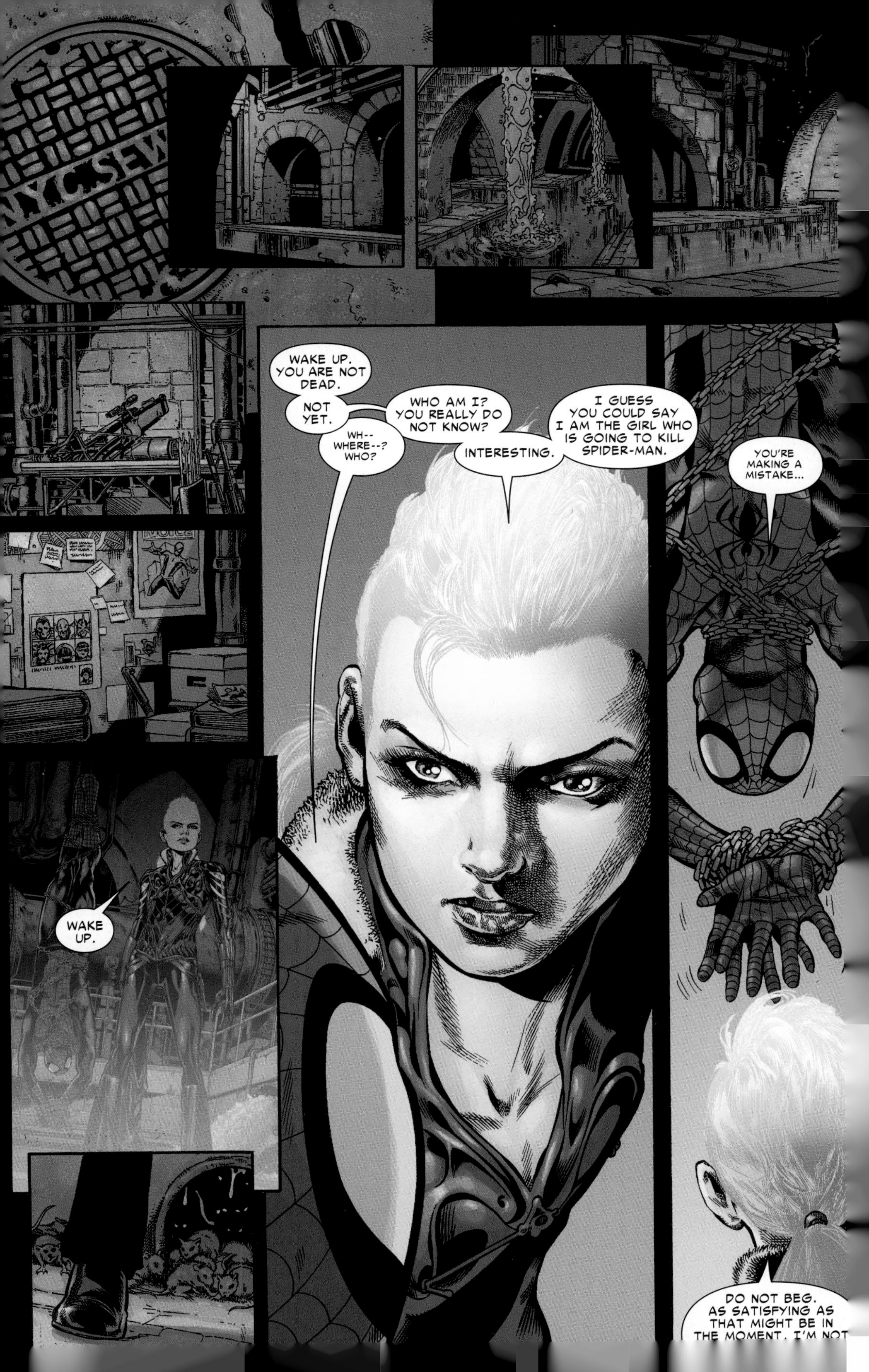
WAKE UP.
WAKE UP. YOU ARE NOT DEAD.
NOT YET.
WH-- WHERE--? WHO?
WHO AM I? YOU REALLY DO NOT KNOW?
INTERESTING.
I GUESS YOU COULD SAY I AM THE GIRL WHO IS GOING TO KILL SPIDER-MAN.
YOU'RE MAKING A MISTAKE...
DO NOT BEG. AS SATISFYING AS THAT MIGHT BE IN THE MOMENT, I'M NOT

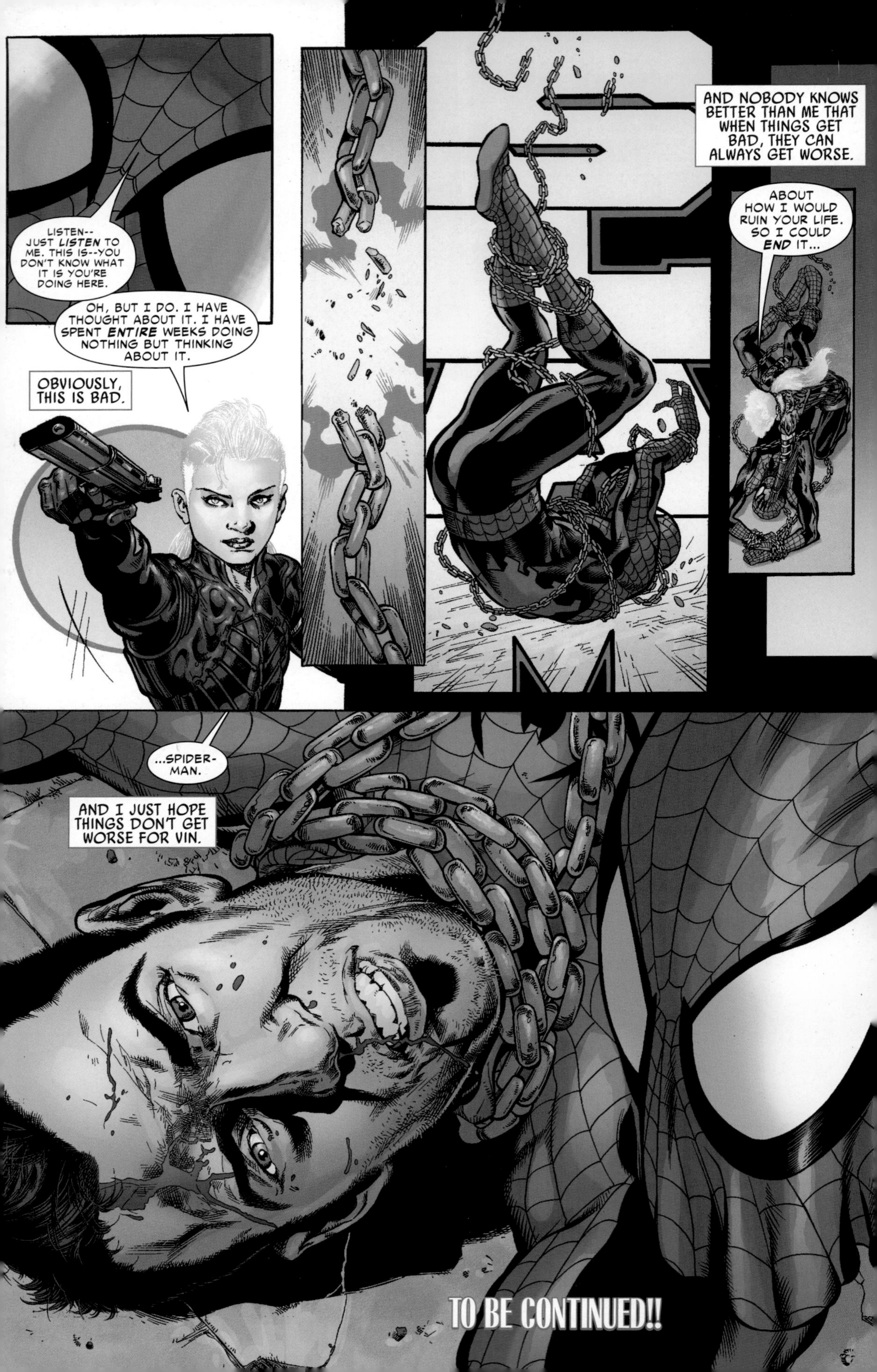
LISTEN-- JUST LISTEN TO ME. THIS IS--YOU DON'T KNOW WHAT IT IS YOU'RE DOING HERE.
OH, BUT I DO. I HAVE THOUGHT ABOUT IT. I HAVE SPENT ENTIRE WEEKS DOING NOTHING BUT THINKING ABOUT IT.
OBVIOUSLY, THIS IS BAD.
AND NOBODY KNOWS BETTER THAN ME THAT WHEN THINGS GET BAD, THEY CAN ALWAYS GET WORSE.
ABOUT HOW I WOULD RUIN YOUR LIFE. SO I COULD END IT...
...SPIDER-MAN.
AND I JUST HOPE THINGS DON'T GET WORSE FOR VIN.
TO BE CONTINUED!!

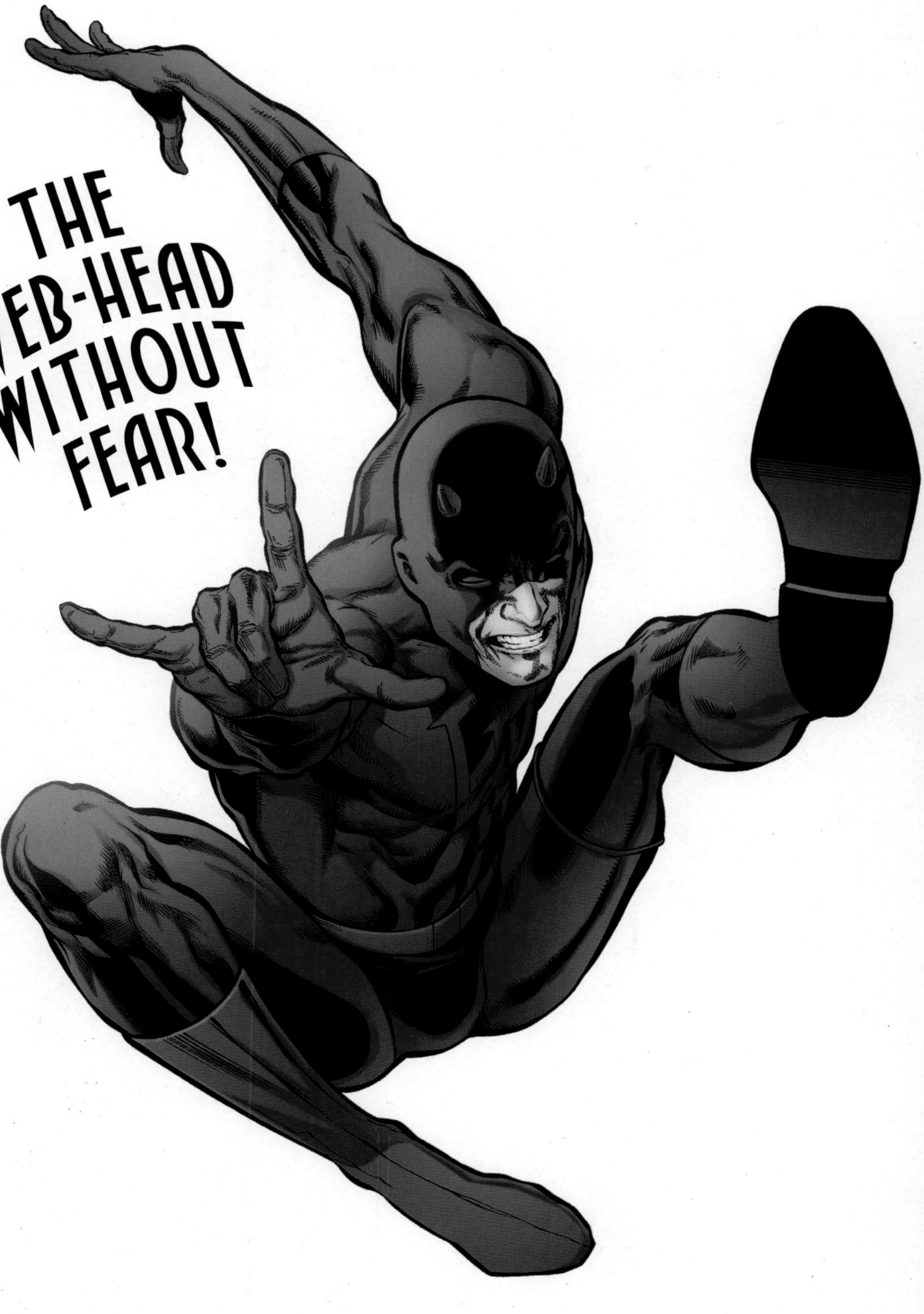
THE WEB-HEAD WITHOUT FEAR!

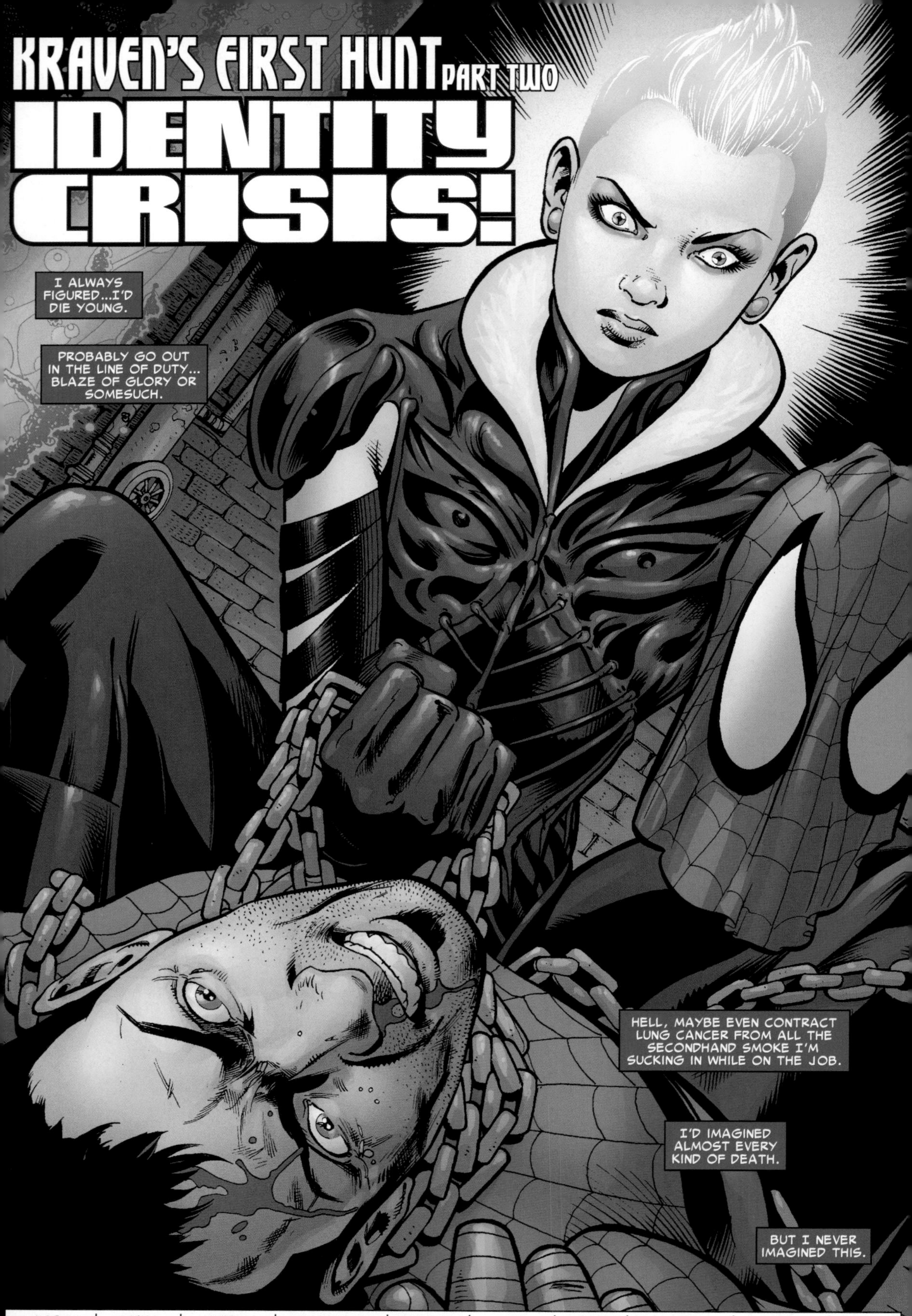
KRAVEN'S FIRST HUNT PART TWO
IDENTITY CRISIS!
I ALWAYS FIGURED...I'D DIE YOUNG.
PROBABLY GO OUT IN THE LINE OF DUTY... BLAZE OF GLORY OR SOMESUCH.
HELL, MAYBE EVEN CONTRACT LUNG CANCER FROM ALL THE SECONDHAND SMOKE I'M SUCKING IN WHILE ON THE JOB.
I'D IMAGINED ALMOST EVERY KIND OF DEATH.
BUT I NEVER IMAGINED THIS.

MARC GUGGENHEIM	PHIL JIMENEZ	MARK PENNINGTON	CHRIS CHUCKRY & JEROMY COX	VC'S CORY PETIT	TOM BRENNAN	STEPHEN WACKER	TOM BREVOORT	JOE QUESADA	DAN BUCKLEY
WRITER	BREAKDOWNS	FINISHES	COLORS	LETTERS	ASST. EDITOR	MELTZER	EXECUTIVE EDITOR	EDITOR IN CHIEF	PUBLISHER

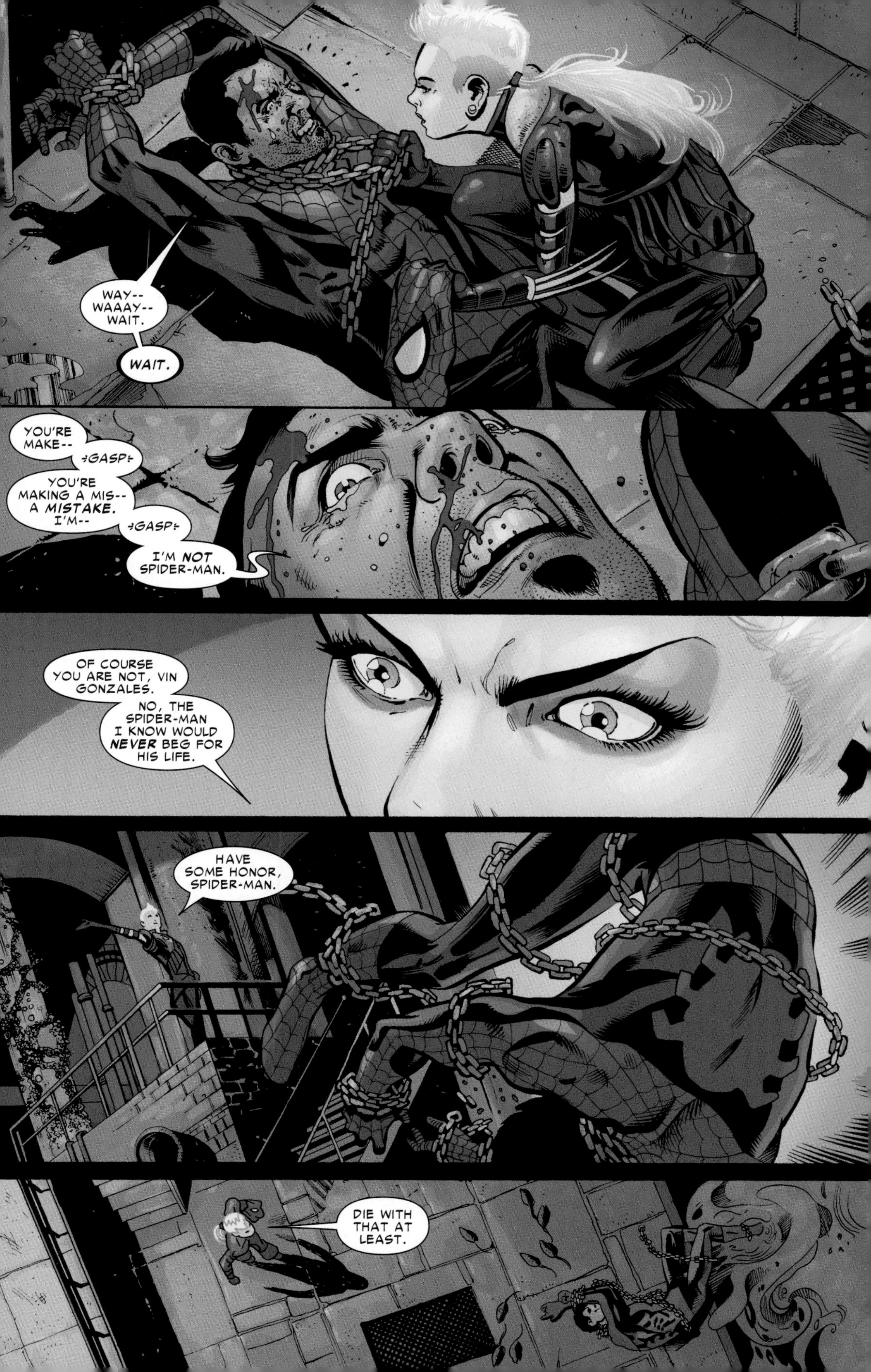
WAY-- WAAAY-- WAIT.
WAIT.
YOU'RE MAKE--
GASP
YOU'RE MAKING A MIS-- A MISTAKE. I'M--
GASP
I'M NOT SPIDER-MAN.
OF COURSE YOU ARE NOT, VIN GONZALES.
NO, THE SPIDER-MAN I KNOW WOULD NEVER BEG FOR HIS LIFE.
HAVE SOME HONOR, SPIDER-MAN.
DIE WITH THAT AT LEAST.

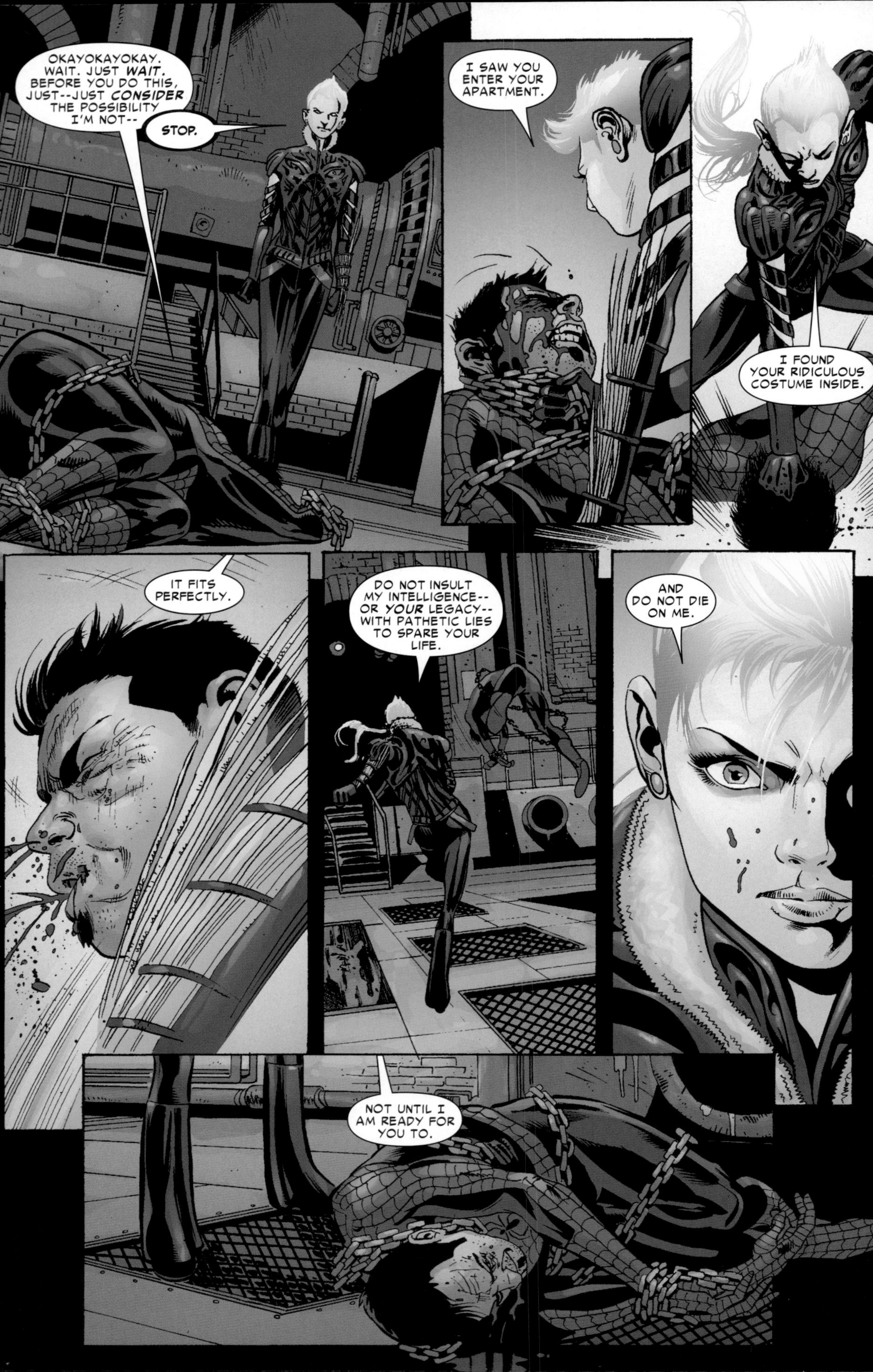

OKAYOKAYOKAY. WAIT. JUST WAIT. BEFORE YOU DO THIS, JUST--JUST CONSIDER THE POSSIBILITY I'M NOT--
STOP.
I SAW YOU ENTER YOUR APARTMENT.
I FOUND YOUR RIDICULOUS COSTUME INSIDE.
IT FITS PERFECTLY.
DO NOT INSULT MY INTELLIGENCE-- OR YOUR LEGACY-- WITH PATHETIC LIES TO SPARE YOUR LIFE.
AND DO NOT DIE ON ME.
NOT UNTIL I AM READY FOR YOU TO.

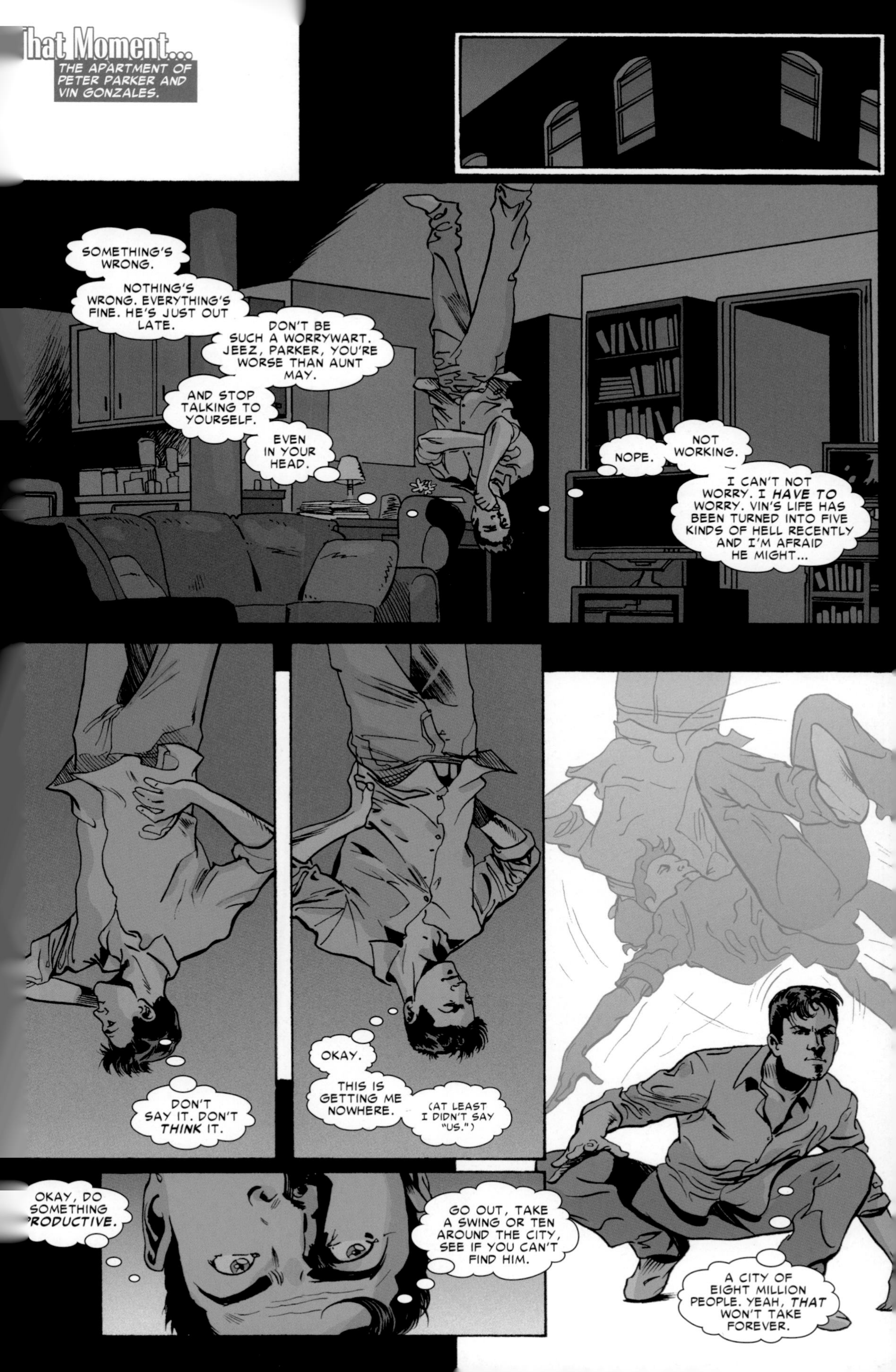

That Moment...
THE APARTMENT OF PETER PARKER AND VIN GONZALES.
SOMETHING'S WRONG.
NOTHING'S WRONG. EVERYTHING'S FINE. HE'S JUST OUT LATE.
DON'T BE SUCH A WORRYWART. JEEZ, PARKER, YOU'RE WORSE THAN AUNT MAY.
AND STOP TALKING TO YOURSELF.
EVEN IN YOUR HEAD.
NOPE.
NOT WORKING.
I CAN'T NOT WORRY. I *HAVE TO* WORRY. VIN'S LIFE HAS BEEN TURNED INTO FIVE KINDS OF HELL RECENTLY AND I'M AFRAID HE MIGHT...
DON'T SAY IT. DON'T *THINK* IT.
OKAY.
THIS IS GETTING ME NOWHERE.
(AT LEAST I DIDN'T SAY "US.")
OKAY, DO SOMETHING *PRODUCTIVE*.
GO OUT, TAKE A SWING OR TEN AROUND THE CITY, SEE IF YOU CAN'T FIND HIM.
A CITY OF EIGHT MILLION PEOPLE. YEAH, *THAT* WON'T TAKE FOREVER.

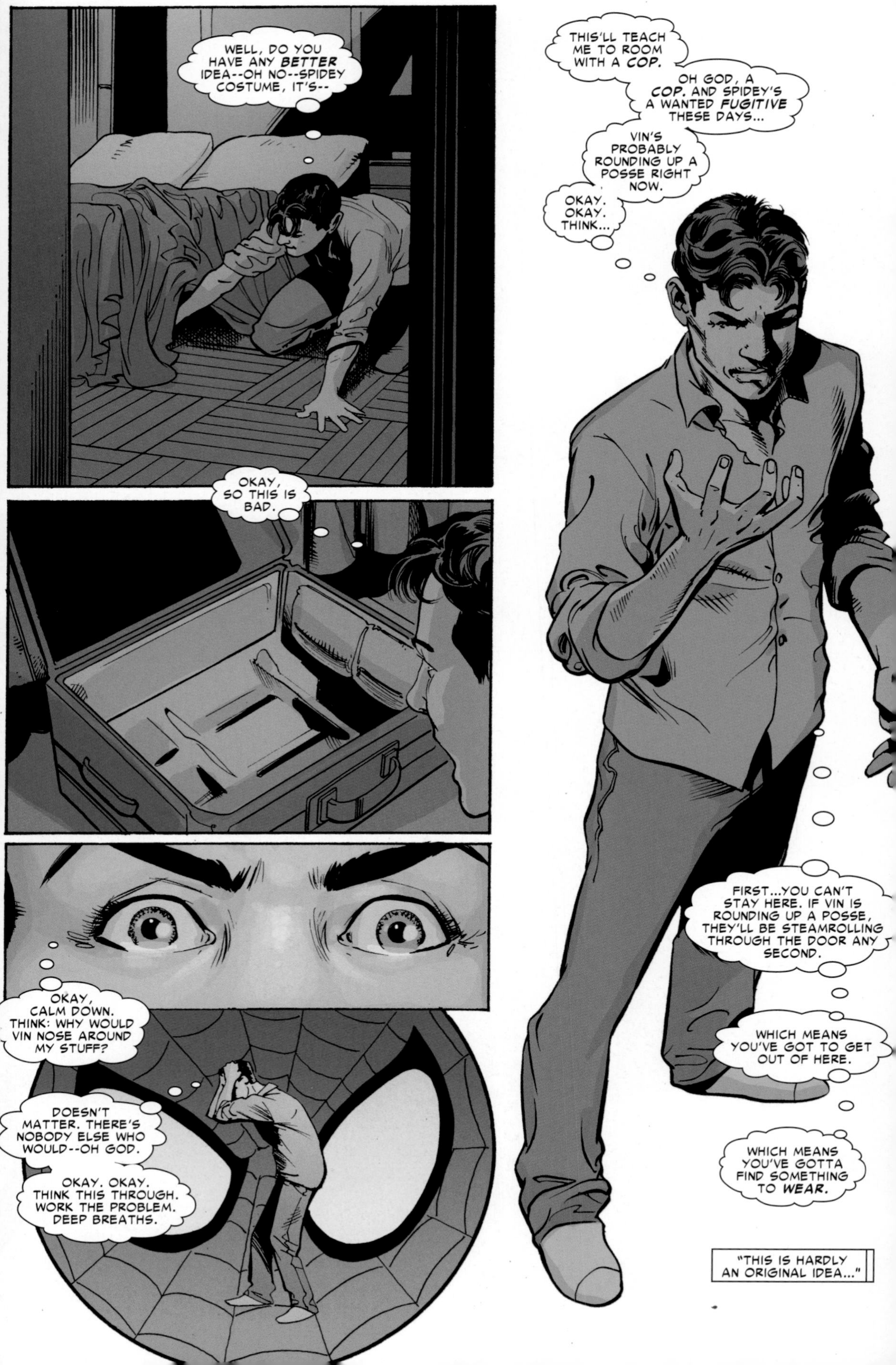
WELL, DO YOU HAVE ANY BETTER IDEA--OH NO--SPIDEY COSTUME, IT'S--
OKAY, SO THIS IS BAD.
OKAY, CALM DOWN. THINK: WHY WOULD VIN NOSE AROUND MY STUFF?
DOESN'T MATTER. THERE'S NOBODY ELSE WHO WOULD--OH GOD.
OKAY. OKAY. THINK THIS THROUGH. WORK THE PROBLEM. DEEP BREATHS.
THIS'LL TEACH ME TO ROOM WITH A COP.
OH GOD, A COP. AND SPIDEY'S A WANTED FUGITIVE THESE DAYS...
VIN'S PROBABLY ROUNDING UP A POSSE RIGHT NOW.
OKAY. OKAY. THINK...
FIRST...YOU CAN'T STAY HERE. IF VIN IS ROUNDING UP A POSSE, THEY'LL BE STEAMROLLING THROUGH THE DOOR ANY SECOND.
WHICH MEANS YOU'VE GOT TO GET OUT OF HERE.
WHICH MEANS YOU'VE GOTTA FIND SOMETHING TO WEAR.
"THIS IS HARDLY AN ORIGINAL IDEA..."

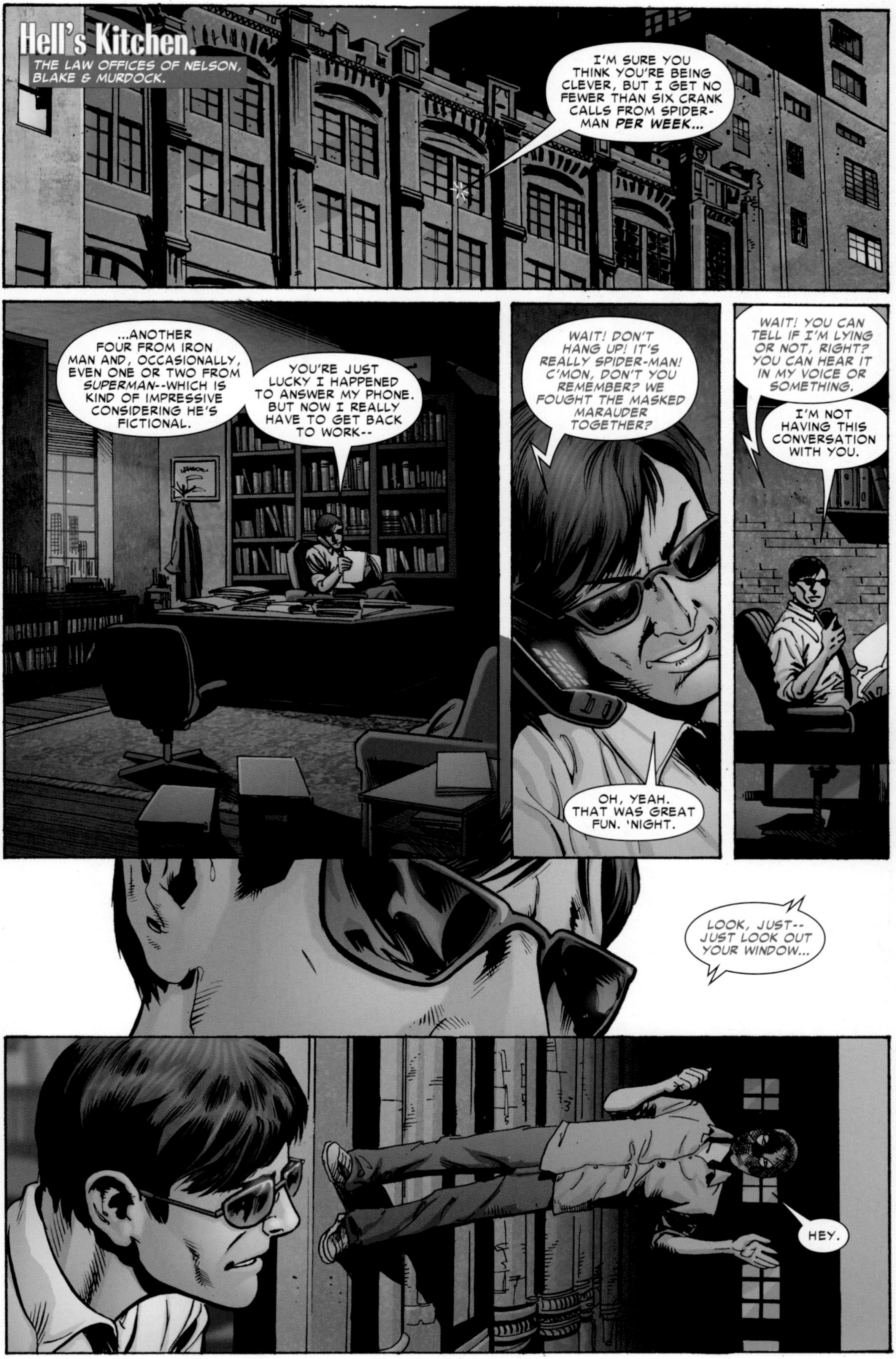
Hell's Kitchen.
THE LAW OFFICES OF NELSON, BLAKE & MURDOCK.
I'M SURE YOU THINK YOU'RE BEING CLEVER, BUT I GET NO FEWER THAN SIX CRANK CALLS FROM SPIDER-MAN PER WEEK...
...ANOTHER FOUR FROM IRON MAN AND, OCCASIONALLY, EVEN ONE OR TWO FROM SUPERMAN--WHICH IS KIND OF IMPRESSIVE CONSIDERING HE'S FICTIONAL.
YOU'RE JUST LUCKY I HAPPENED TO ANSWER MY PHONE. BUT NOW I REALLY HAVE TO GET BACK TO WORK--
WAIT! DON'T HANG UP! IT'S REALLY SPIDER-MAN! C'MON, DON'T YOU REMEMBER? WE FOUGHT THE MASKED MARAUDER TOGETHER?
OH, YEAH. THAT WAS GREAT FUN. 'NIGHT.
WAIT! YOU CAN TELL IF I'M LYING OR NOT, RIGHT? YOU CAN HEAR IT IN MY VOICE OR SOMETHING.
I'M NOT HAVING THIS CONVERSATION WITH YOU.
LOOK, JUST-- JUST LOOK OUT YOUR WINDOW...
HEY.

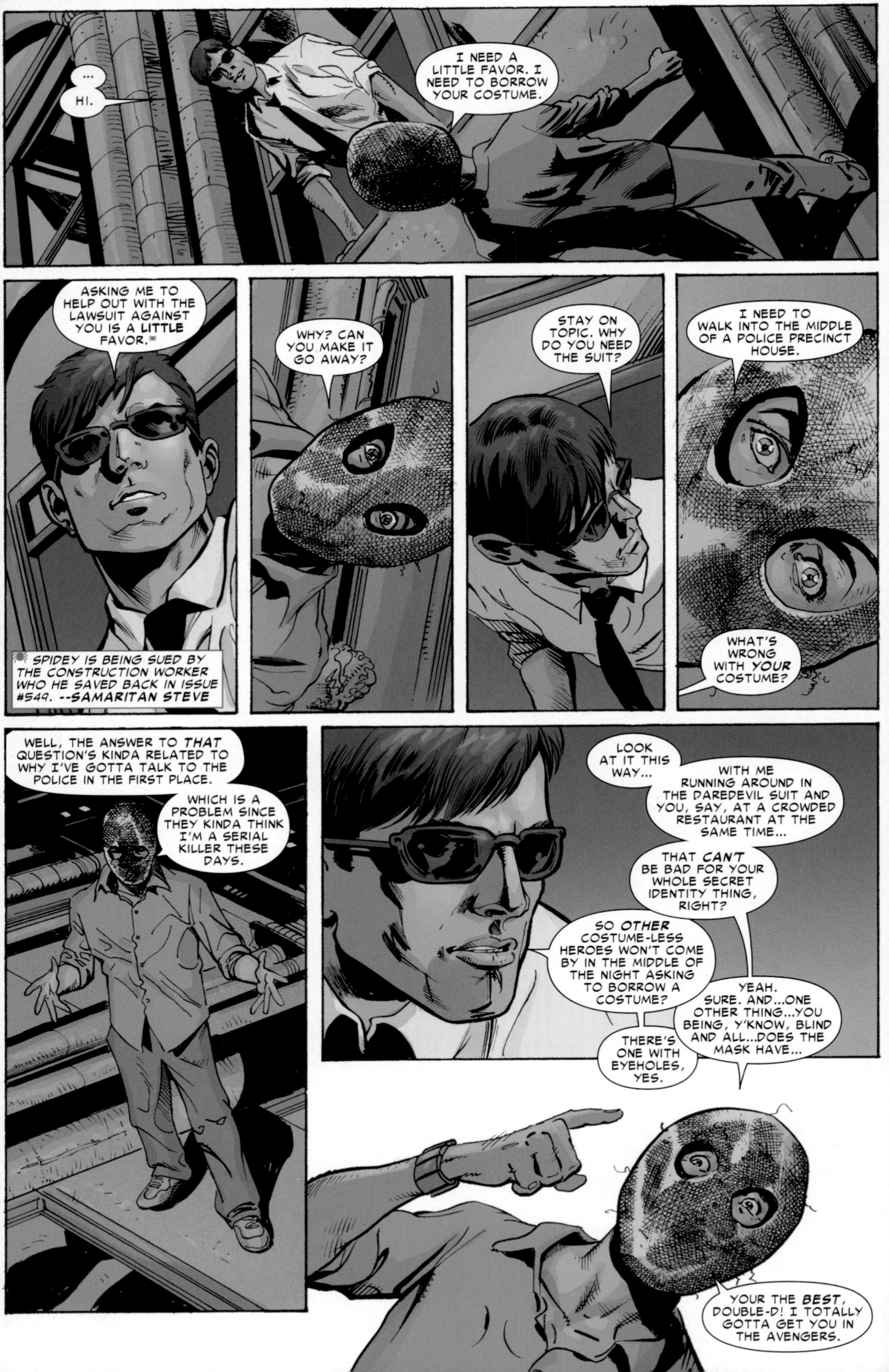
...
HI.
I NEED A LITTLE FAVOR. I NEED TO BORROW YOUR COSTUME.
ASKING ME TO HELP OUT WITH THE LAWSUIT AGAINST YOU IS A LITTLE FAVOR.*
*SPIDEY IS BEING SUED BY THE CONSTRUCTION WORKER WHO HE SAVED BACK IN ISSUE #549. --SAMARITAN STEVE
WHY? CAN YOU MAKE IT GO AWAY?
STAY ON TOPIC. WHY DO YOU NEED THE SUIT?
I NEED TO WALK INTO THE MIDDLE OF A POLICE PRECINCT HOUSE.
WHAT'S WRONG WITH YOUR COSTUME?
WELL, THE ANSWER TO THAT QUESTION'S KINDA RELATED TO WHY I'VE GOTTA TALK TO THE POLICE IN THE FIRST PLACE.
WHICH IS A PROBLEM SINCE THEY KINDA THINK I'M A SERIAL KILLER THESE DAYS.
LOOK AT IT THIS WAY...
WITH ME RUNNING AROUND IN THE DAREDEVIL SUIT AND YOU, SAY, AT A CROWDED RESTAURANT AT THE SAME TIME...
THAT CAN'T BE BAD FOR YOUR WHOLE SECRET IDENTITY THING, RIGHT?
SO OTHER COSTUME-LESS HEROES WON'T COME BY IN THE MIDDLE OF THE NIGHT ASKING TO BORROW A COSTUME?
YEAH. SURE. AND...ONE OTHER THING...YOU BEING, Y'KNOW, BLIND AND ALL...DOES THE MASK HAVE...
THERE'S ONE WITH EYEHOLES, YES.
YOUR THE BEST, DOUBLE-D! I TOTALLY GOTTA GET YOU IN THE AVENGERS.

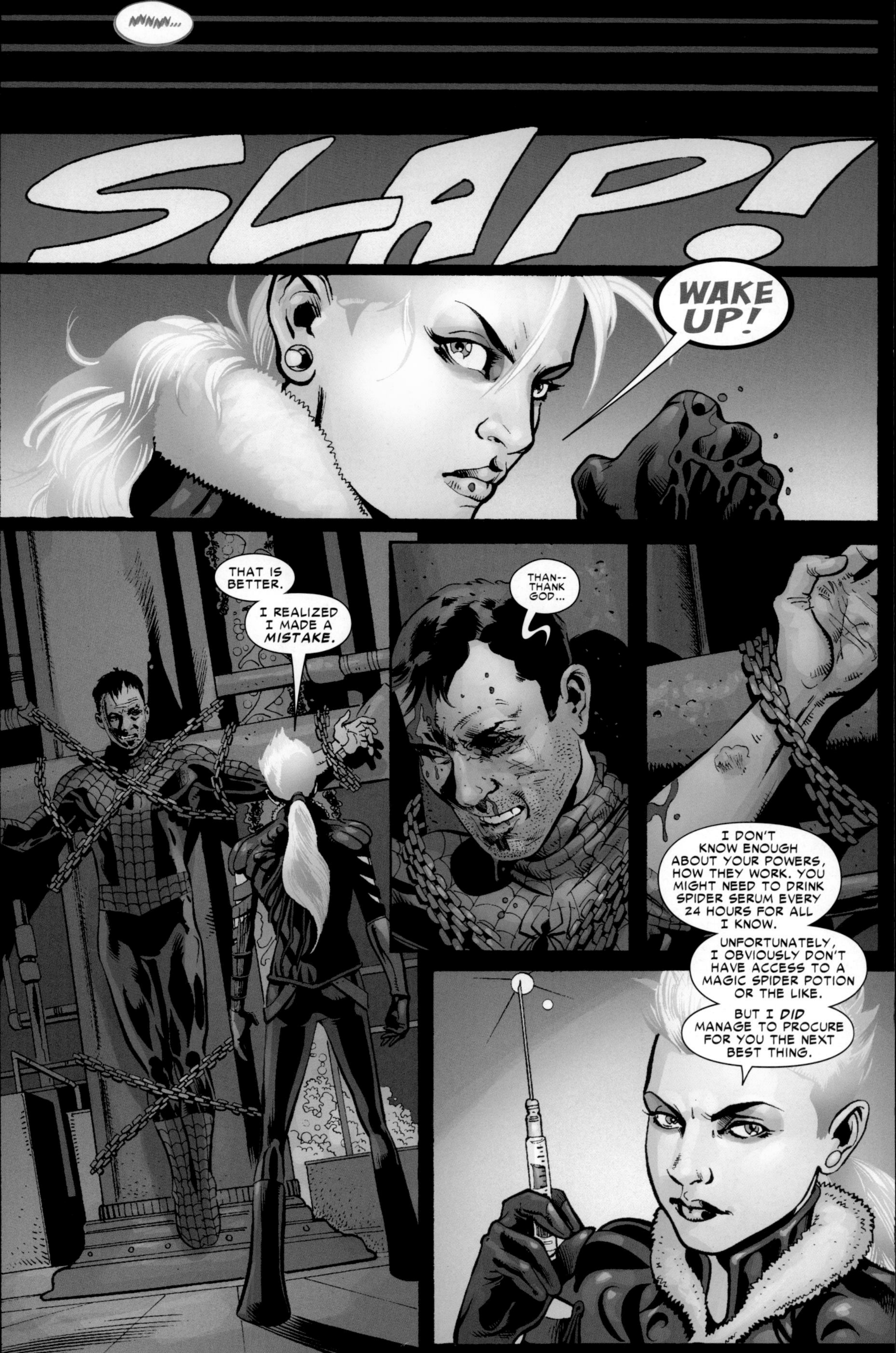
NNNNN...
SLAP!
WAKE UP!
THAT IS BETTER.
I REALIZED I MADE A MISTAKE.
THAN-- THANK GOD...
I DON'T KNOW ENOUGH ABOUT YOUR POWERS, HOW THEY WORK. YOU MIGHT NEED TO DRINK SPIDER SERUM EVERY 24 HOURS FOR ALL I KNOW.
UNFORTUNATELY, I OBVIOUSLY DON'T HAVE ACCESS TO A MAGIC SPIDER POTION OR THE LIKE.
BUT I DID MANAGE TO PROCURE FOR YOU THE NEXT BEST THING.

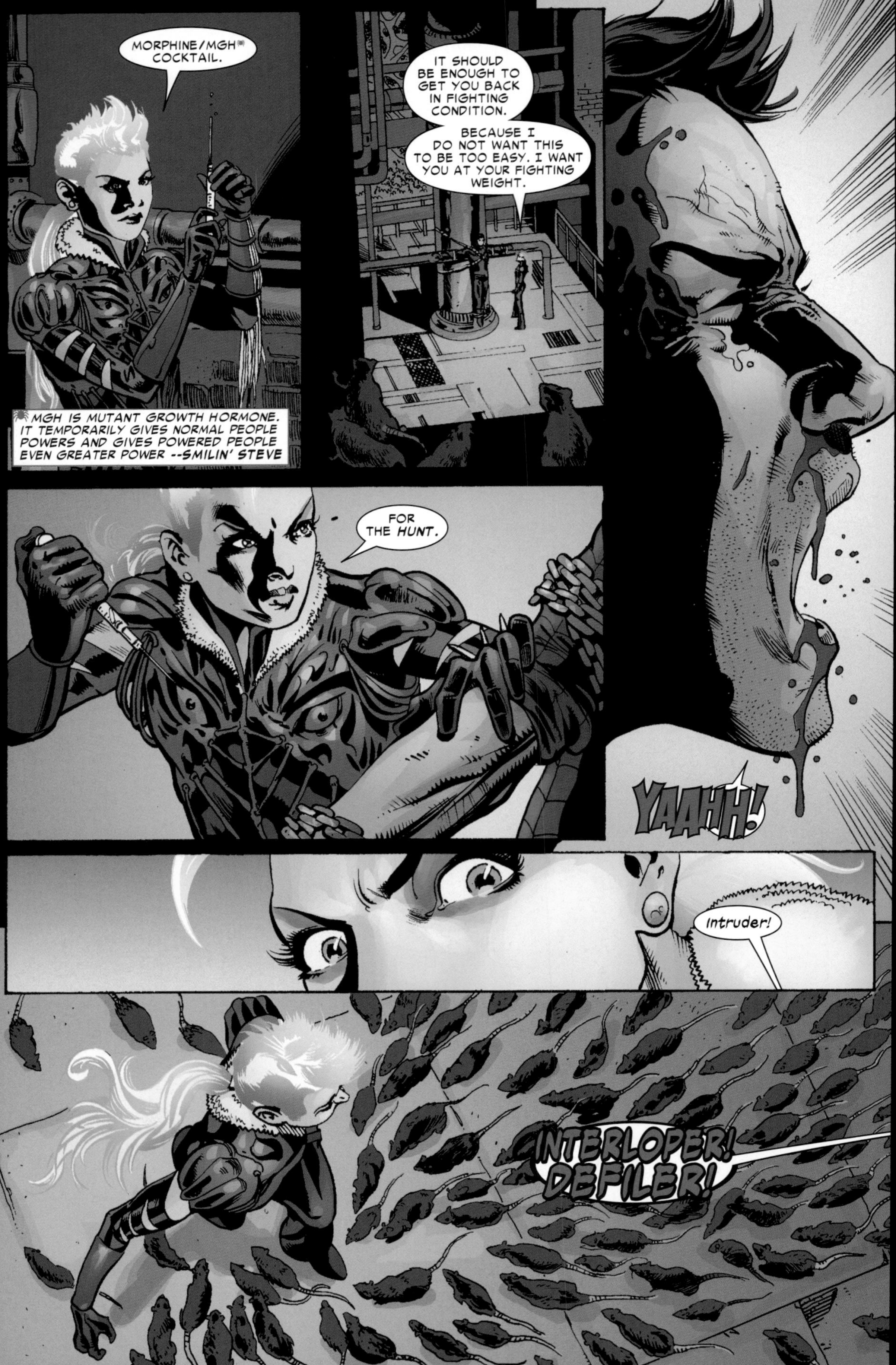

MORPHINE/MGH* COCKTAIL.
*MGH IS MUTANT GROWTH HORMONE. IT TEMPORARILY GIVES NORMAL PEOPLE POWERS AND GIVES POWERED PEOPLE EVEN GREATER POWER --SMILIN' STEVE
IT SHOULD BE ENOUGH TO GET YOU BACK IN FIGHTING CONDITION.
BECAUSE I DO NOT WANT THIS TO BE TOO EASY. I WANT YOU AT YOUR FIGHTING WEIGHT.
FOR THE HUNT.
YAAHH!
Intruder!
INTERLOPER! DEFILER!

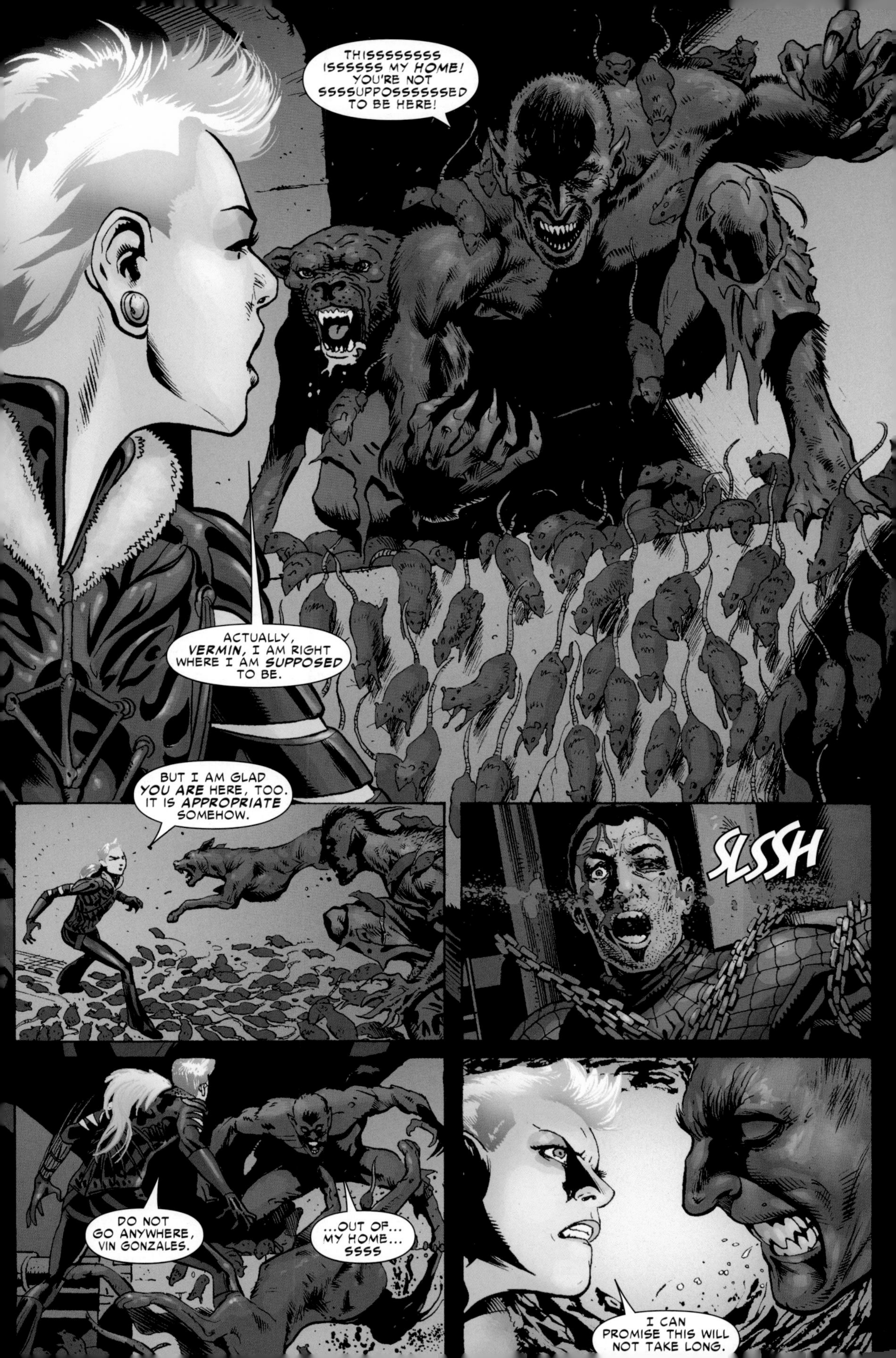
THISSSSSSSS ISSSSSS MY HOME! YOU'RE NOT SSSSUPPOSSSSSSSED TO BE HERE!
ACTUALLY, VERMIN, I AM RIGHT WHERE I AM SUPPOSED TO BE.
BUT I AM GLAD YOU ARE HERE, TOO. IT IS APPROPRIATE SOMEHOW.
SLSSH
DO NOT GO ANYWHERE, VIN GONZALES.
...OUT OF... MY HOME... SSSS
I CAN PROMISE THIS WILL NOT TAKE LONG.

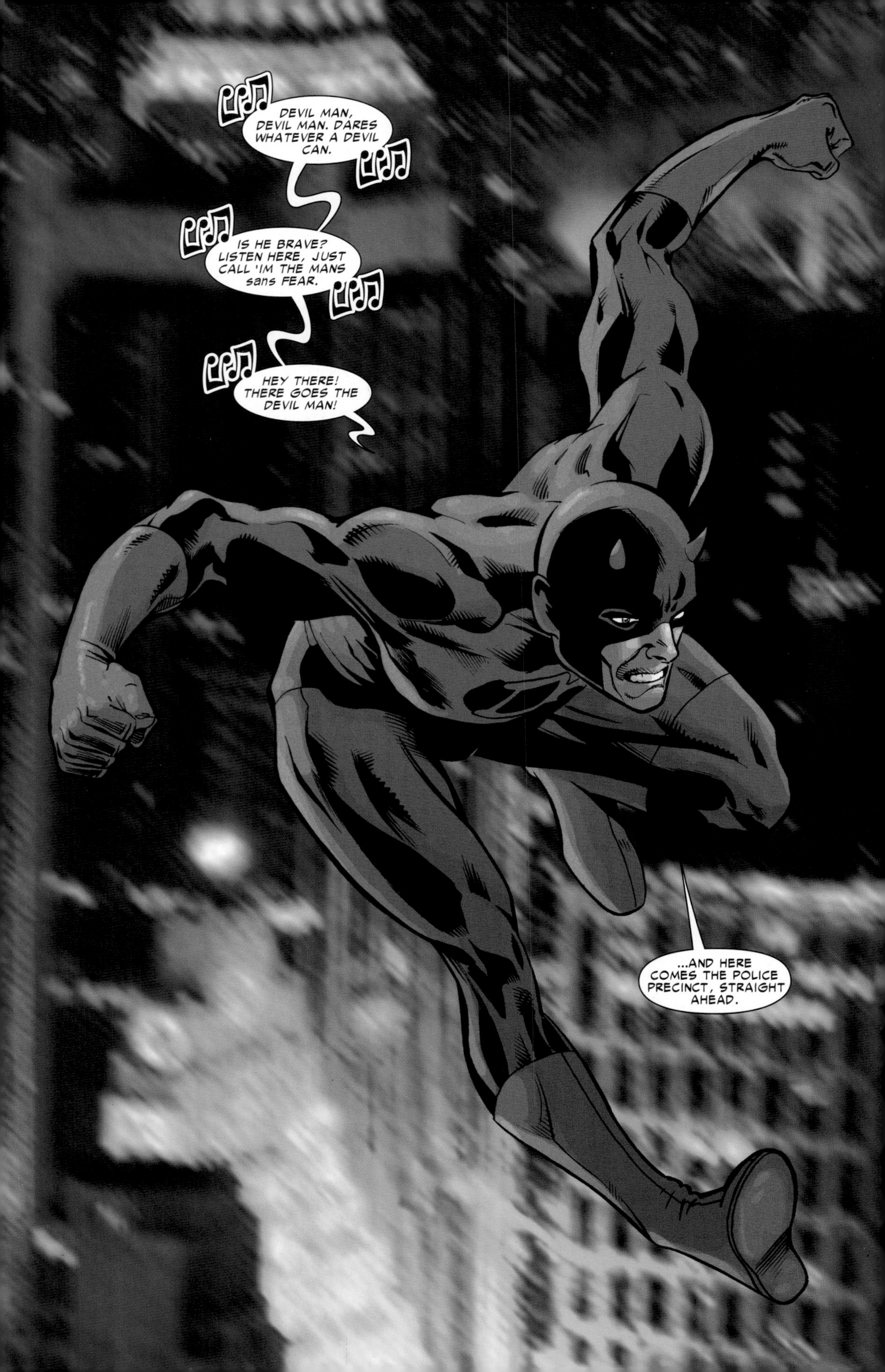
DEVIL MAN, DEVIL MAN. DARES WHATEVER A DEVIL CAN.
IS HE BRAVE? LISTEN HERE, JUST CALL 'IM THE MANS sans FEAR.
HEY THERE! THERE GOES THE DEVIL MAN!
...AND HERE COMES THE POLICE PRECINCT, STRAIGHT AHEAD.

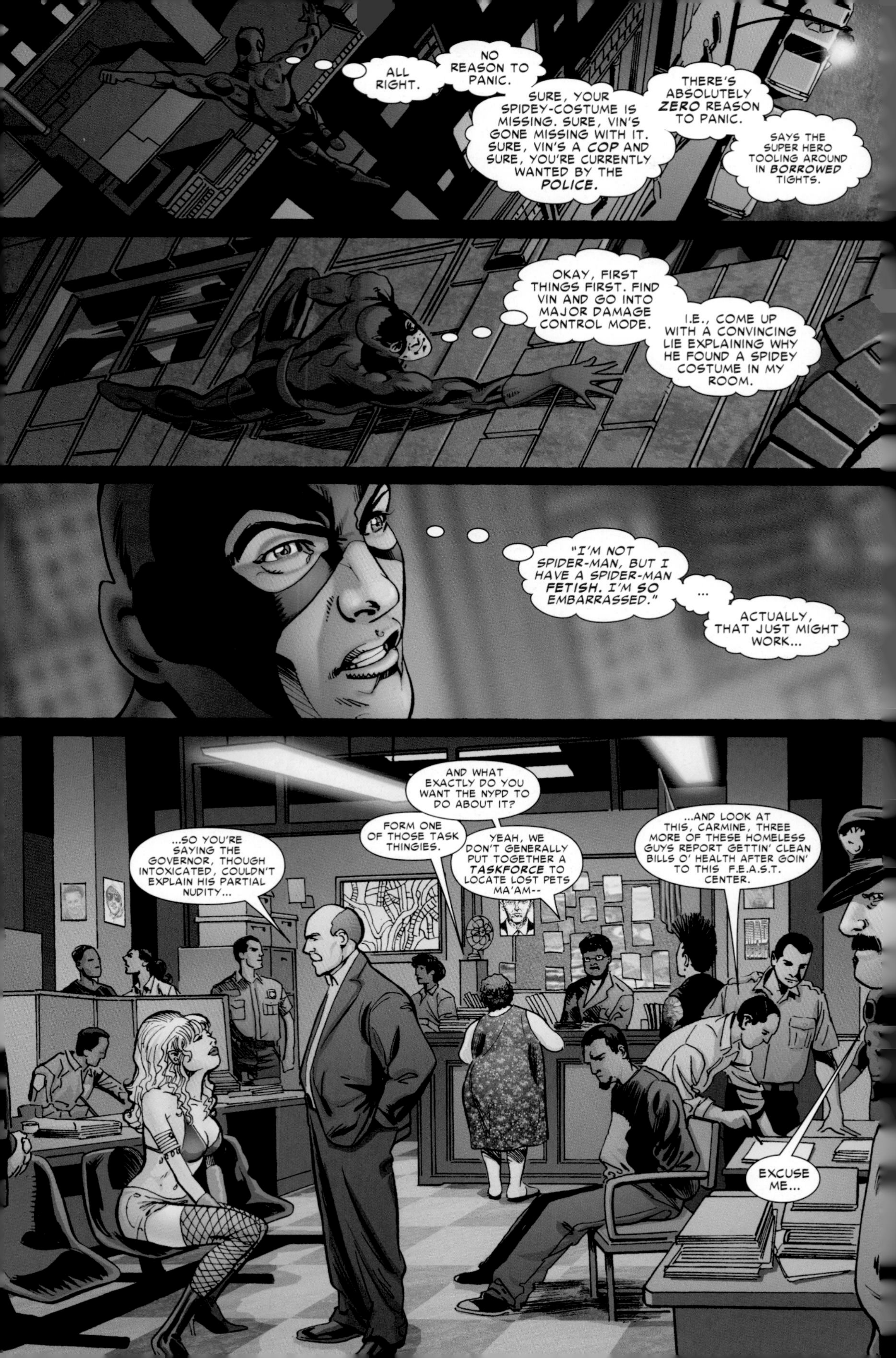
ALL RIGHT.
NO REASON TO PANIC.
SURE, YOUR SPIDEY-COSTUME IS MISSING. SURE, VIN'S GONE MISSING WITH IT. SURE, VIN'S A COP AND SURE, YOU'RE CURRENTLY WANTED BY THE POLICE.
THERE'S ABSOLUTELY ZERO REASON TO PANIC.
SAYS THE SUPER HERO TOOLING AROUND IN BORROWED TIGHTS.
OKAY, FIRST THINGS FIRST. FIND VIN AND GO INTO MAJOR DAMAGE CONTROL MODE.
I.E., COME UP WITH A CONVINCING LIE EXPLAINING WHY HE FOUND A SPIDEY COSTUME IN MY ROOM.
"I'M NOT SPIDER-MAN, BUT I HAVE A SPIDER-MAN FETISH. I'M SO EMBARRASSED."
...
ACTUALLY, THAT JUST MIGHT WORK...
...SO YOU'RE SAYING THE GOVERNOR, THOUGH INTOXICATED, COULDN'T EXPLAIN HIS PARTIAL NUDITY...
AND WHAT EXACTLY DO YOU WANT THE NYPD TO DO ABOUT IT?
FORM ONE OF THOSE TASK THINGIES.
YEAH, WE DON'T GENERALLY PUT TOGETHER A TASKFORCE TO LOCATE LOST PETS MA'AM--
...AND LOOK AT THIS, CARMINE, THREE MORE OF THESE HOMELESS GUYS REPORT GETTIN' CLEAN BILLS O' HEALTH AFTER GOIN' TO THIS F.E.A.S.T. CENTER.
EXCUSE ME...

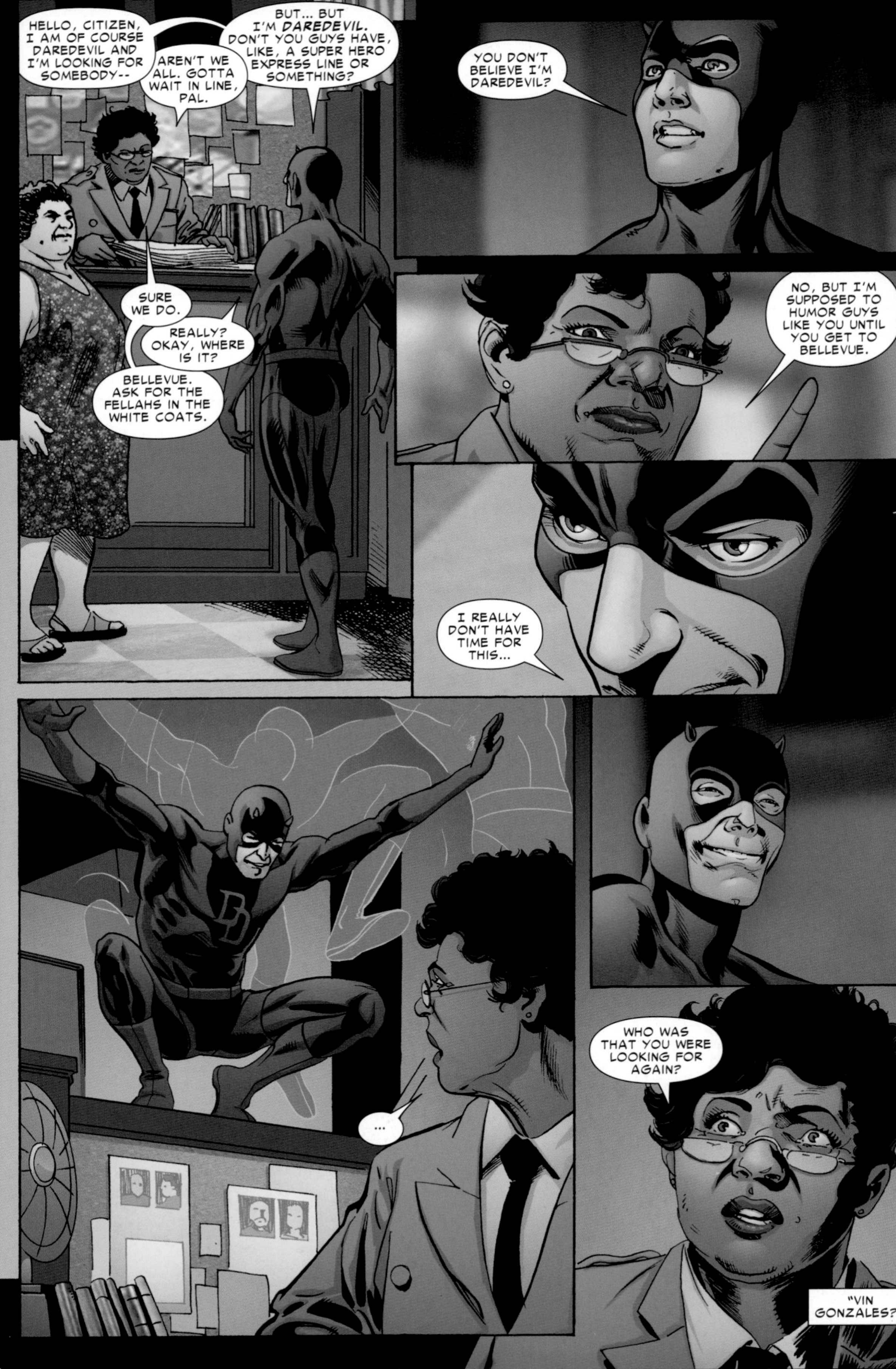
HELLO, CITIZEN, I AM OF COURSE DAREDEVIL AND I'M LOOKING FOR SOMEBODY--
AREN'T WE ALL. GOTTA WAIT IN LINE, PAL.
BUT... BUT I'M DAREDEVIL. DON'T YOU GUYS HAVE, LIKE, A SUPER HERO EXPRESS LINE OR SOMETHING?
SURE WE DO.
REALLY? OKAY, WHERE IS IT?
BELLEVUE. ASK FOR THE FELLAHS IN THE WHITE COATS.
YOU DON'T BELIEVE I'M DAREDEVIL?
NO, BUT I'M SUPPOSED TO HUMOR GUYS LIKE YOU UNTIL YOU GET TO BELLEVUE.
I REALLY DON'T HAVE TIME FOR THIS...
...
WHO WAS THAT YOU WERE LOOKING FOR AGAIN?
"VIN GONZALES?"

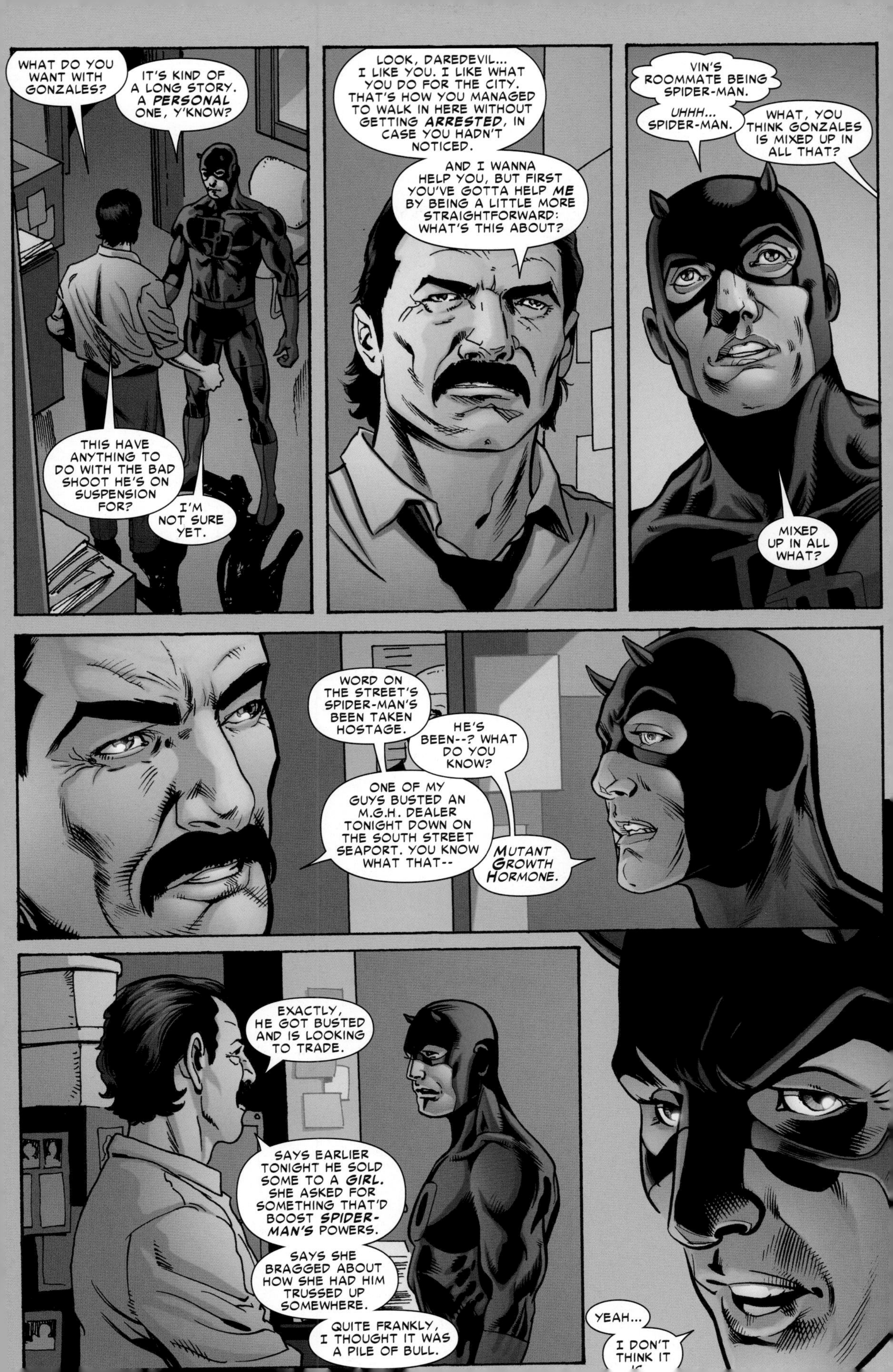

WHAT DO YOU WANT WITH GONZALES?
IT'S KIND OF A LONG STORY. A *PERSONAL* ONE, Y'KNOW?
THIS HAVE ANYTHING TO DO WITH THE BAD SHOOT HE'S ON SUSPENSION FOR?
I'M NOT SURE YET.
LOOK, DAREDEVIL... I LIKE YOU. I LIKE WHAT YOU DO FOR THE CITY. THAT'S HOW YOU MANAGED TO WALK IN HERE WITHOUT GETTING *ARRESTED*, IN CASE YOU HADN'T NOTICED.
AND I WANNA HELP YOU, BUT FIRST YOU'VE GOTTA HELP *ME* BY BEING A LITTLE MORE STRAIGHTFORWARD: WHAT'S THIS ABOUT?
VIN'S ROOMMATE BEING SPIDER-MAN.
UHHH... SPIDER-MAN.
WHAT, YOU THINK GONZALES IS MIXED UP IN ALL THAT?
MIXED UP IN ALL WHAT?
WORD ON THE STREET'S SPIDER-MAN'S BEEN TAKEN HOSTAGE.
HE'S BEEN--? WHAT DO YOU KNOW?
ONE OF MY GUYS BUSTED AN M.G.H. DEALER TONIGHT DOWN ON THE SOUTH STREET SEAPORT. YOU KNOW WHAT THAT--
MUTANT GROWTH HORMONE.
EXACTLY, HE GOT BUSTED AND IS LOOKING TO TRADE.
SAYS EARLIER TONIGHT HE SOLD SOME TO A *GIRL.* SHE ASKED FOR SOMETHING THAT'D BOOST *SPIDER-MAN'S* POWERS.
SAYS SHE BRAGGED ABOUT HOW SHE HAD HIM TRUSSED UP SOMEWHERE.
QUITE FRANKLY, I THOUGHT IT WAS A PILE OF BULL.
YEAH...
I DON'T THINK IT

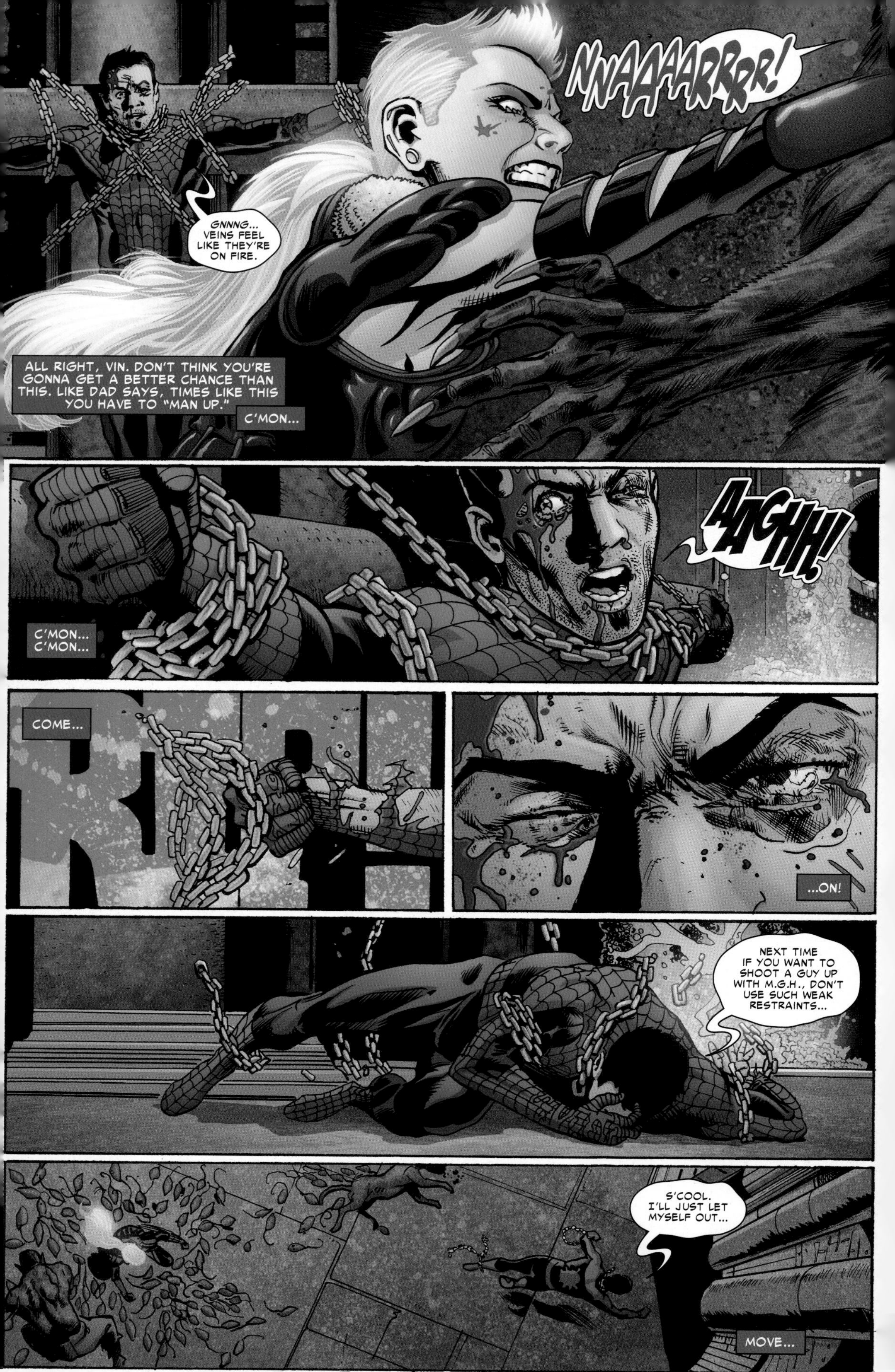
NNAAAARRRR!
GNNNG... VEINS FEEL LIKE THEY'RE ON FIRE.
ALL RIGHT, VIN. DON'T THINK YOU'RE GONNA GET A BETTER CHANCE THAN THIS. LIKE DAD SAYS, TIMES LIKE THIS YOU HAVE TO "MAN UP."
C'MON...
AAGHH!
C'MON... C'MON...
COME...
...ON!
NEXT TIME IF YOU WANT TO SHOOT A GUY UP WITH M.G.H., DON'T USE SUCH WEAK RESTRAINTS...
S'COOL. I'LL JUST LET MYSELF OUT...
MOVE...

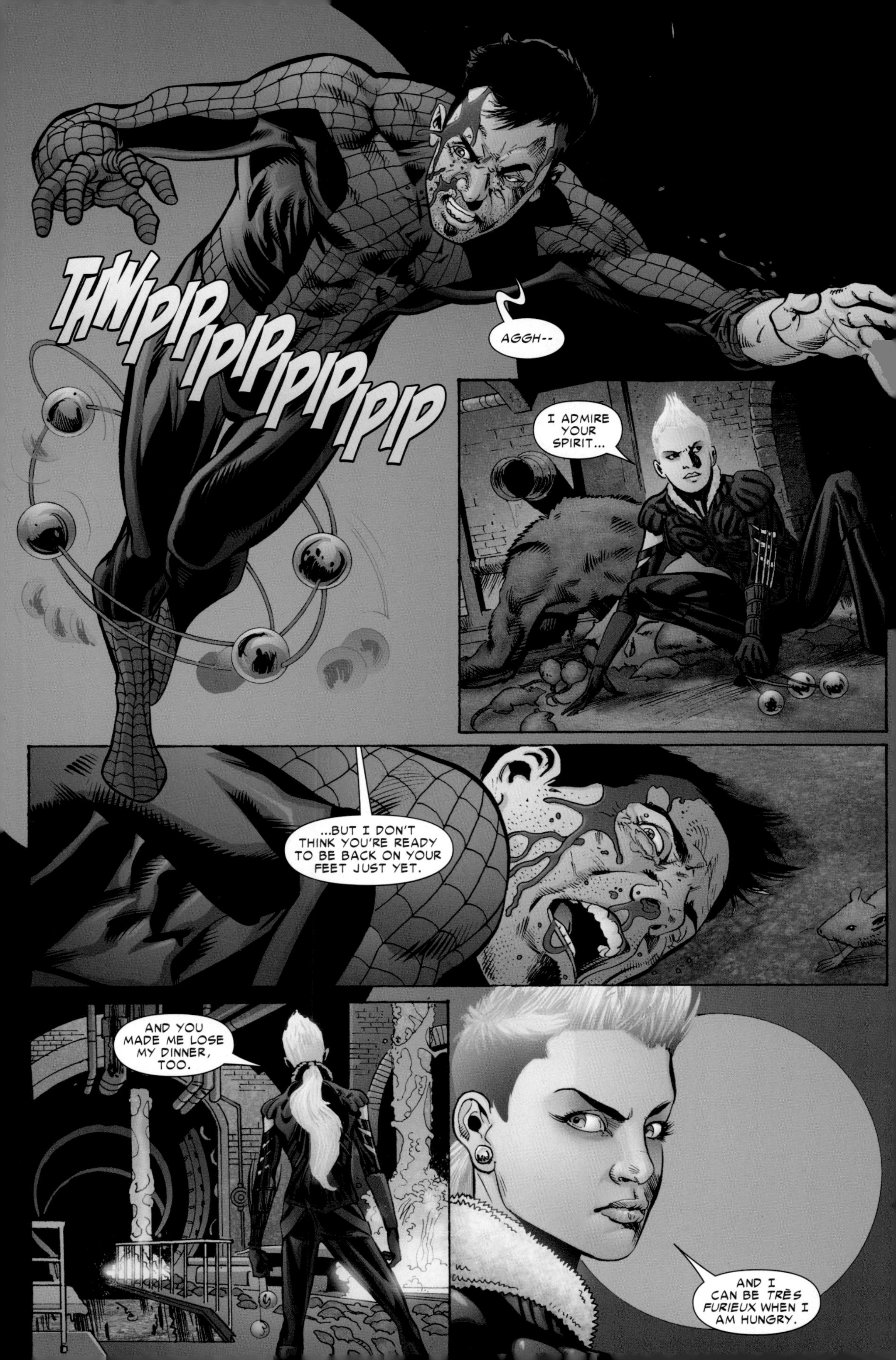
THWIPIPIPIPIPIPIPIPIP
AGGH--
I ADMIRE YOUR SPIRIT...
...BUT I DON'T THINK YOU'RE READY TO BE BACK ON YOUR FEET JUST YET.
AND YOU MADE ME LOSE MY DINNER, TOO.
AND I CAN BE *TRÈS FURIEUX* WHEN I AM HUNGRY.

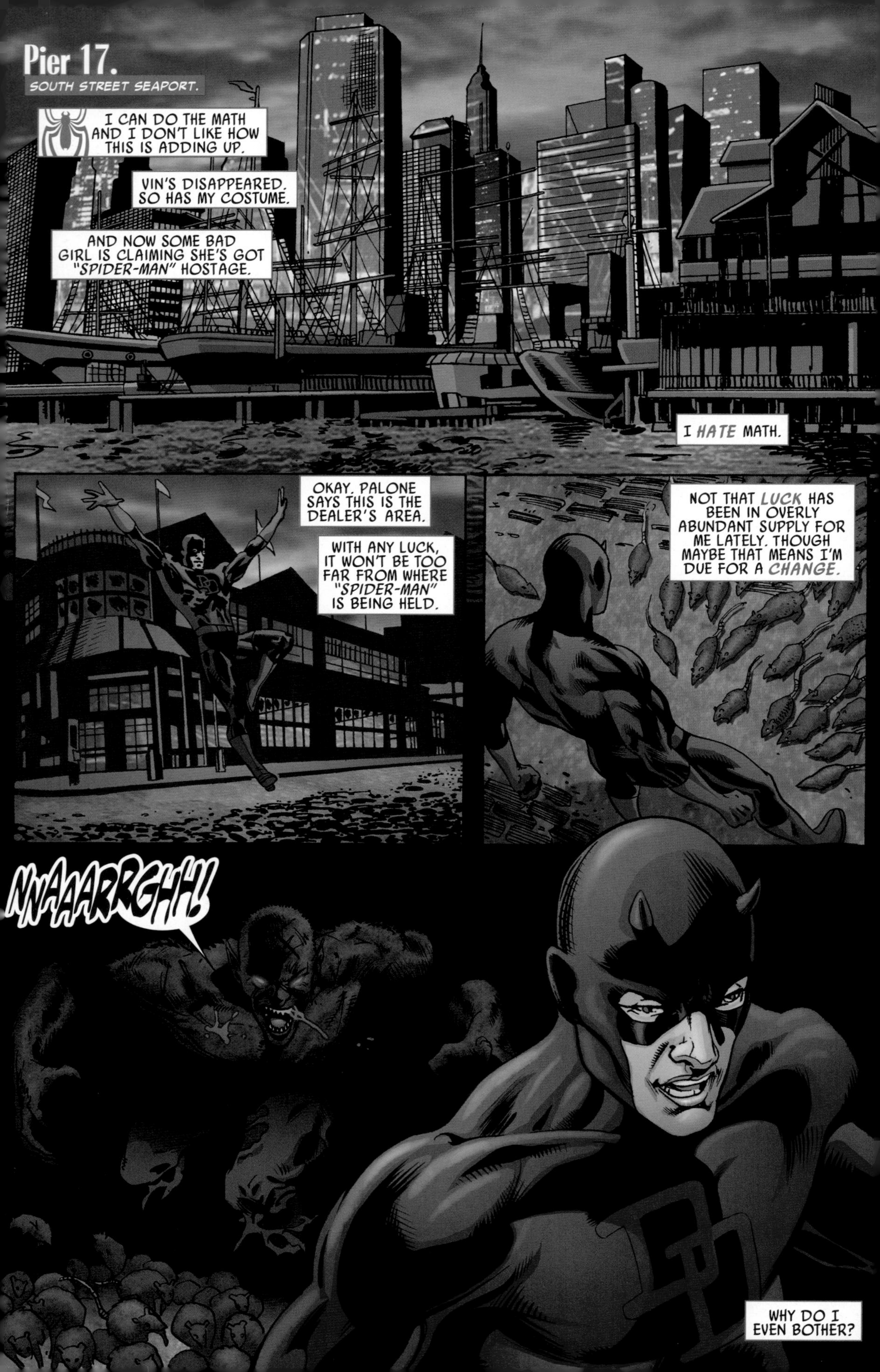
Pier 17.
SOUTH STREET SEAPORT.
I CAN DO THE MATH AND I DON'T LIKE HOW THIS IS ADDING UP.
VIN'S DISAPPEARED. SO HAS MY COSTUME.
AND NOW SOME BAD GIRL IS CLAIMING SHE'S GOT "SPIDER-MAN" HOSTAGE.
I HATE MATH.
OKAY. PALONE SAYS THIS IS THE DEALER'S AREA.
WITH ANY LUCK, IT WON'T BE TOO FAR FROM WHERE "SPIDER-MAN" IS BEING HELD.
NOT THAT LUCK HAS BEEN IN OVERLY ABUNDANT SUPPLY FOR ME LATELY. THOUGH MAYBE THAT MEANS I'M DUE FOR A CHANGE.
NNAAARRGHH!
WHY DO I EVEN BOTHER?

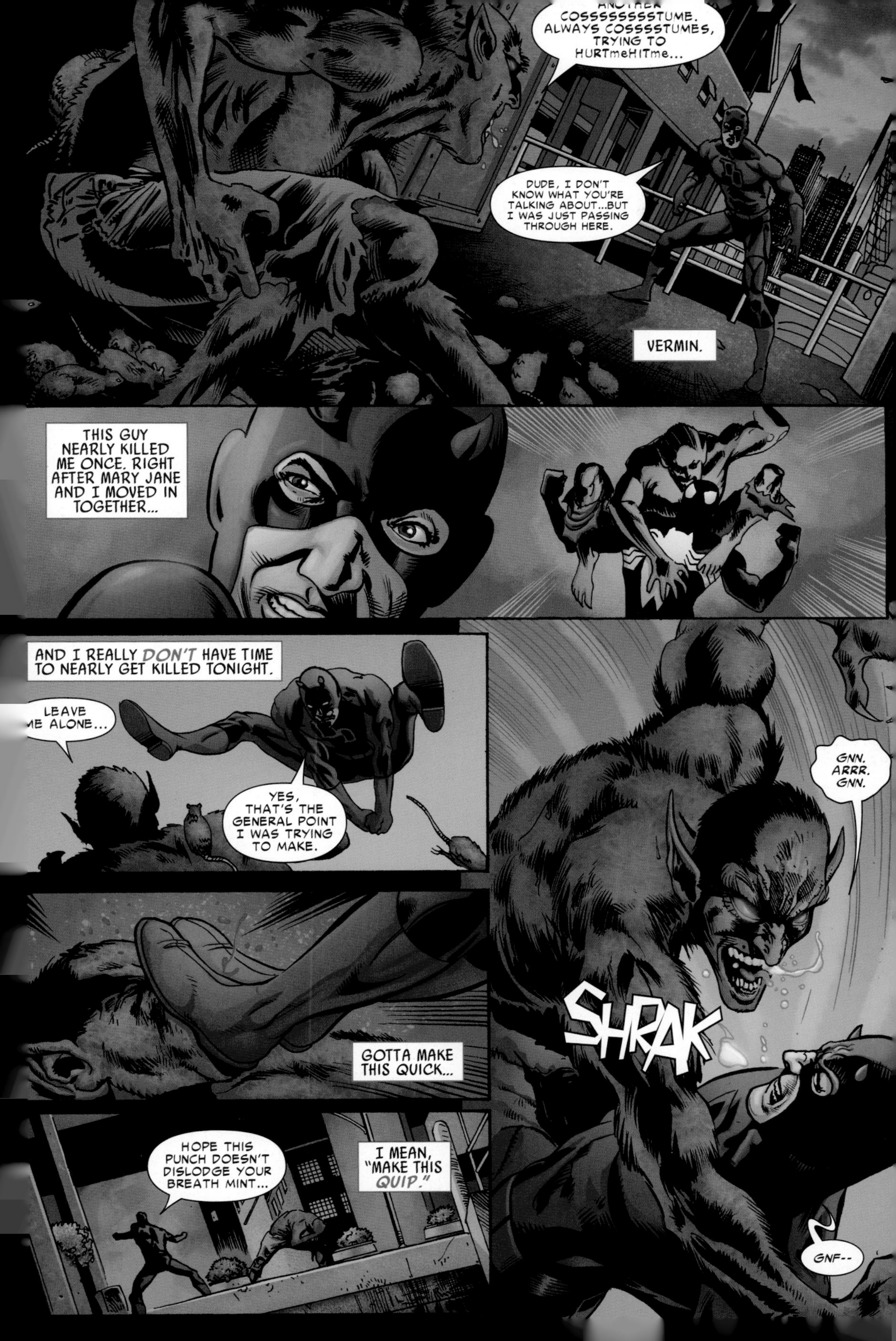
COSSSSSSSSSTUME. ALWAYS COSSSSSTUMES, TRYING TO HURTmeHITme...
DUDE, I DON'T KNOW WHAT YOU'RE TALKING ABOUT...BUT I WAS JUST PASSING THROUGH HERE.
VERMIN.
THIS GUY NEARLY KILLED ME ONCE. RIGHT AFTER MARY JANE AND I MOVED IN TOGETHER...
AND I REALLY DON'T HAVE TIME TO NEARLY GET KILLED TONIGHT.
LEAVE ME ALONE...
YES, THAT'S THE GENERAL POINT I WAS TRYING TO MAKE.
GOTTA MAKE THIS QUICK...
HOPE THIS PUNCH DOESN'T DISLODGE YOUR BREATH MINT...
I MEAN, "MAKE THIS QUIP."
GNN. ARRR. GNN.
SHRAK
GNF--

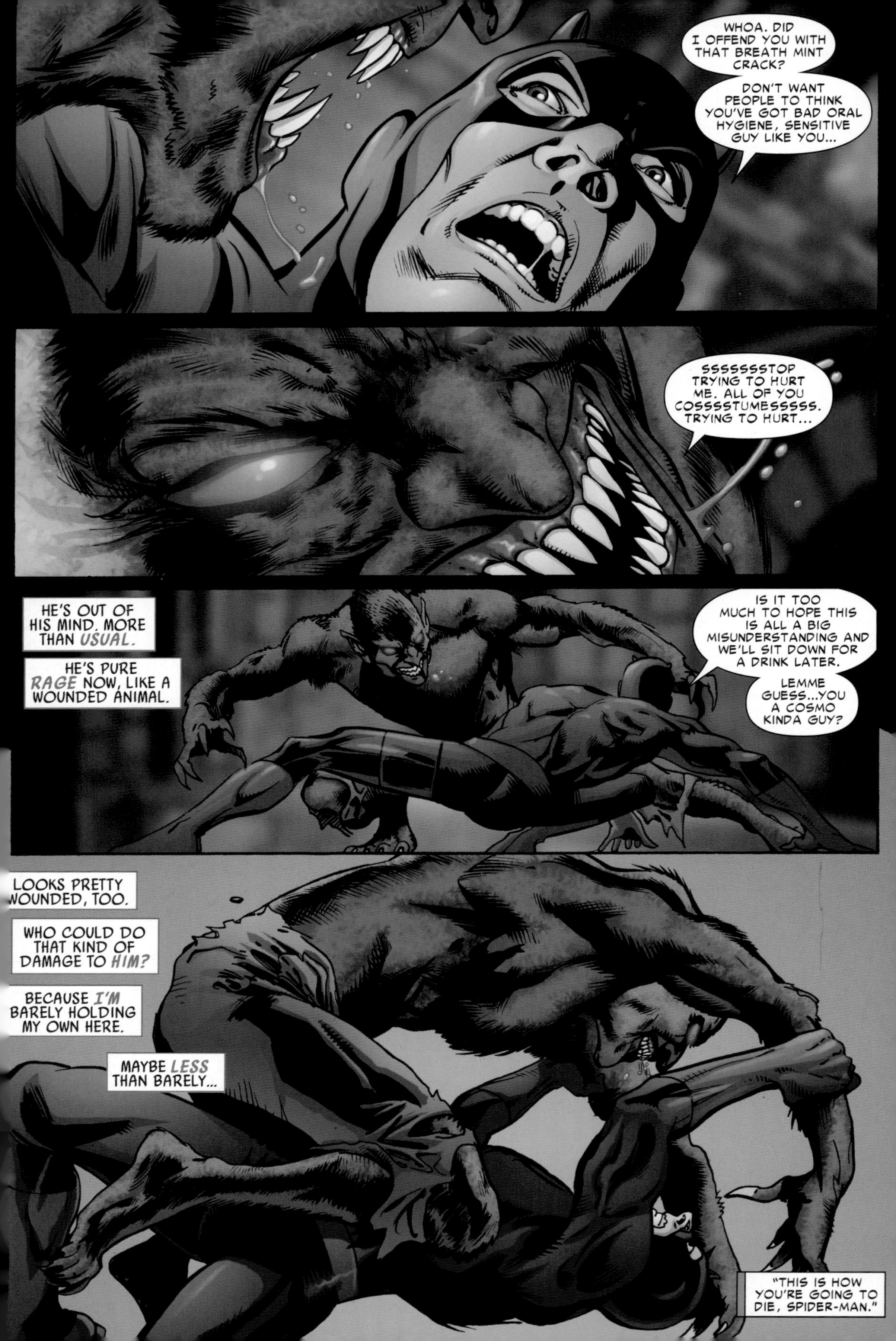

WHOA. DID I OFFEND YOU WITH THAT BREATH MINT CRACK?
DON'T WANT PEOPLE TO THINK YOU'VE GOT BAD ORAL HYGIENE, SENSITIVE GUY LIKE YOU...
SSSSSSSTOP TRYING TO HURT ME. ALL OF YOU COSSSSTUMESSSSS. TRYING TO HURT...
HE'S OUT OF HIS MIND. MORE THAN USUAL.
HE'S PURE RAGE NOW, LIKE A WOUNDED ANIMAL.
IS IT TOO MUCH TO HOPE THIS IS ALL A BIG MISUNDERSTANDING AND WE'LL SIT DOWN FOR A DRINK LATER.
LEMME GUESS...YOU A COSMO KINDA GUY?
LOOKS PRETTY WOUNDED, TOO.
WHO COULD DO THAT KIND OF DAMAGE TO HIM?
BECAUSE I'M BARELY HOLDING MY OWN HERE.
MAYBE LESS THAN BARELY...
"THIS IS HOW YOU'RE GOING TO DIE, SPIDER-MAN."

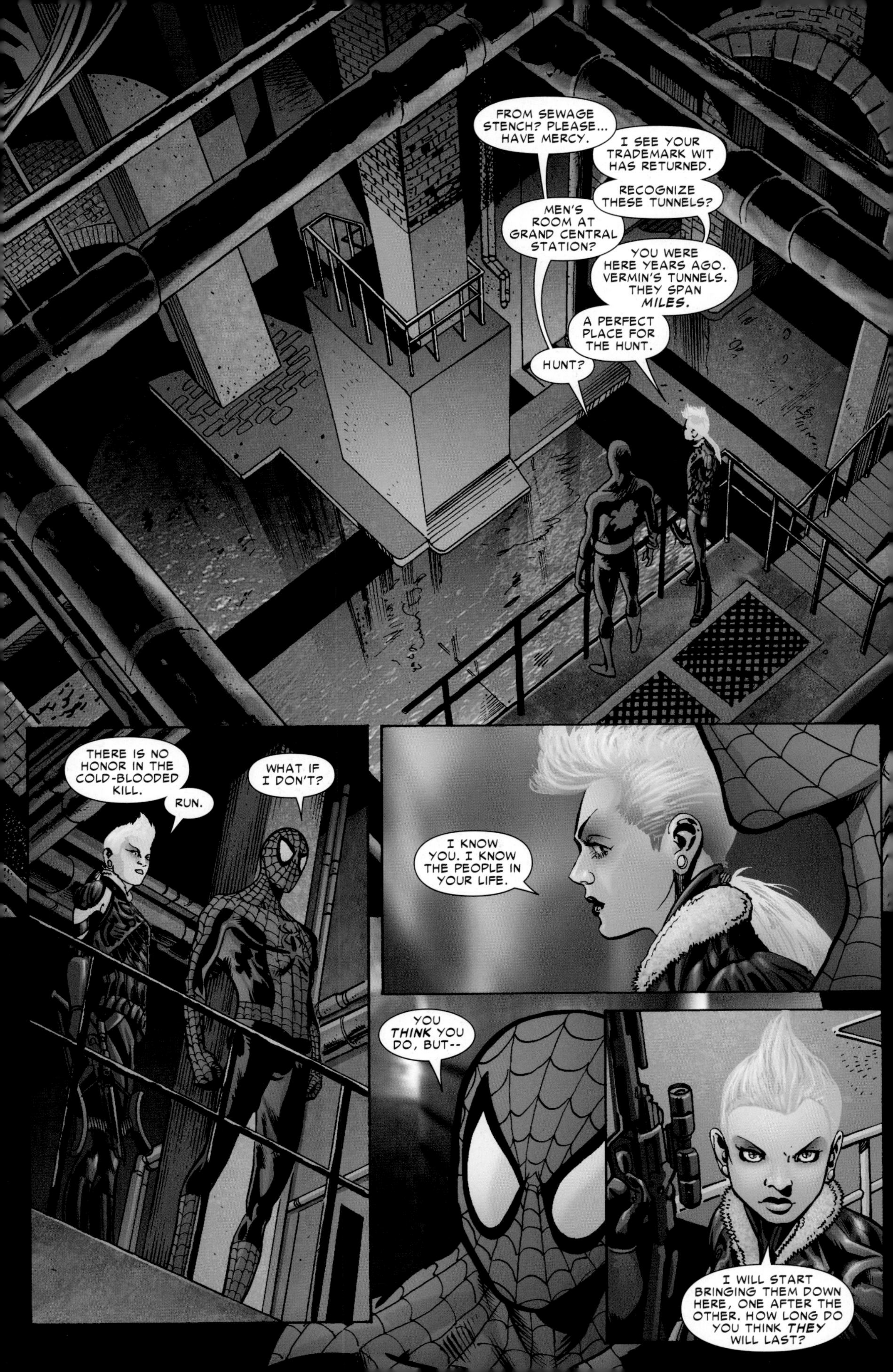
FROM SEWAGE STENCH? PLEASE... HAVE MERCY.
I SEE YOUR TRADEMARK WIT HAS RETURNED.
RECOGNIZE THESE TUNNELS?
MEN'S ROOM AT GRAND CENTRAL STATION?
YOU WERE HERE YEARS AGO. VERMIN'S TUNNELS. THEY SPAN *MILES.*
A PERFECT PLACE FOR THE HUNT.
HUNT?
THERE IS NO HONOR IN THE COLD-BLOODED KILL.
RUN.
WHAT IF I DON'T?
I KNOW YOU. I KNOW THE PEOPLE IN YOUR LIFE.
YOU *THINK* YOU DO, BUT--
I WILL START BRINGING THEM DOWN HERE, ONE AFTER THE OTHER. HOW LONG DO YOU THINK *THEY* WILL LAST?

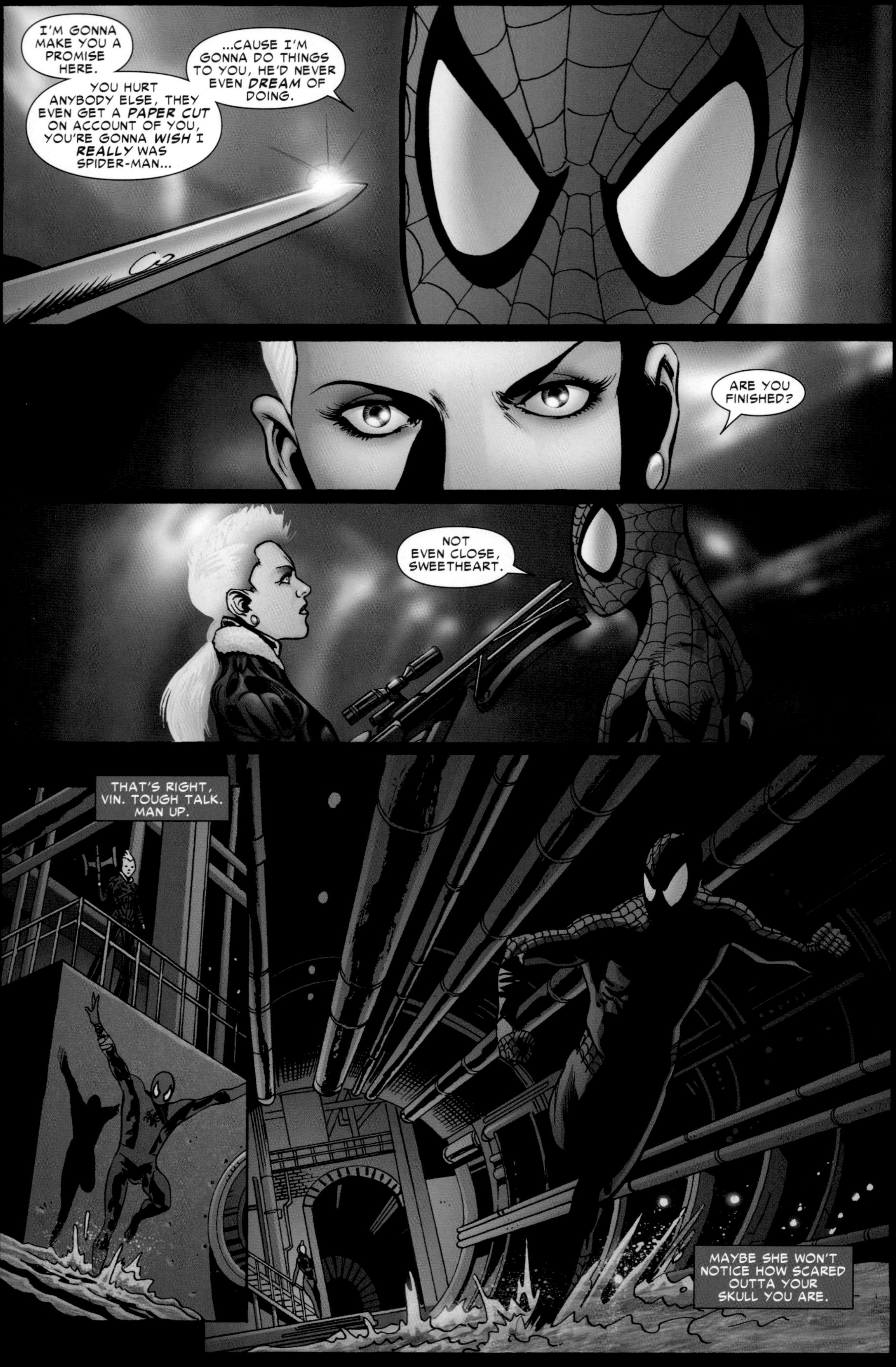
I'M GONNA MAKE YOU A PROMISE HERE.
YOU HURT ANYBODY ELSE, THEY EVEN GET A PAPER CUT ON ACCOUNT OF YOU, YOU'RE GONNA WISH I REALLY WAS SPIDER-MAN...
...CAUSE I'M GONNA DO THINGS TO YOU, HE'D NEVER EVEN DREAM OF DOING.
ARE YOU FINISHED?
NOT EVEN CLOSE, SWEETHEART.
THAT'S RIGHT, VIN. TOUGH TALK. MAN UP.
MAYBE SHE WON'T NOTICE HOW SCARED OUTTA YOUR SKULL YOU ARE.

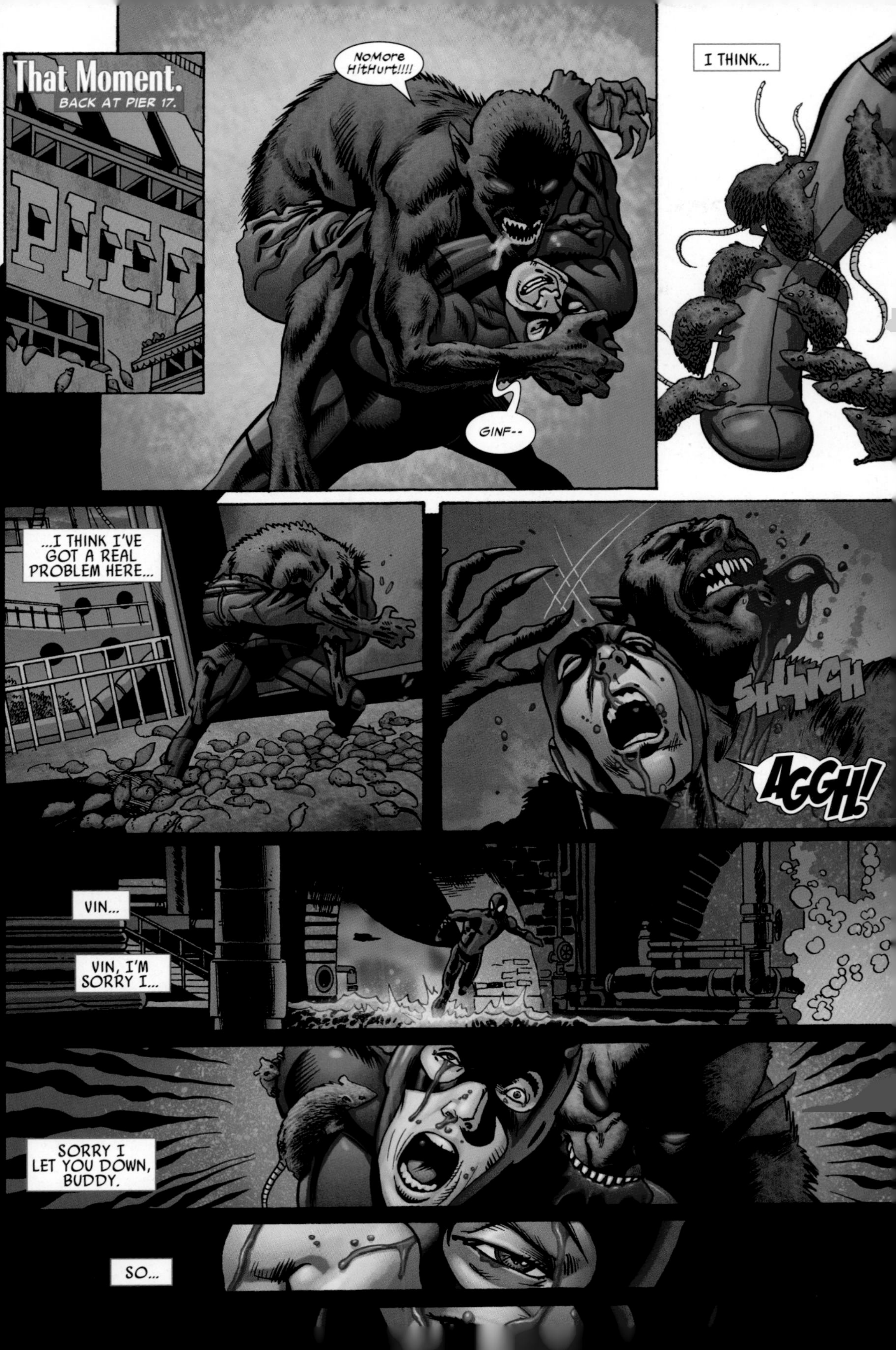
That Moment.
BACK AT PIER 17.
NoMore HitHurt!!!!
GINF--
I THINK...
...I THINK I'VE GOT A REAL PROBLEM HERE...
SHLUNCH
AGGH!
VIN...
VIN, I'M SORRY I...
SORRY I LET YOU DOWN, BUDDY.
SO...

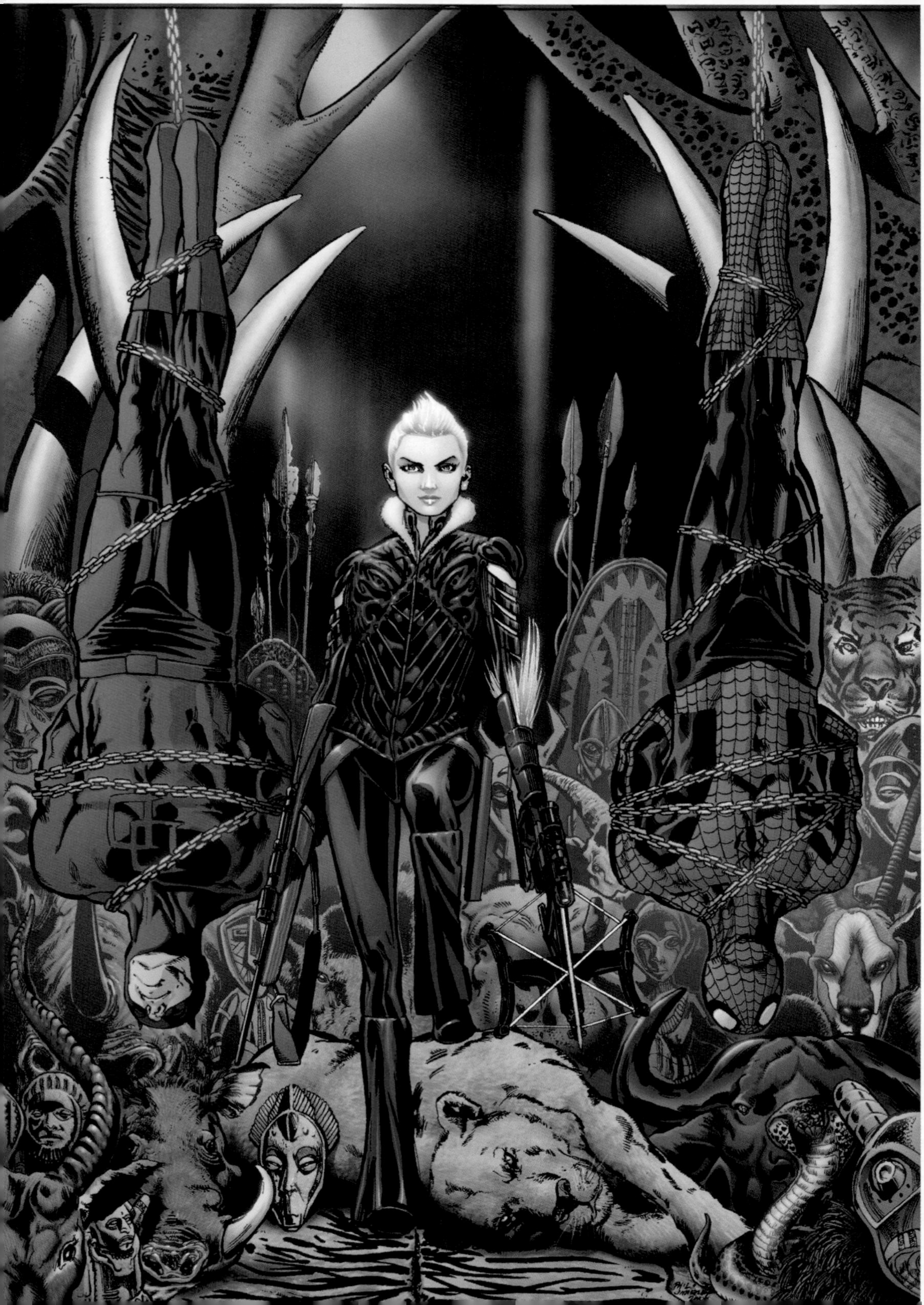

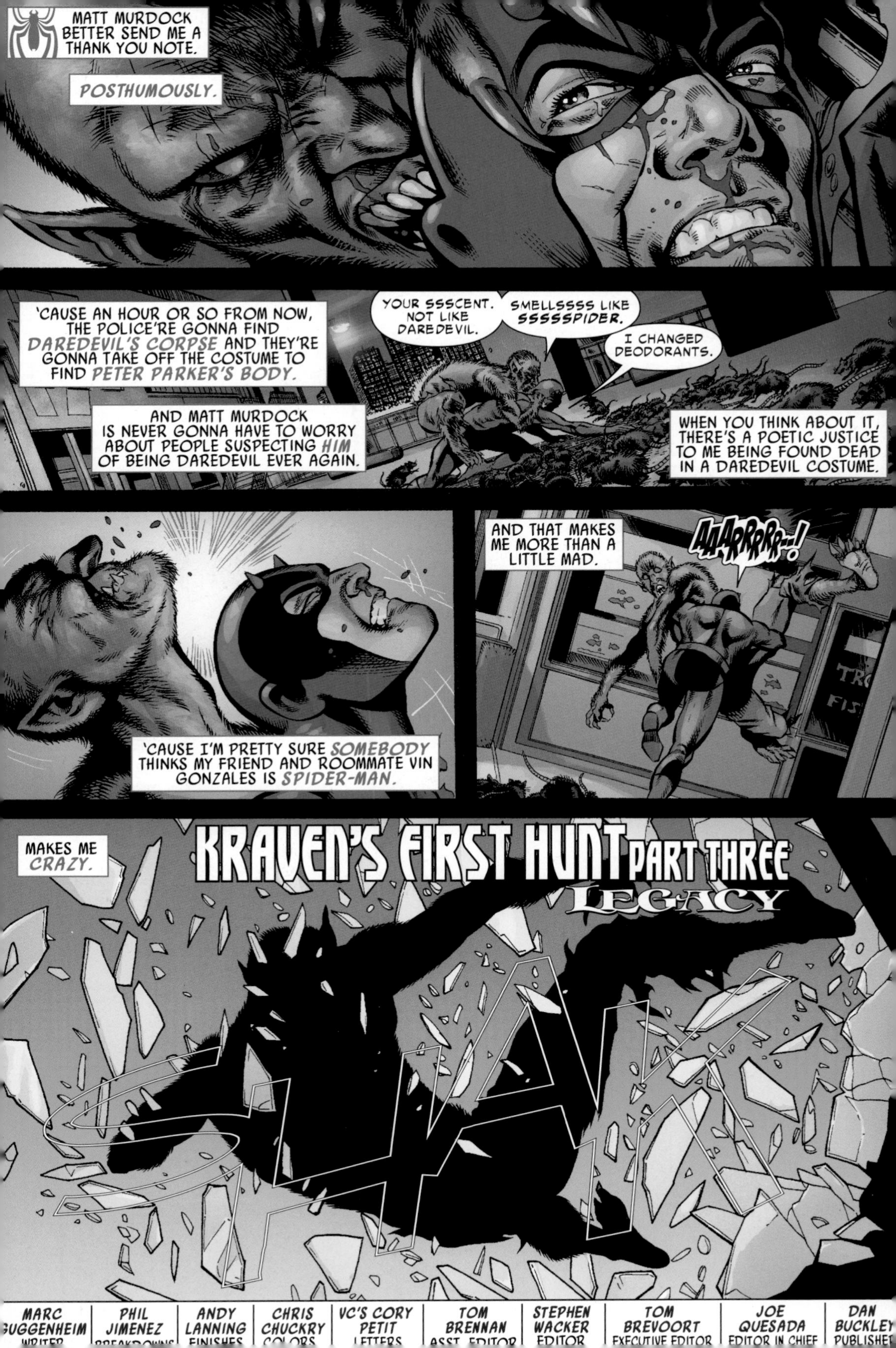
MATT MURDOCK BETTER SEND ME A THANK YOU NOTE.
POSTHUMOUSLY.
'CAUSE AN HOUR OR SO FROM NOW, THE POLICE'RE GONNA FIND DAREDEVIL'S CORPSE AND THEY'RE GONNA TAKE OFF THE COSTUME TO FIND PETER PARKER'S BODY.
YOUR SSSCENT. NOT LIKE DAREDEVIL.
SMELLSSSS LIKE SSSSSPIDER.
I CHANGED DEODORANTS.
AND MATT MURDOCK IS NEVER GONNA HAVE TO WORRY ABOUT PEOPLE SUSPECTING HIM OF BEING DAREDEVIL EVER AGAIN.
WHEN YOU THINK ABOUT IT, THERE'S A POETIC JUSTICE TO ME BEING FOUND DEAD IN A DAREDEVIL COSTUME.
'CAUSE I'M PRETTY SURE SOMEBODY THINKS MY FRIEND AND ROOMMATE VIN GONZALES IS SPIDER-MAN.
AND THAT MAKES ME MORE THAN A LITTLE MAD.
AAARRRRR--!
MAKES ME CRAZY.
KRAVEN'S FIRST HUNT PART THREE
LEGACY
MARC GUGGENHEIM WRITER
PHIL JIMENEZ BREAKDOWNS
ANDY LANNING FINISHES
CHRIS CHUCKRY COLORS
VC'S CORY PETIT LETTERS
TOM BRENNAN ASST. EDITOR
STEPHEN WACKER EDITOR
TOM BREVOORT EXECUTIVE EDITOR
JOE QUESADA EDITOR IN CHIEF
DAN BUCKLEY PUBLISHER

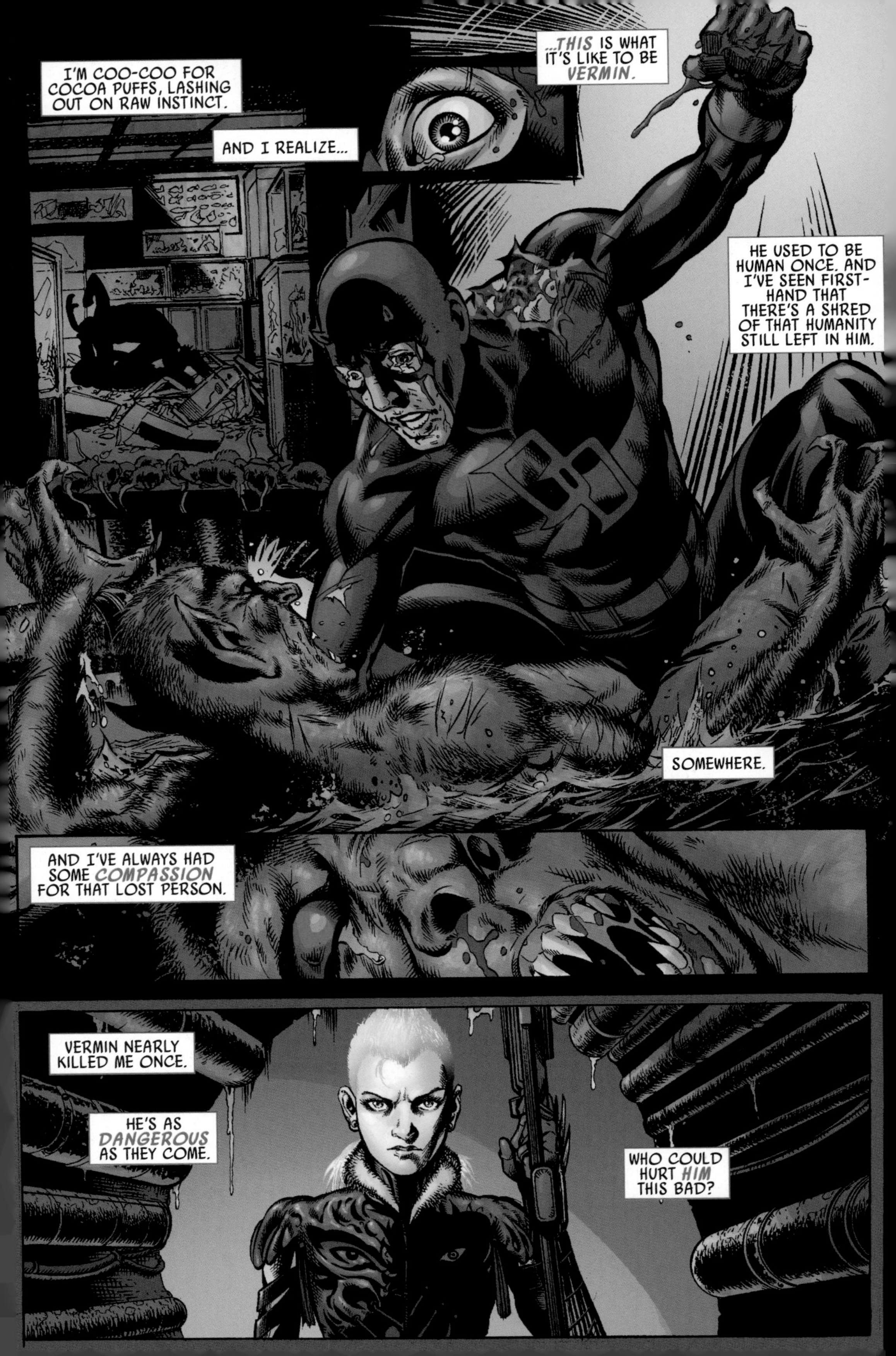
I'M COO-COO FOR COCOA PUFFS, LASHING OUT ON RAW INSTINCT.
AND I REALIZE...
...THIS IS WHAT IT'S LIKE TO BE VERMIN.
HE USED TO BE HUMAN ONCE. AND I'VE SEEN FIRST-HAND THAT THERE'S A SHRED OF THAT HUMANITY STILL LEFT IN HIM.
SOMEWHERE.
AND I'VE ALWAYS HAD SOME COMPASSION FOR THAT LOST PERSON.
VERMIN NEARLY KILLED ME ONCE.
HE'S AS DANGEROUS AS THEY COME.
WHO COULD HURT HIM THIS BAD?

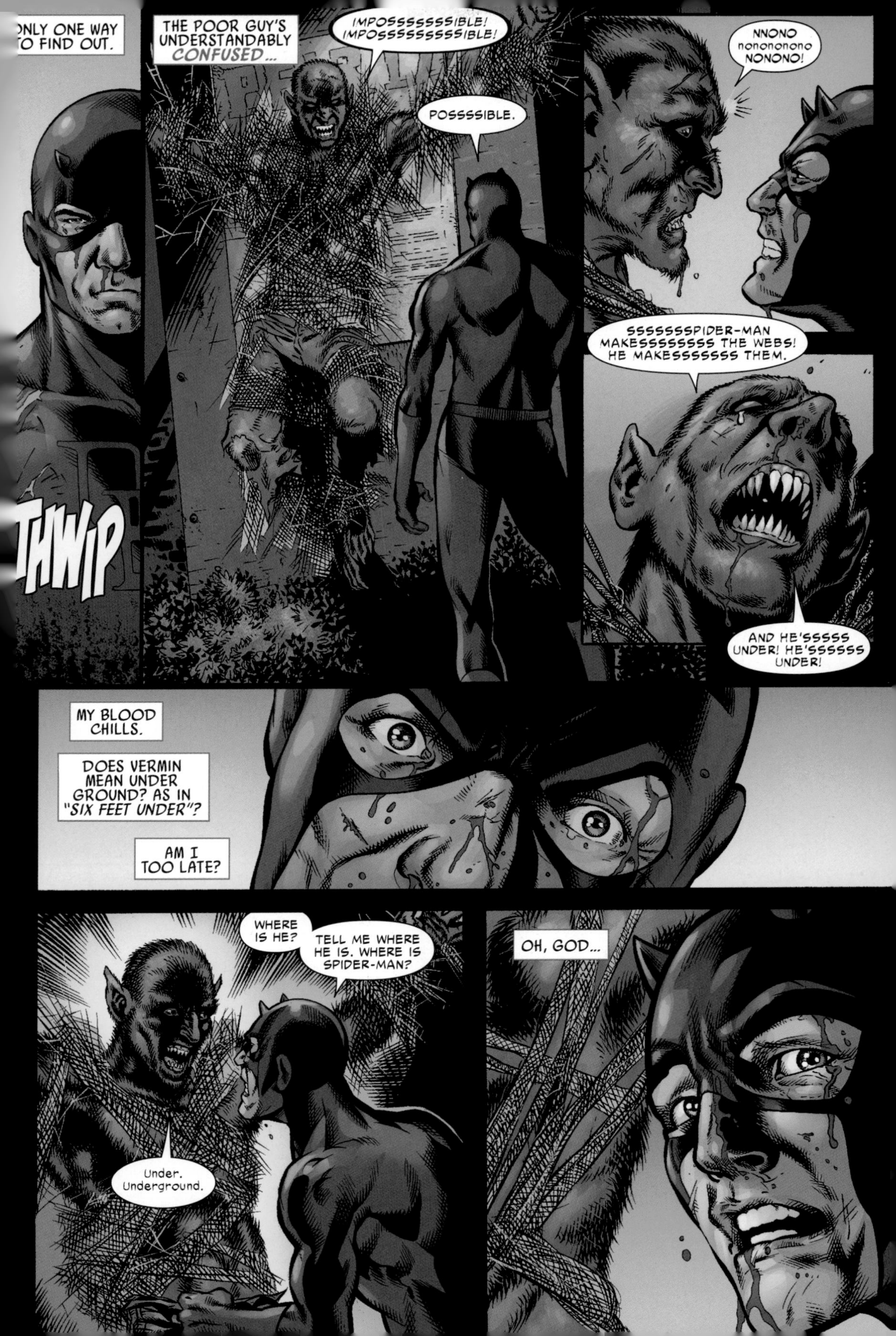
ONLY ONE WAY TO FIND OUT.
THWIP
THE POOR GUY'S UNDERSTANDABLY CONFUSED...
IMPOSSSSSSSIBLE! IMPOSSSSSSSSSSIBLE!
POSSSSIBLE.
NNONO nononnonono NONONO!
SSSSSSSPIDER-MAN MAKESSSSSSSSS THE WEBS! HE MAKESSSSSSSS THEM.
AND HE'SSSSS UNDER! HE'SSSSSS UNDER!
MY BLOOD CHILLS.
DOES VERMIN MEAN UNDER GROUND? AS IN "SIX FEET UNDER"?
AM I TOO LATE?
WHERE IS HE?
TELL ME WHERE HE IS. WHERE IS SPIDER-MAN?
Under. Underground.
OH, GOD...

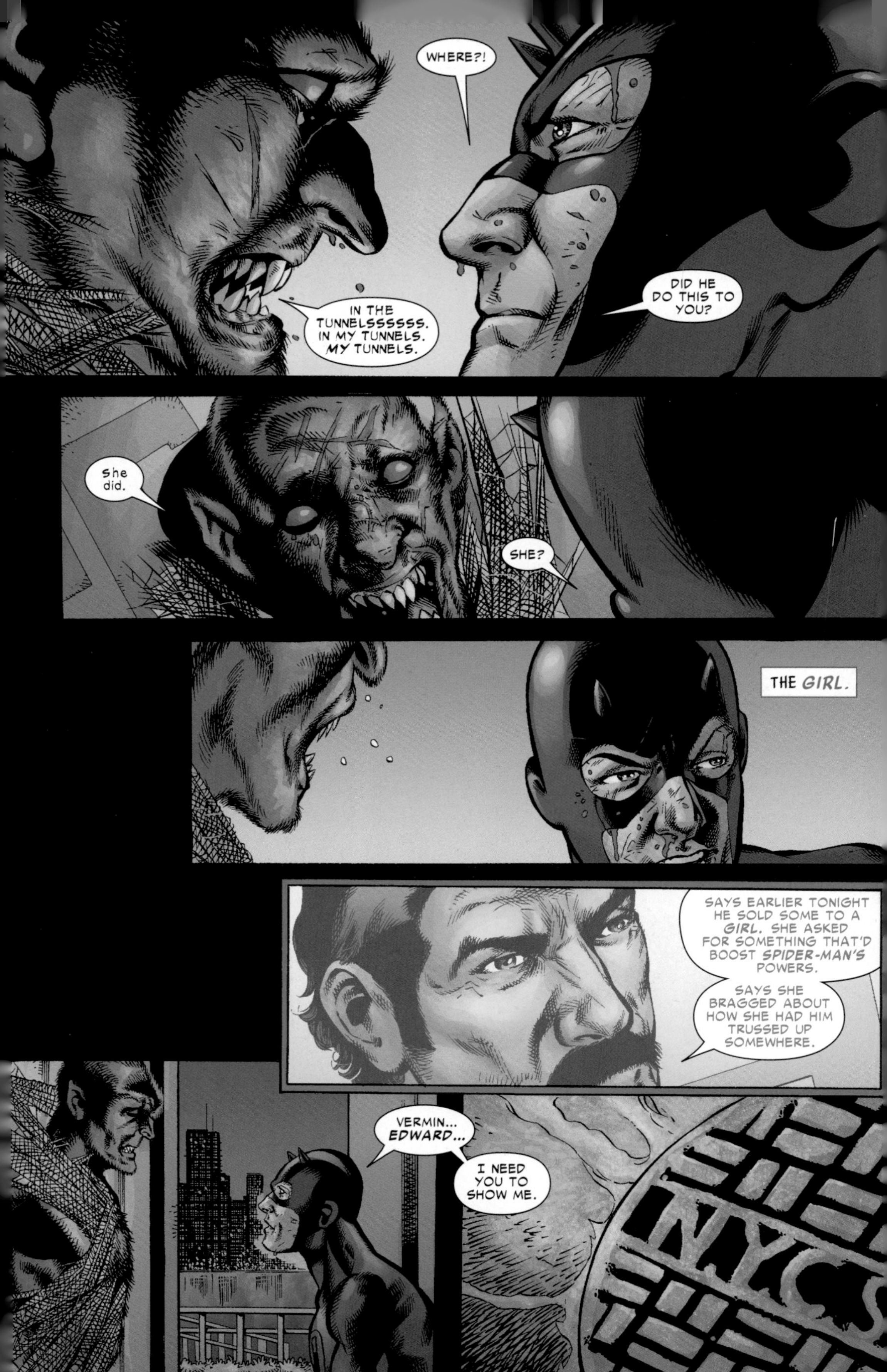
WHERE?!
IN THE TUNNELSSSSSS. IN MY TUNNELS. MY TUNNELS.
DID HE DO THIS TO YOU?
She did.
SHE?
THE GIRL.
SAYS EARLIER TONIGHT HE SOLD SOME TO A GIRL. SHE ASKED FOR SOMETHING THAT'D BOOST SPIDER-MAN'S POWERS.
SAYS SHE BRAGGED ABOUT HOW SHE HAD HIM TRUSSED UP SOMEWHERE.
VERMIN... EDWARD...
I NEED YOU TO SHOW ME.
NYC

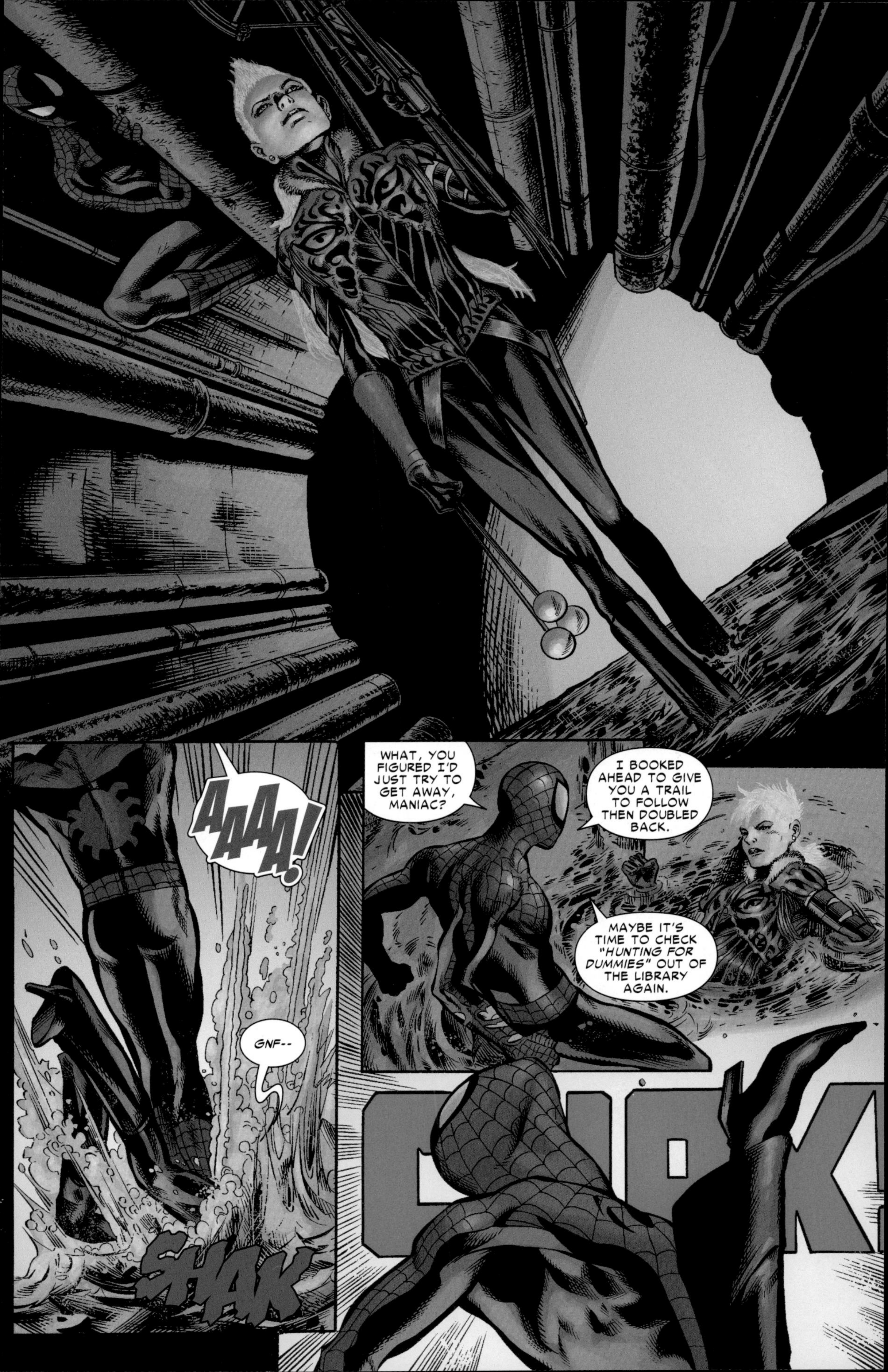
AAAAA!
GNF--
SHAK
WHAT, YOU FIGURED I'D JUST TRY TO GET AWAY, MANIAC?
I BOOKED AHEAD TO GIVE YOU A TRAIL TO FOLLOW THEN DOUBLED BACK.
MAYBE IT'S TIME TO CHECK "HUNTING FOR DUMMIES" OUT OF THE LIBRARY AGAIN.

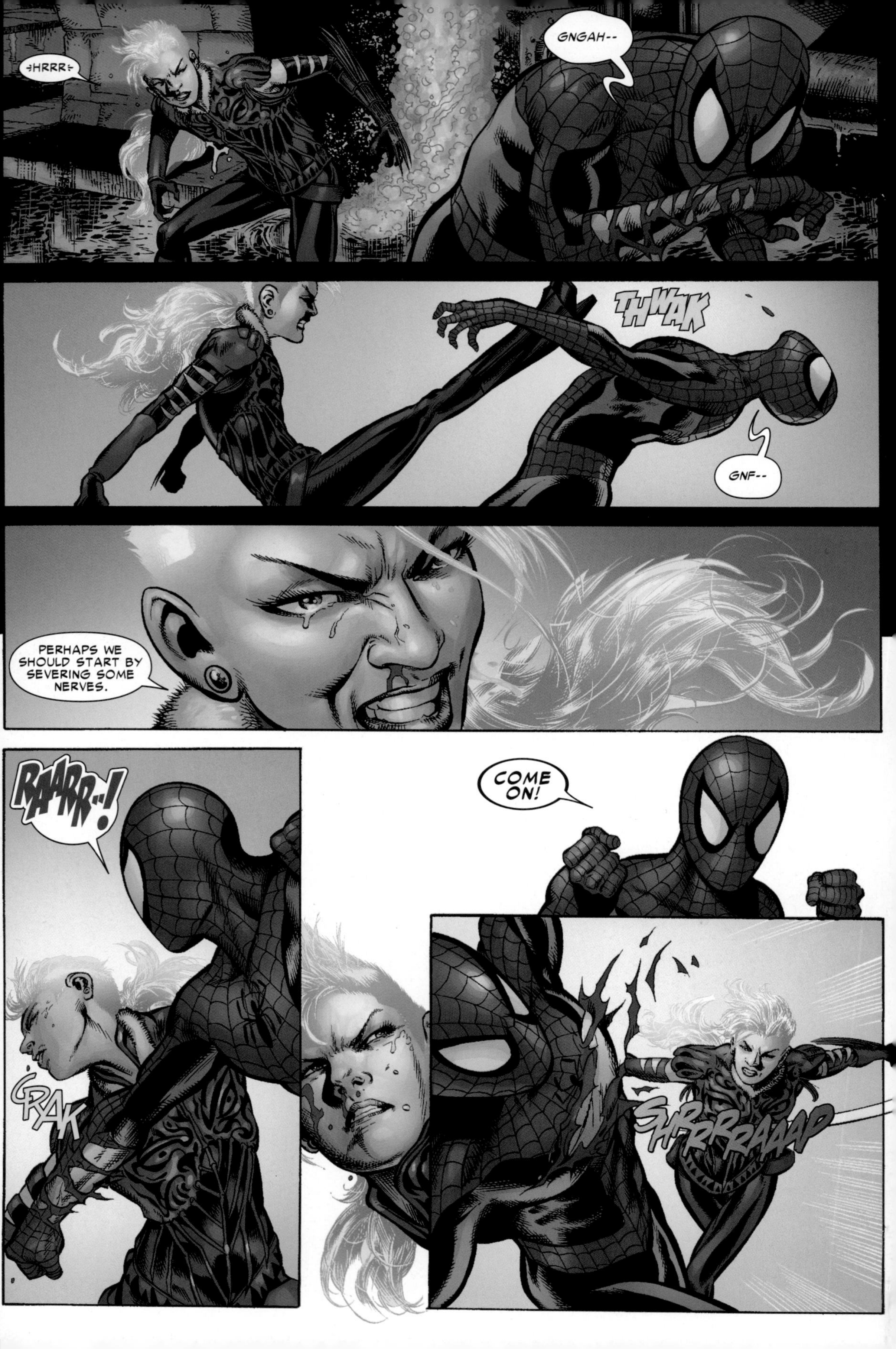

=HRRR=
GNGAH--
THWAK
GNF--
PERHAPS WE SHOULD START BY SEVERING SOME NERVES.
RAAARR--!
CRAK
COME ON!
SHRRRAAAP

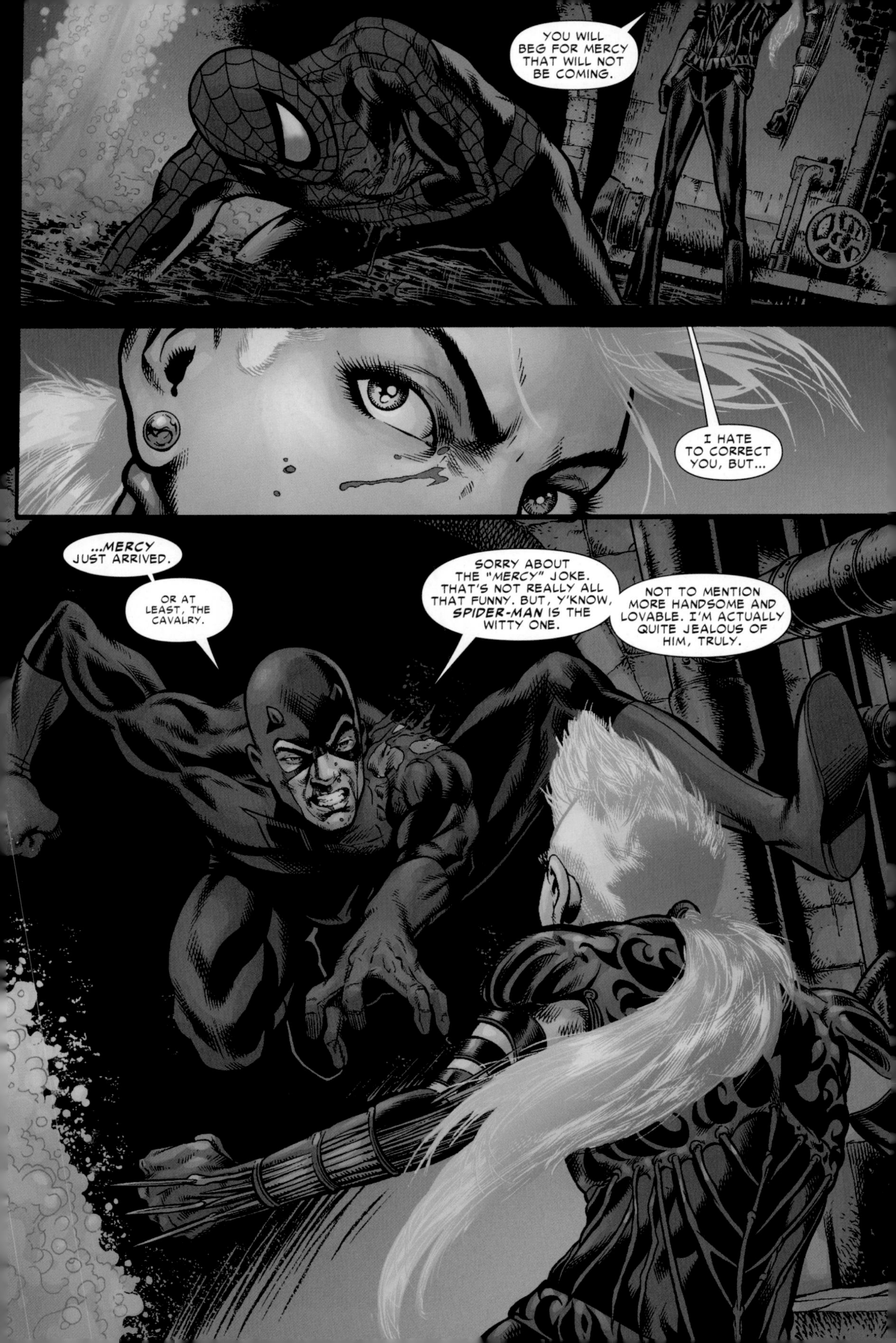
YOU WILL BEG FOR MERCY THAT WILL NOT BE COMING.
I HATE TO CORRECT YOU, BUT...
...MERCY JUST ARRIVED.
OR AT LEAST, THE CAVALRY.
SORRY ABOUT THE "MERCY" JOKE. THAT'S NOT REALLY ALL THAT FUNNY. BUT, Y'KNOW, SPIDER-MAN IS THE WITTY ONE.
NOT TO MENTION MORE HANDSOME AND LOVABLE. I'M ACTUALLY QUITE JEALOUS OF HIM, TRULY.

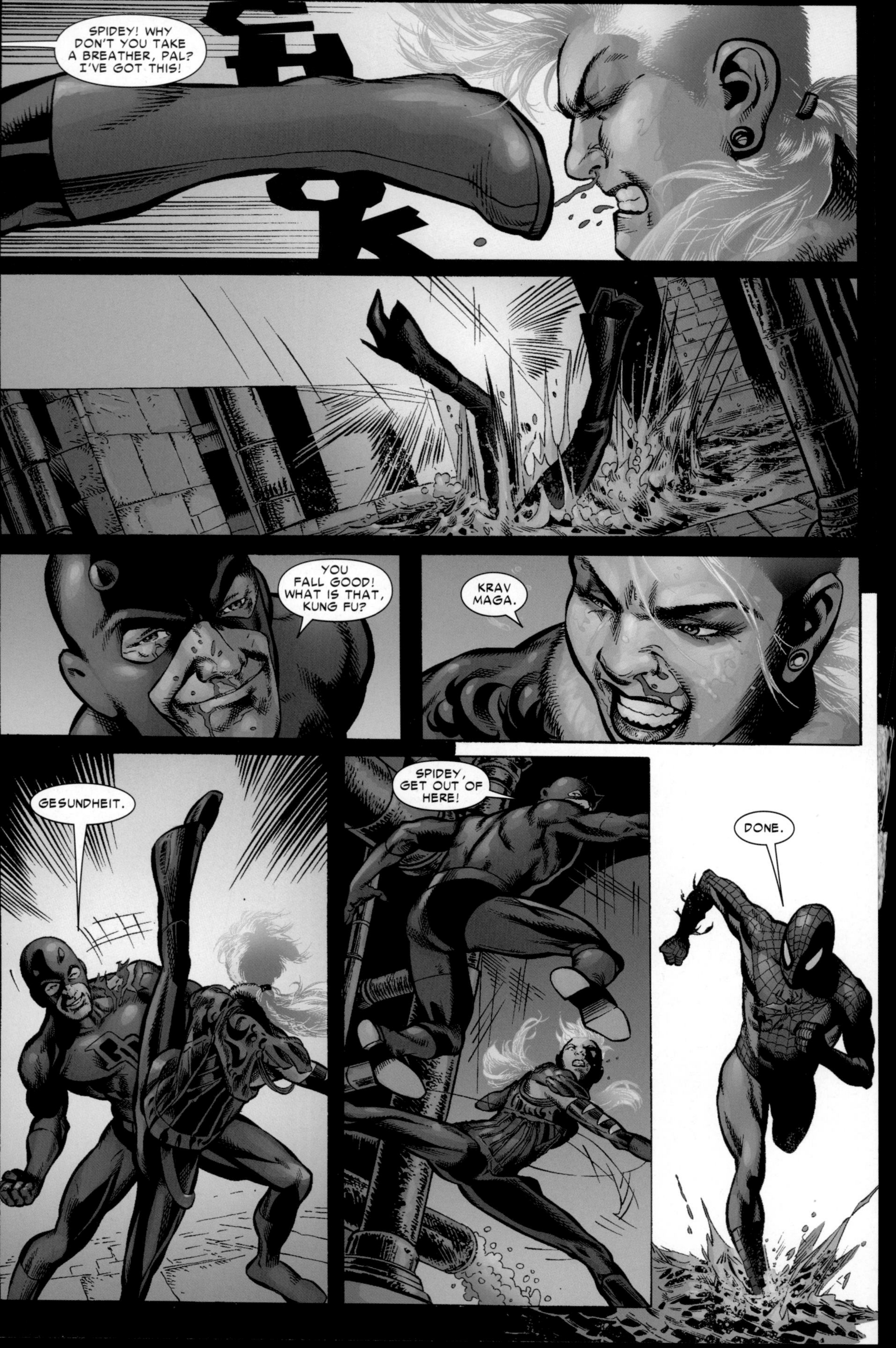
SPIDEY! WHY DON'T YOU TAKE A BREATHER, PAL? I'VE GOT THIS!
CHK
YOU FALL GOOD! WHAT IS THAT, KUNG FU?
KRAV MAGA.
GESUNDHEIT.
SPIDEY, GET OUT OF HERE!
DONE.

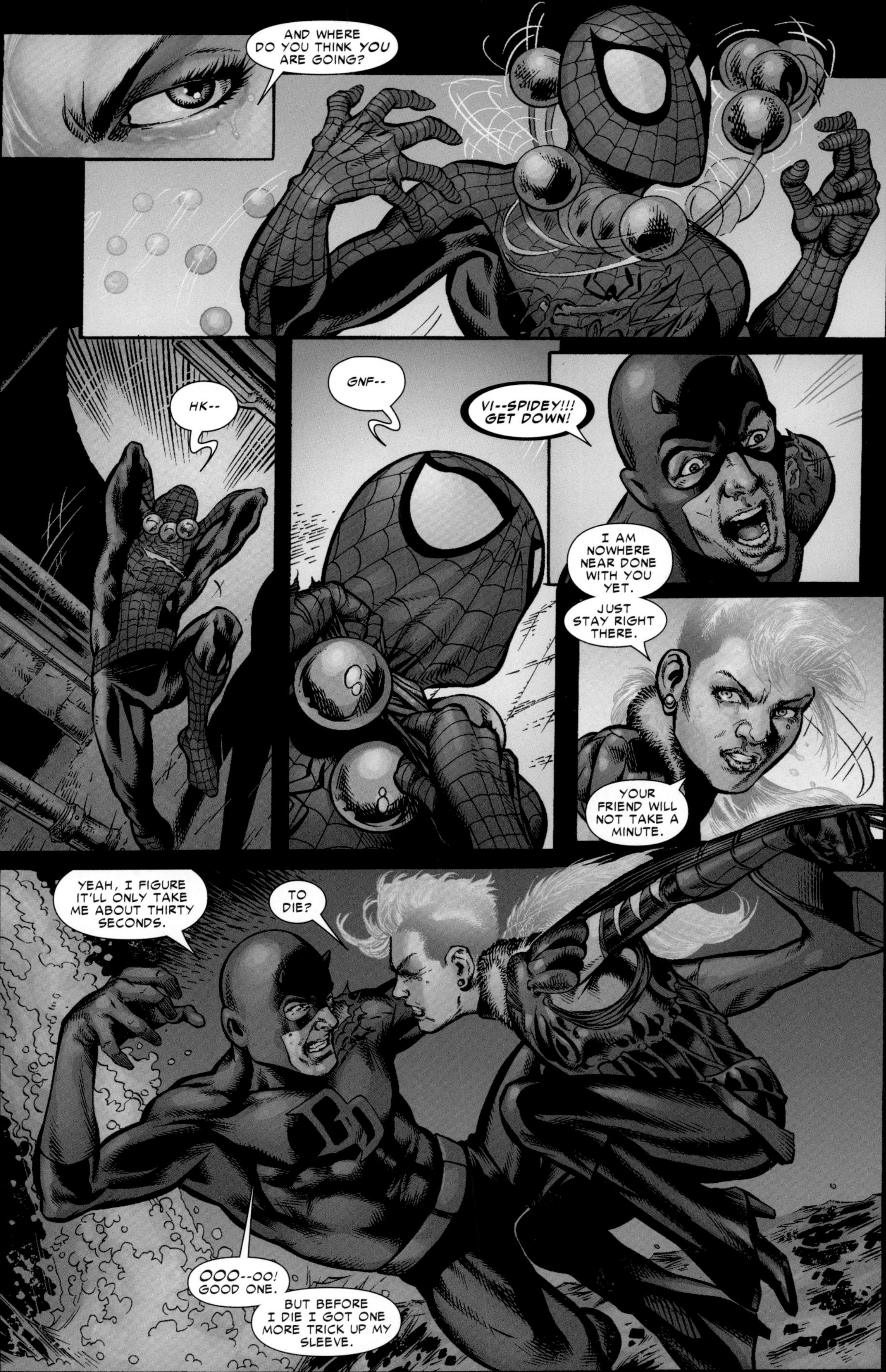
AND WHERE DO YOU THINK YOU ARE GOING?
HK--
GNF--
VI--SPIDEY!!! GET DOWN!
I AM NOWHERE NEAR DONE WITH YOU YET.
JUST STAY RIGHT THERE.
YOUR FRIEND WILL NOT TAKE A MINUTE.
YEAH, I FIGURE IT'LL ONLY TAKE ME ABOUT THIRTY SECONDS.
TO DIE?
OOO--OO! GOOD ONE.
BUT BEFORE I DIE I GOT ONE MORE TRICK UP MY SLEEVE.

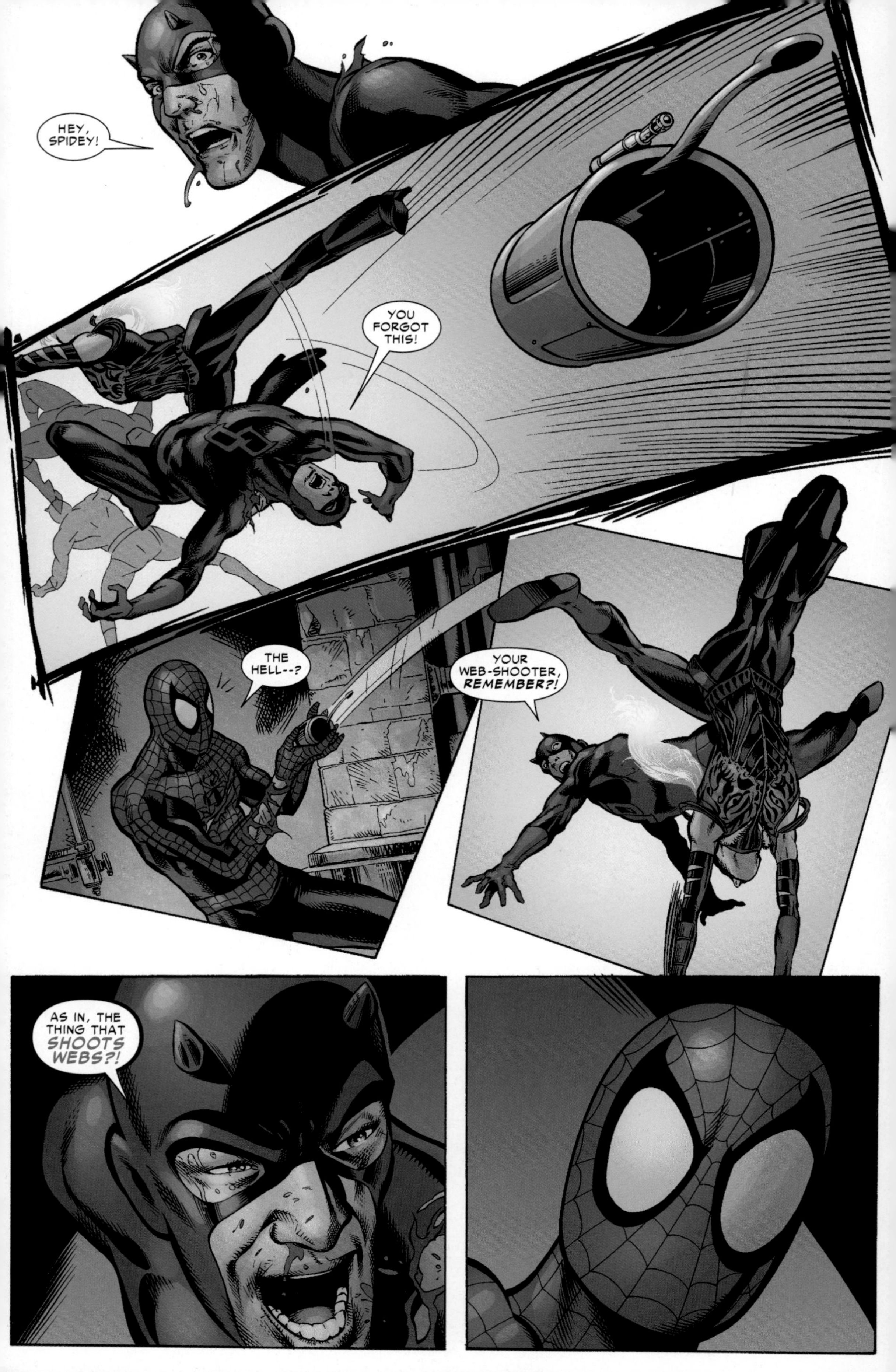
HEY, SPIDEY!
YOU FORGOT THIS!
THE HELL--?
YOUR WEB-SHOOTER, REMEMBER?!
AS IN, THE THING THAT SHOOTS WEBS?!

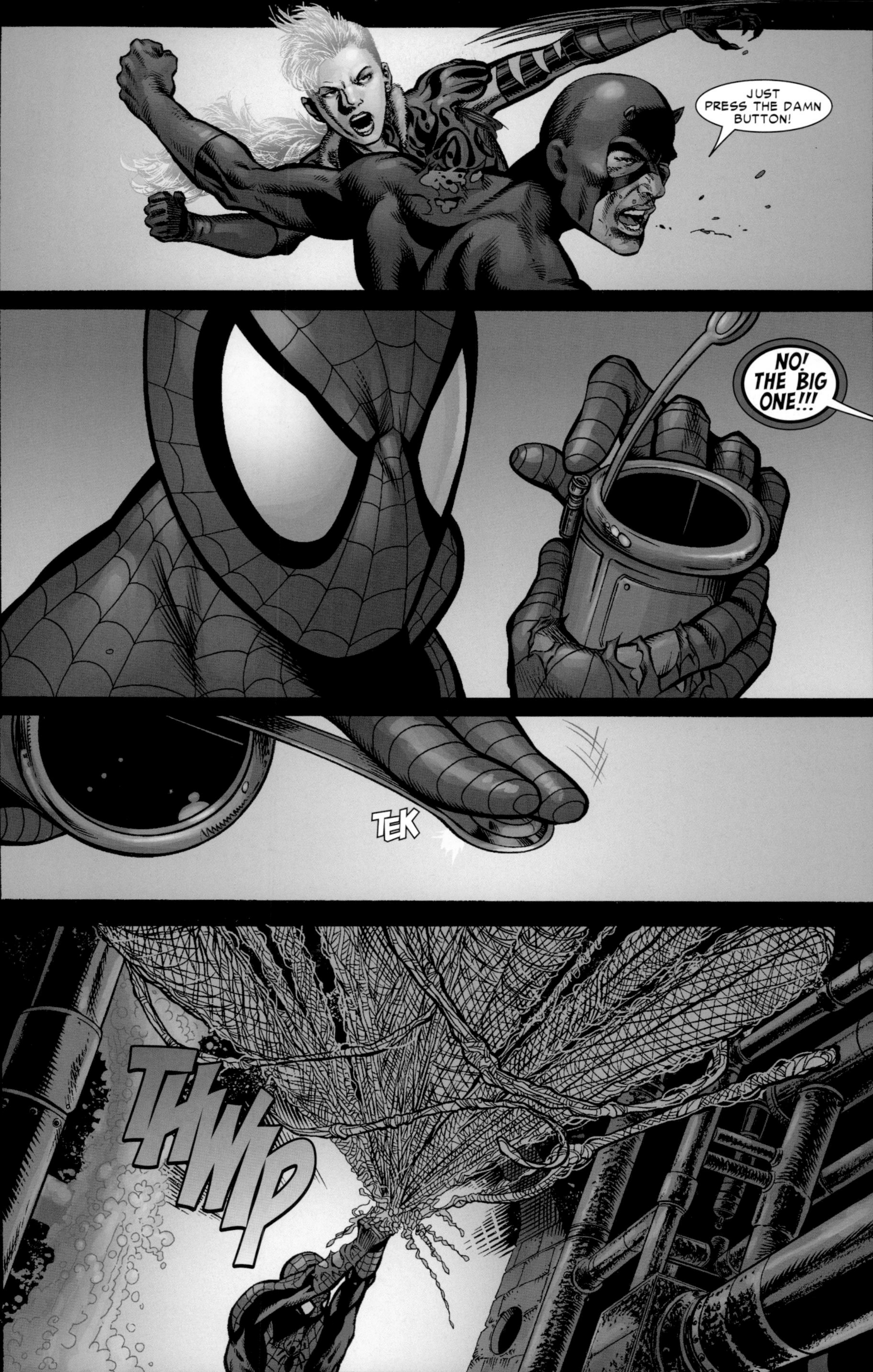
JUST PRESS THE DAMN BUTTON!
NO! THE BIG ONE!!!
TEK
THMP

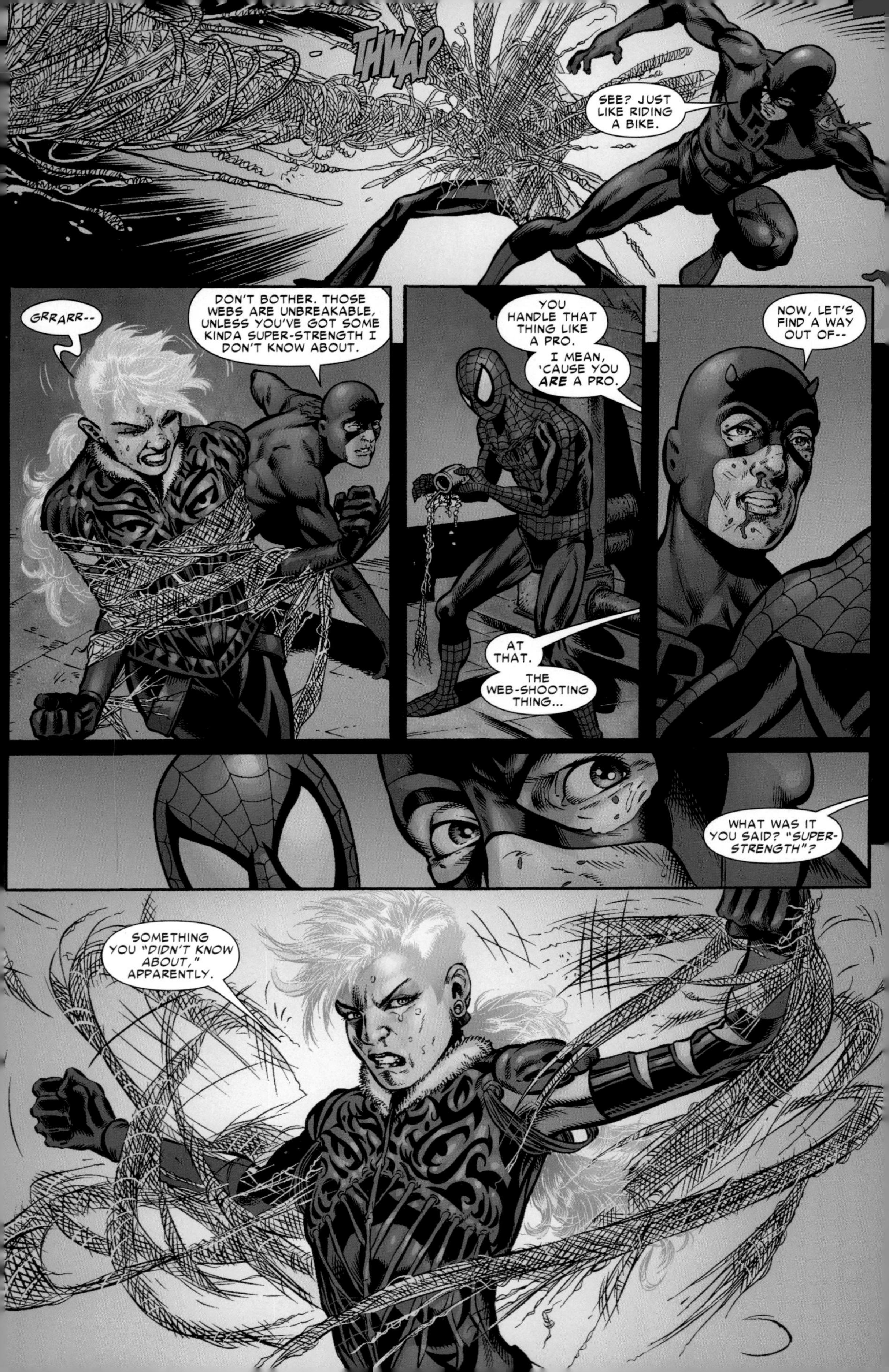
THWAP
SEE? JUST LIKE RIDING A BIKE.
GRRARR--
DON'T BOTHER. THOSE WEBS ARE UNBREAKABLE, UNLESS YOU'VE GOT SOME KINDA SUPER-STRENGTH I DON'T KNOW ABOUT.
YOU HANDLE THAT THING LIKE A PRO.
I MEAN, 'CAUSE YOU ARE A PRO.
AT THAT.
THE WEB-SHOOTING THING...
NOW, LET'S FIND A WAY OUT OF--
WHAT WAS IT YOU SAID? "SUPER-STRENGTH"?
SOMETHING YOU "DIDN'T KNOW ABOUT," APPARENTLY.

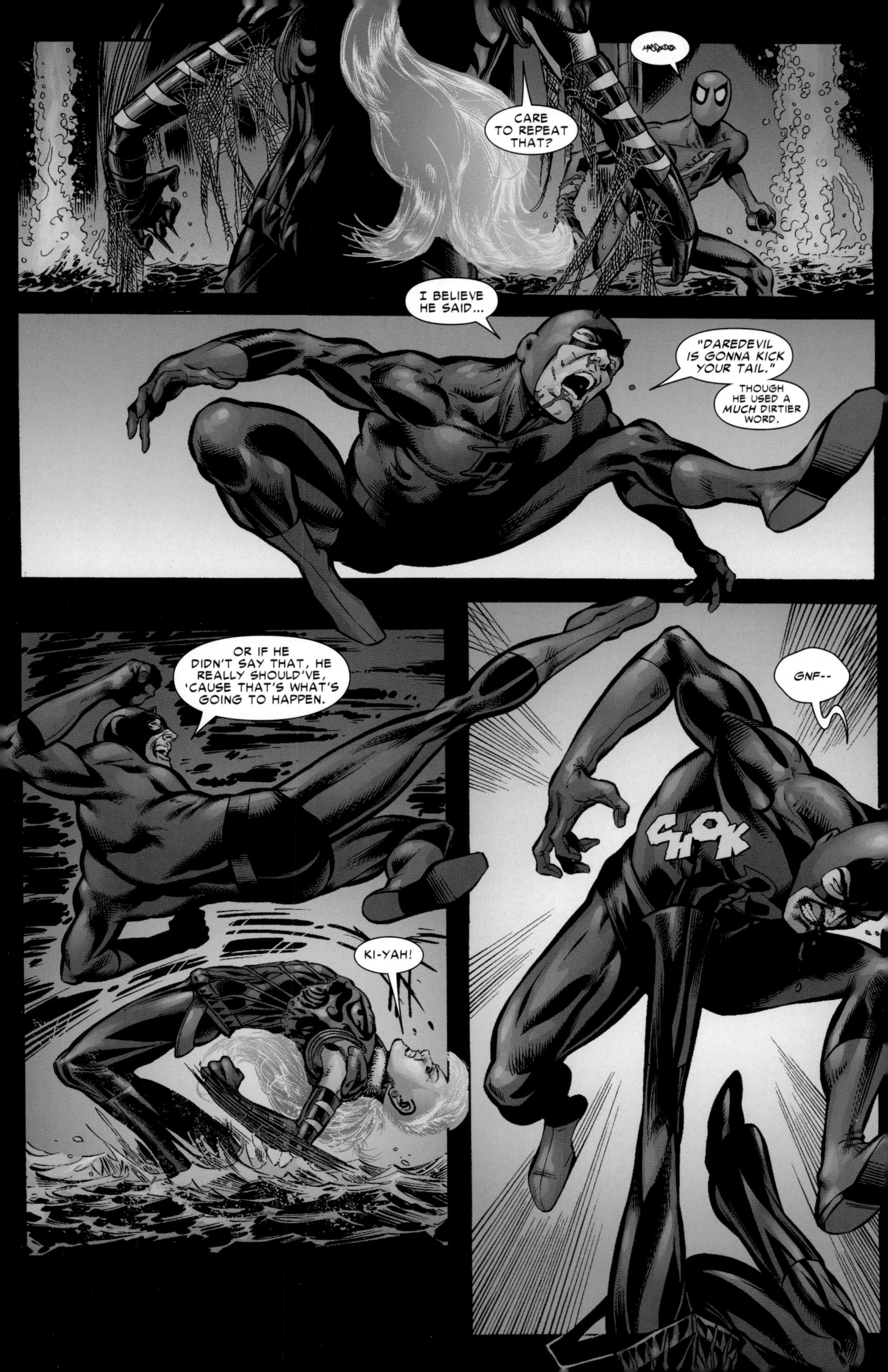
CARE TO REPEAT THAT?
I BELIEVE HE SAID...
"DAREDEVIL IS GONNA KICK YOUR TAIL."
THOUGH HE USED A MUCH DIRTIER WORD.
OR IF HE DIDN'T SAY THAT, HE REALLY SHOULD'VE, 'CAUSE THAT'S WHAT'S GOING TO HAPPEN.
KI-YAH!
GNF--
CHOK

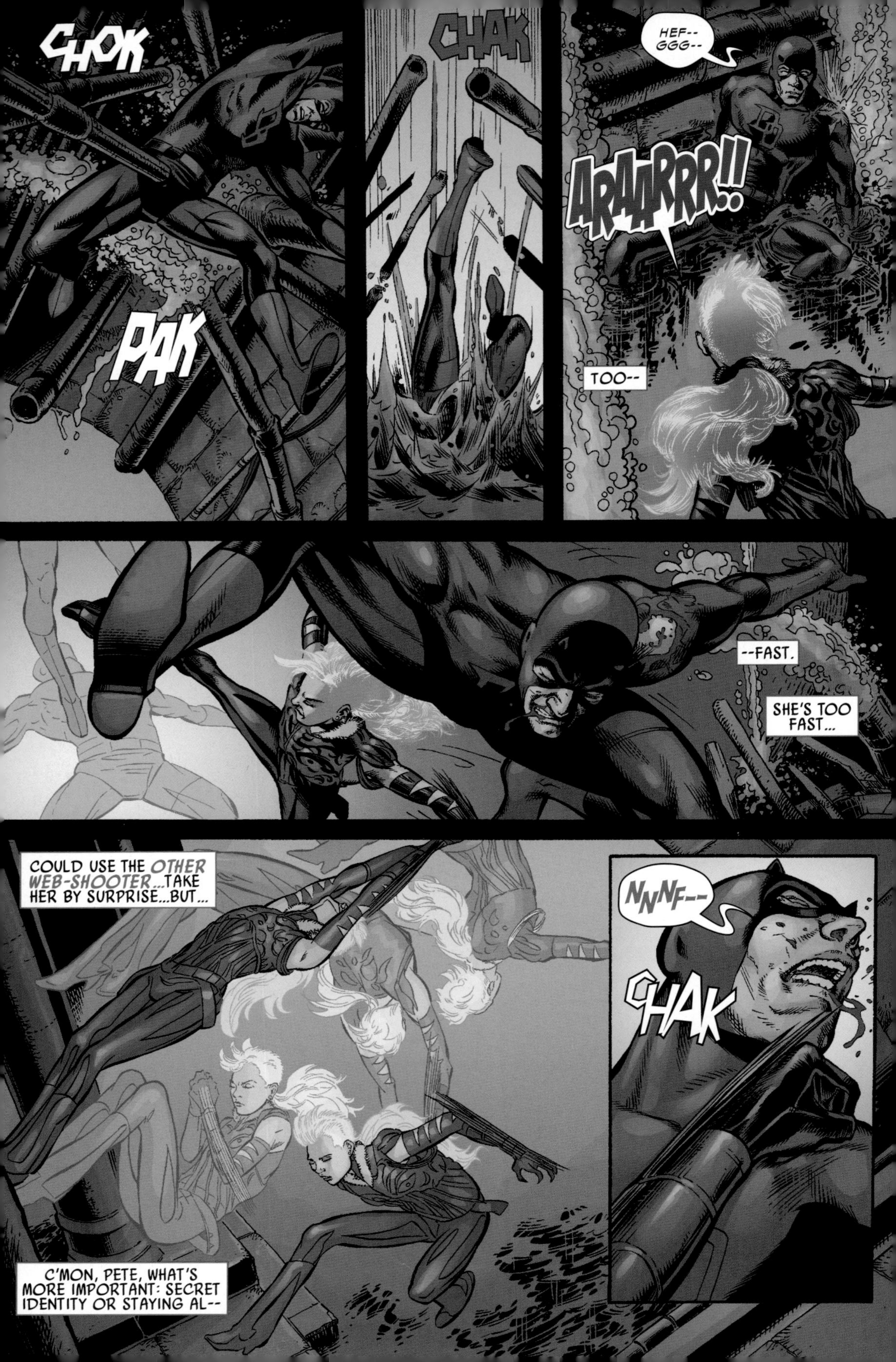
CHOK
PAK
CHAK
HEF-- GGG--
ARAAARRR!!
TOO--
--FAST.
SHE'S TOO FAST...
COULD USE THE OTHER WEB-SHOOTER...TAKE HER BY SURPRISE...BUT...
C'MON, PETE, WHAT'S MORE IMPORTANT: SECRET IDENTITY OR STAYING AL--
NNNF--
CHAK

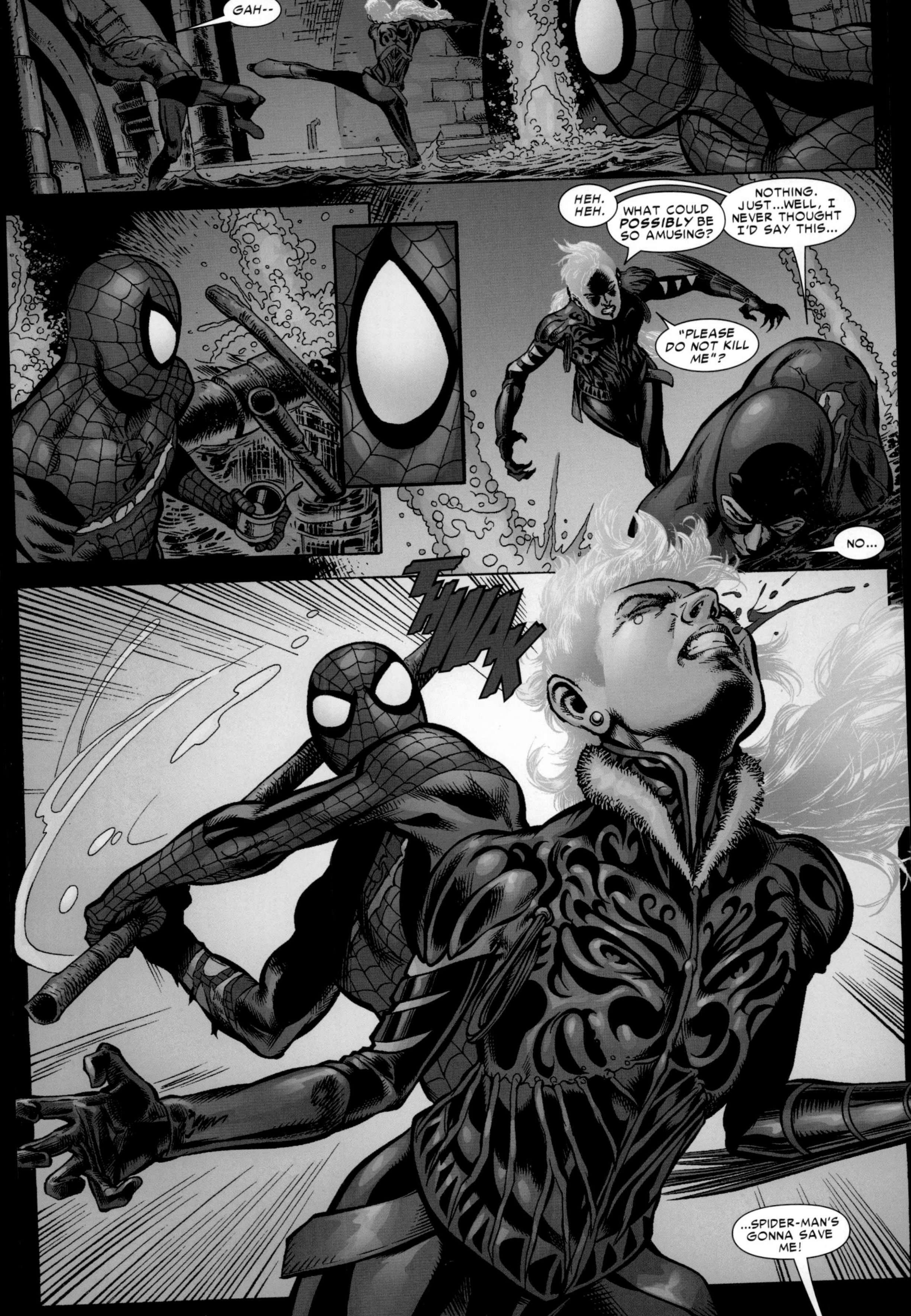
GAH--
HEH. HEH.
WHAT COULD POSSIBLY BE SO AMUSING?
NOTHING. JUST...WELL, I NEVER THOUGHT I'D SAY THIS...
"PLEASE DO NOT KILL ME"?
NO...
THWAK
...SPIDER-MAN'S GONNA SAVE ME!

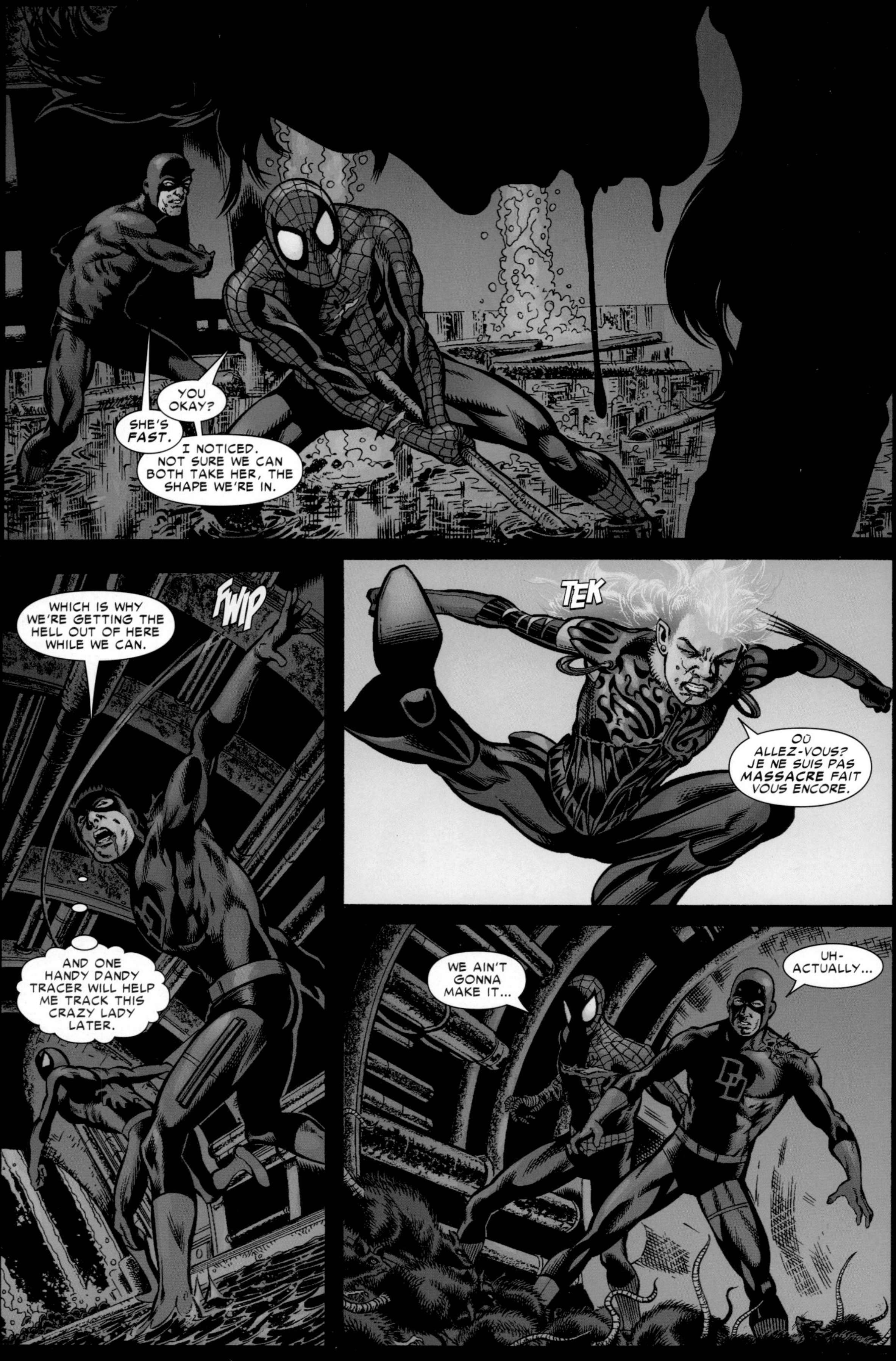
YOU OKAY?
SHE'S FAST.
I NOTICED. NOT SURE WE CAN BOTH TAKE HER, THE SHAPE WE'RE IN.
WHICH IS WHY WE'RE GETTING THE HELL OUT OF HERE WHILE WE CAN.
FWIP
AND ONE HANDY DANDY TRACER WILL HELP ME TRACK THIS CRAZY LADY LATER.
TEK
OÙ ALLEZ-VOUS? JE NE SUIS PAS MASSACRE FAIT VOUS ENCORE.
WE AIN'T GONNA MAKE IT...
UH-ACTUALLY...

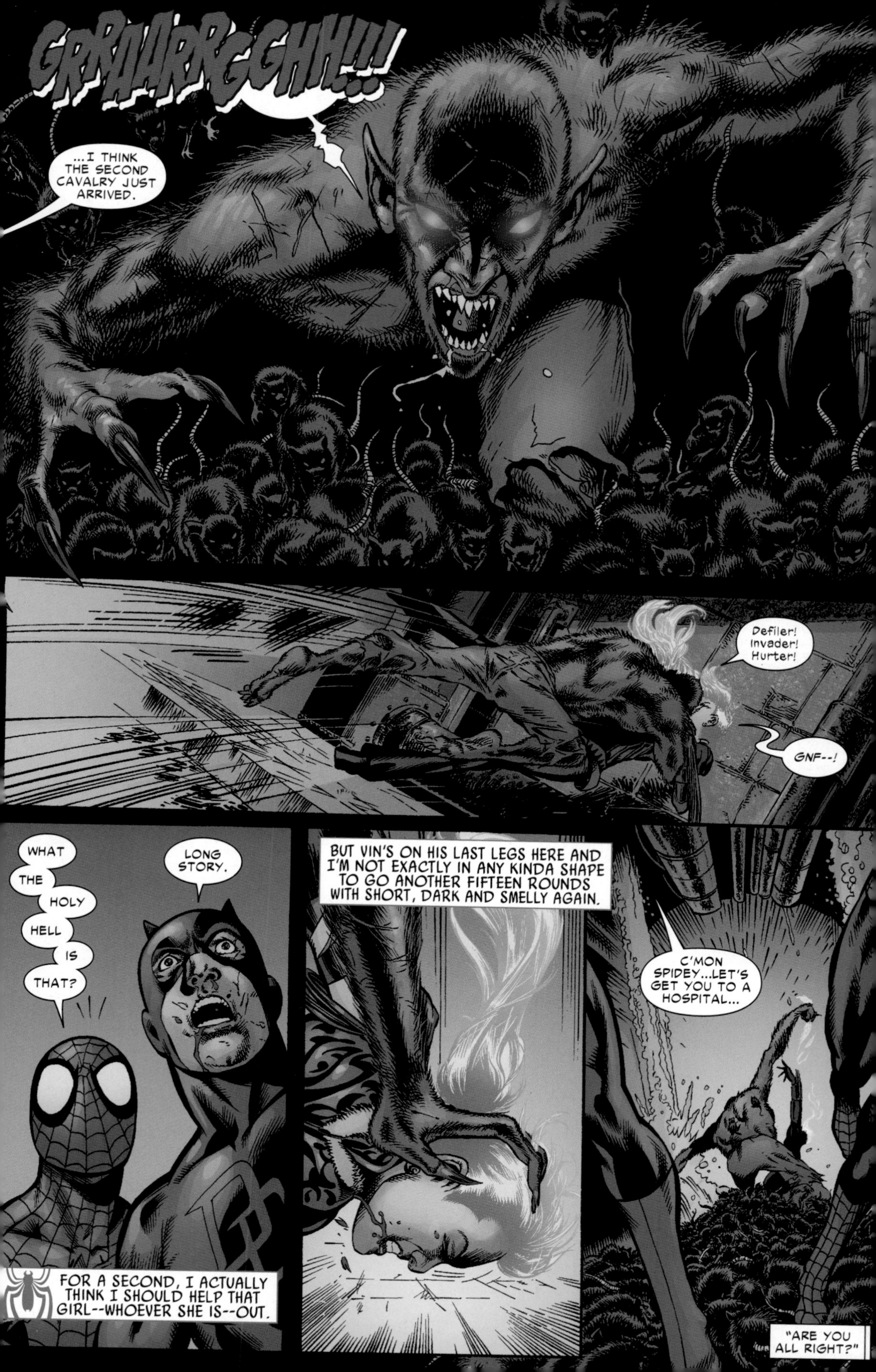
GRRAARRGGHH!!!
...I THINK THE SECOND CAVALRY JUST ARRIVED.
Defiler! Invader! Hurter!
GNF--!
WHAT THE HOLY HELL IS THAT?
LONG STORY.
FOR A SECOND, I ACTUALLY THINK I SHOULD HELP THAT GIRL--WHOEVER SHE IS--OUT.
BUT VIN'S ON HIS LAST LEGS HERE AND I'M NOT EXACTLY IN ANY KINDA SHAPE TO GO ANOTHER FIFTEEN ROUNDS WITH SHORT, DARK AND SMELLY AGAIN.
C'MON SPIDEY...LET'S GET YOU TO A HOSPITAL...
"ARE YOU ALL RIGHT?"

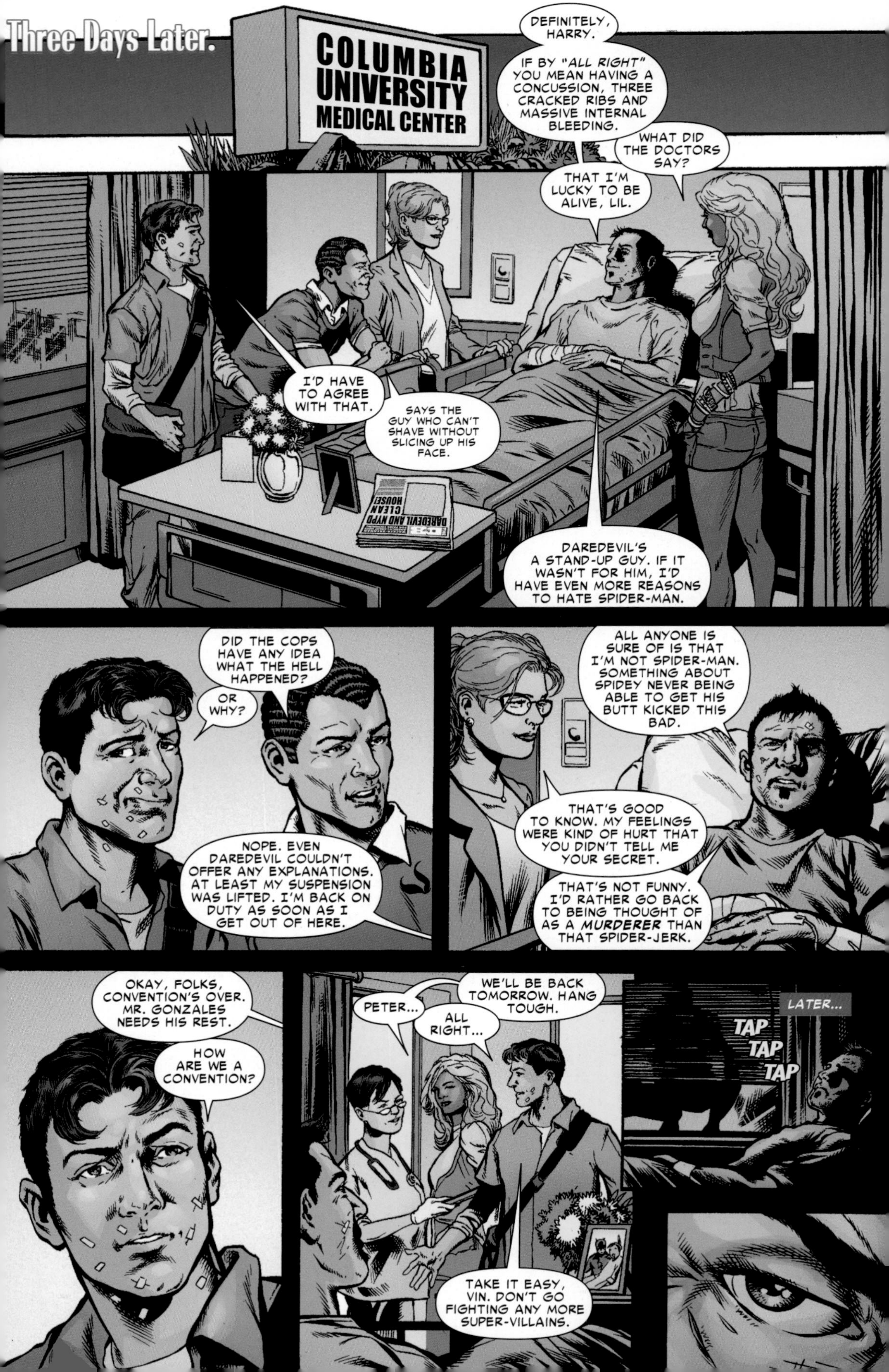

Three Days Later.
COLUMBIA UNIVERSITY MEDICAL CENTER
DEFINITELY, HARRY.
IF BY "ALL RIGHT" YOU MEAN HAVING A CONCUSSION, THREE CRACKED RIBS AND MASSIVE INTERNAL BLEEDING.
WHAT DID THE DOCTORS SAY?
THAT I'M LUCKY TO BE ALIVE, LIL.
I'D HAVE TO AGREE WITH THAT.
SAYS THE GUY WHO CAN'T SHAVE WITHOUT SLICING UP HIS FACE.
DAREDEVIL AND NYPD CLEAN HOUSE!
DAREDEVIL'S A STAND-UP GUY. IF IT WASN'T FOR HIM, I'D HAVE EVEN MORE REASONS TO HATE SPIDER-MAN.
DID THE COPS HAVE ANY IDEA WHAT THE HELL HAPPENED?
OR WHY?
NOPE. EVEN DAREDEVIL COULDN'T OFFER ANY EXPLANATIONS. AT LEAST MY SUSPENSION WAS LIFTED. I'M BACK ON DUTY AS SOON AS I GET OUT OF HERE.
ALL ANYONE IS SURE OF IS THAT I'M NOT SPIDER-MAN. SOMETHING ABOUT SPIDEY NEVER BEING ABLE TO GET HIS BUTT KICKED THIS BAD.
THAT'S GOOD TO KNOW. MY FEELINGS WERE KIND OF HURT THAT YOU DIDN'T TELL ME YOUR SECRET.
THAT'S NOT FUNNY. I'D RATHER GO BACK TO BEING THOUGHT OF AS A MURDERER THAN THAT SPIDER-JERK.
OKAY, FOLKS, CONVENTION'S OVER. MR. GONZALES NEEDS HIS REST.
HOW ARE WE A CONVENTION?
PETER...
ALL RIGHT...
WE'LL BE BACK TOMORROW. HANG TOUGH.
TAKE IT EASY, VIN. DON'T GO FIGHTING ANY MORE SUPER-VILLAINS.
LATER...
TAP
TAP
TAP

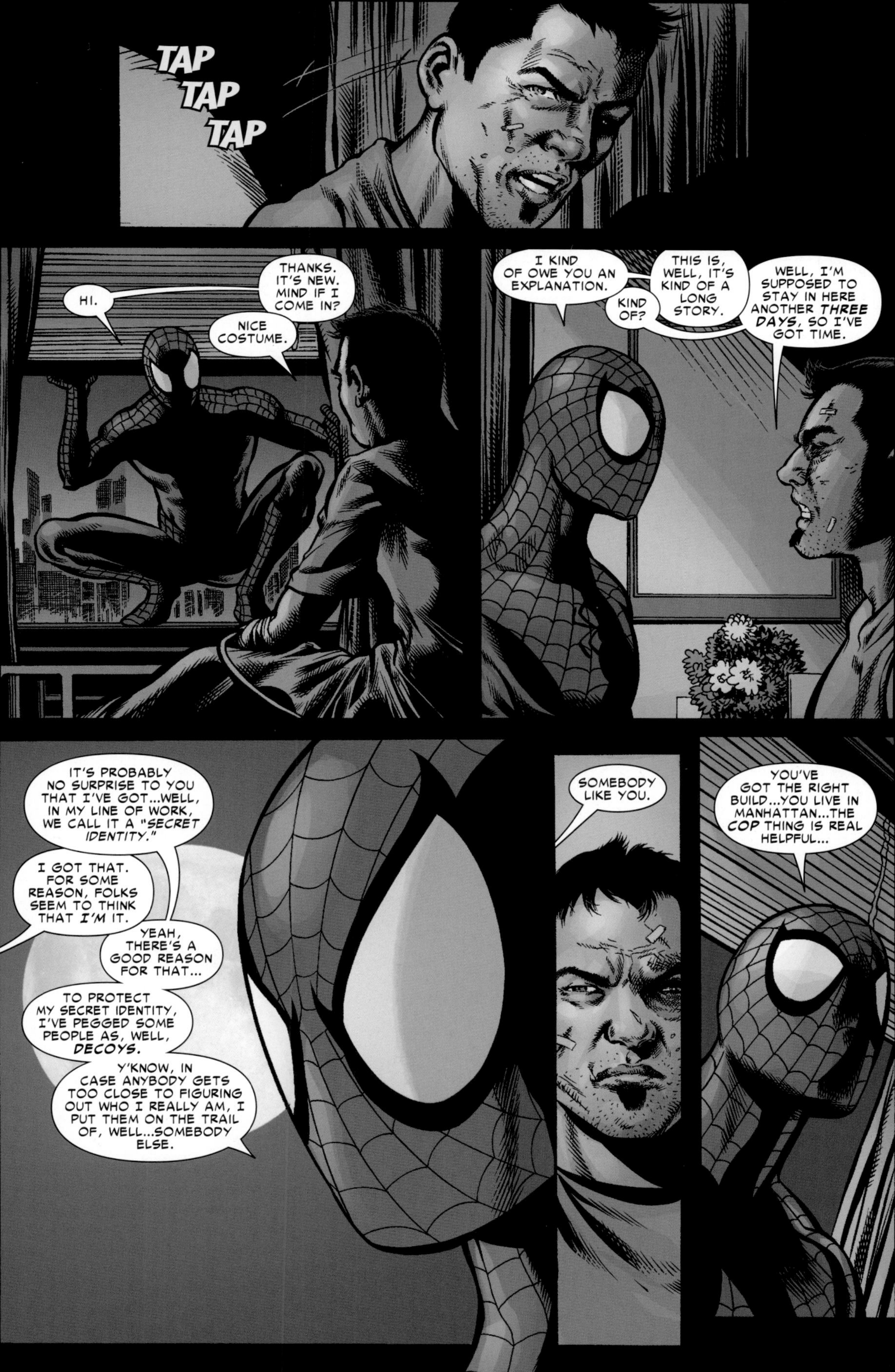

TAP TAP TAP
HI.
NICE COSTUME.
THANKS. IT'S NEW. MIND IF I COME IN?
I KIND OF OWE YOU AN EXPLANATION.
KIND OF?
THIS IS, WELL, IT'S KIND OF A LONG STORY.
WELL, I'M SUPPOSED TO STAY IN HERE ANOTHER *THREE DAYS*, SO I'VE GOT TIME.
IT'S PROBABLY NO SURPRISE TO YOU THAT I'VE GOT...WELL, IN MY LINE OF WORK, WE CALL IT A "*SECRET IDENTITY*."
I GOT THAT. FOR SOME REASON, FOLKS SEEM TO THINK THAT *I'M* IT.
YEAH, THERE'S A GOOD REASON FOR THAT...
TO PROTECT MY SECRET IDENTITY, I'VE PEGGED SOME PEOPLE AS, WELL, **DECOYS.**
Y'KNOW, IN CASE ANYBODY GETS TOO CLOSE TO FIGURING OUT WHO I REALLY AM, I PUT THEM ON THE TRAIL OF, WELL...SOMEBODY ELSE.
SOMEBODY LIKE YOU.
YOU'VE GOT THE RIGHT BUILD...YOU LIVE IN MANHATTAN...THE *COP* THING IS REAL HELPFUL...

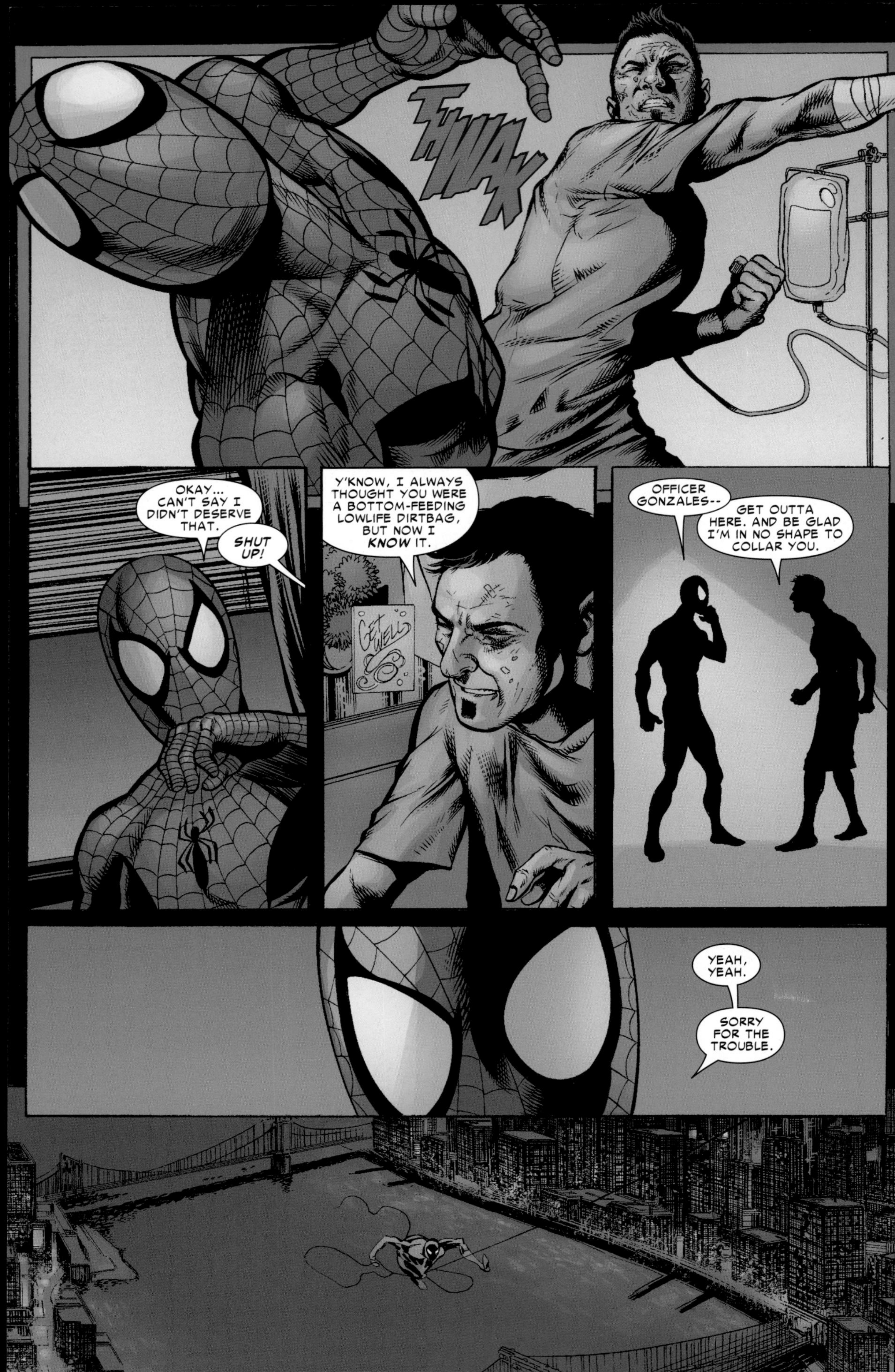

THWAK
OKAY... CAN'T SAY I DIDN'T DESERVE THAT.
SHUT UP!
Y'KNOW, I ALWAYS THOUGHT YOU WERE A BOTTOM-FEEDING LOWLIFE DIRTBAG, BUT NOW I KNOW IT.
GET WELL
OFFICER GONZALES--
GET OUTTA HERE. AND BE GLAD I'M IN NO SHAPE TO COLLAR YOU.
YEAH, YEAH.
SORRY FOR THE TROUBLE.

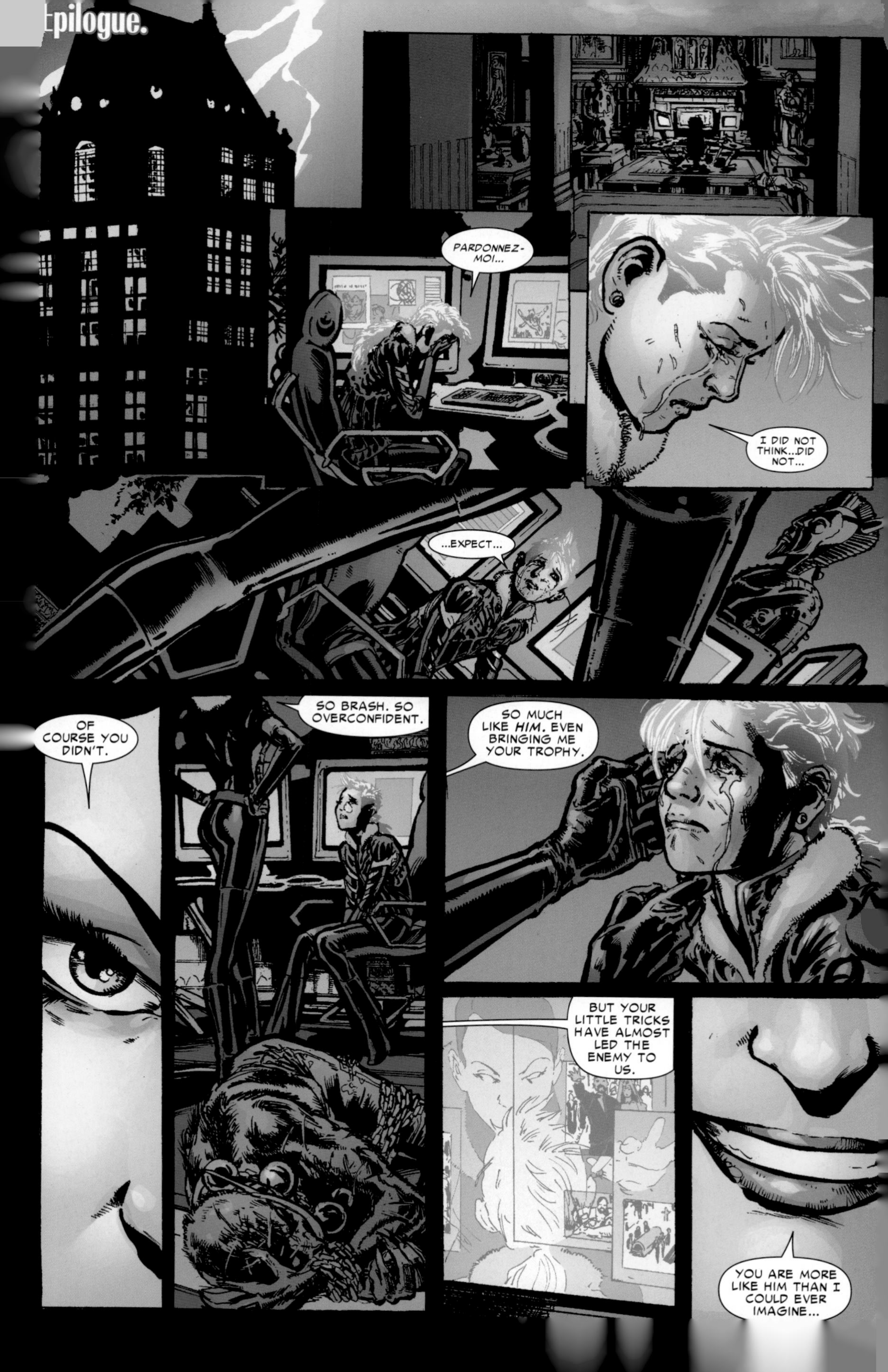
Epilogue.
PARDONNEZ-MOI...
I DID NOT THINK...DID NOT...
...EXPECT...
OF COURSE YOU DIDN'T.
SO BRASH. SO OVERCONFIDENT.
SO MUCH LIKE HIM. EVEN BRINGING ME YOUR TROPHY.
BUT YOUR LITTLE TRICKS HAVE ALMOST LED THE ENEMY TO US.
YOU ARE MORE LIKE HIM THAN I COULD EVER IMAGINE...

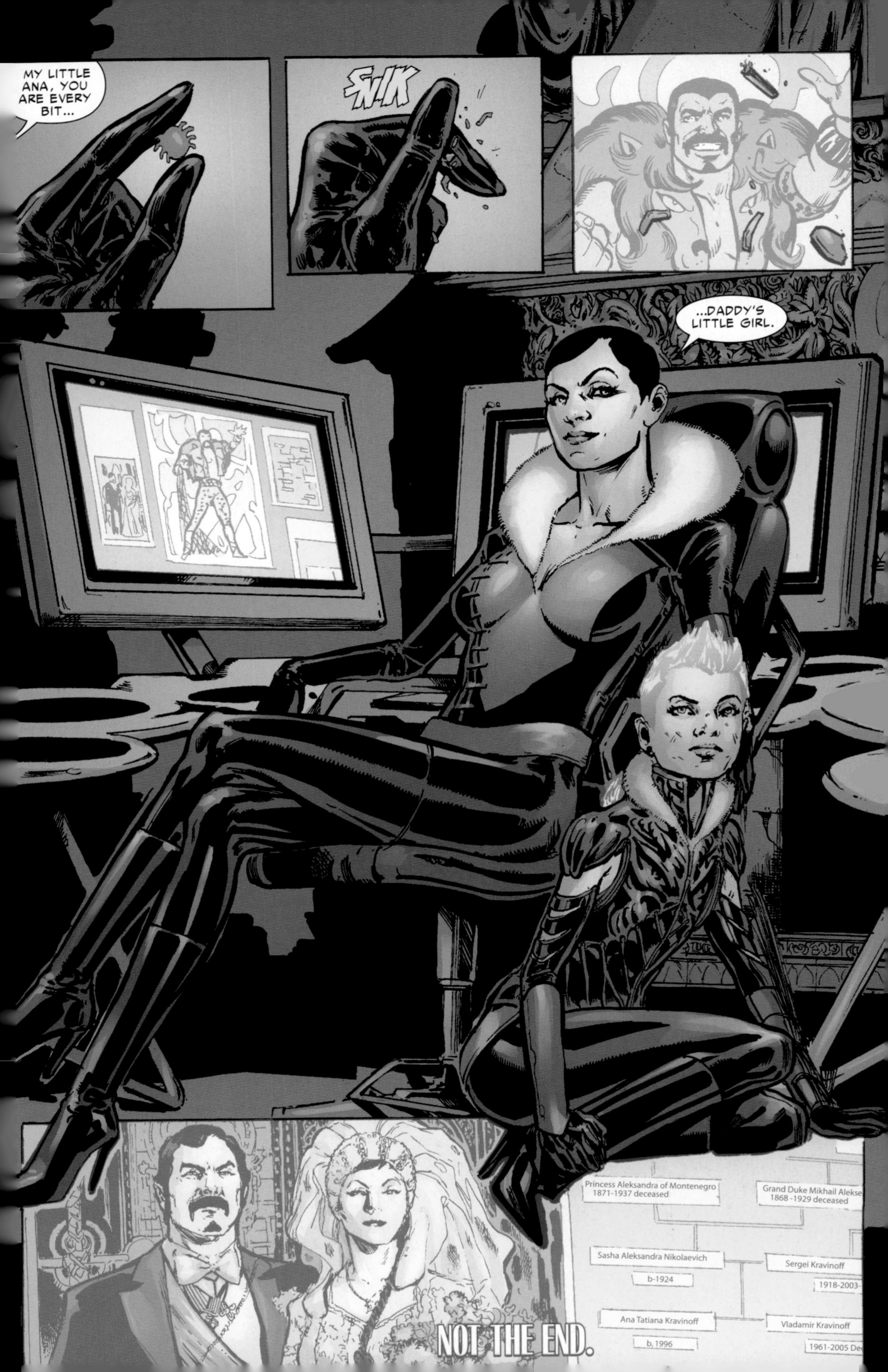
MY LITTLE ANA, YOU ARE EVERY BIT...
SNIK
...DADDY'S LITTLE GIRL.
Princess Aleksandra of Montenegro
1871-1937 deceased
Grand Duke Mikhail Alekse
1868 -1929 deceased
Sasha Aleksandra Nikolaevich
b-1924
Sergei Kravinoff
1918-2003-
Ana Tatiana Kravinoff
b. 1996
Vladamir Kravinoff
1961-2005 De
NOT THE END.

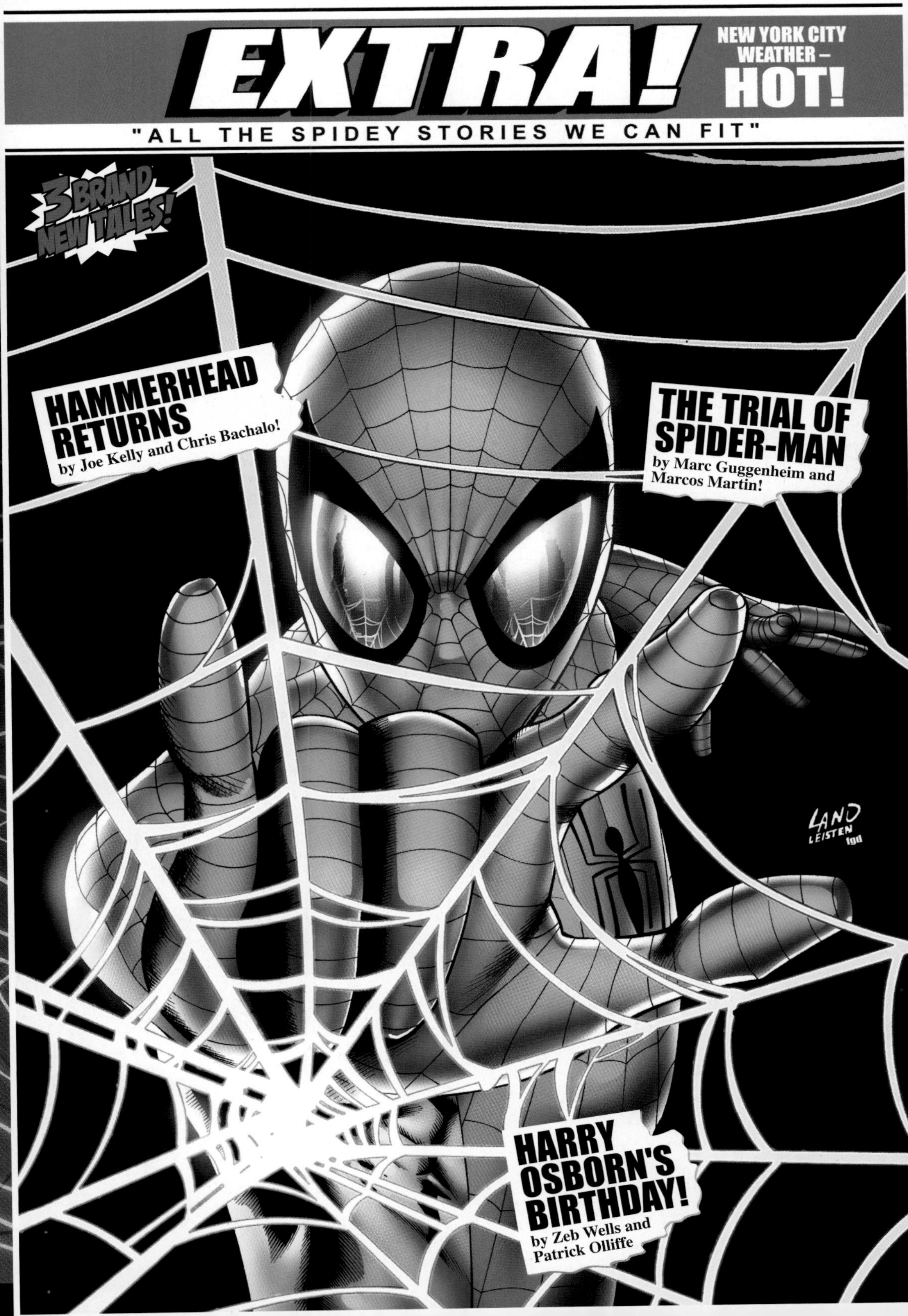

EXTRA!
NEW YORK CITY WEATHER – HOT!
"ALL THE SPIDEY STORIES WE CAN FIT"
3 BRAND NEW TALES!
HAMMERHEAD RETURNS
by Joe Kelly and Chris Bachalo!
THE TRIAL OF SPIDER-MAN
by Marc Guggenheim and Marcos Martin!
HARRY OSBORN'S BIRTHDAY!
by Zeb Wells and Patrick Olliffe
LAND LEISTEN

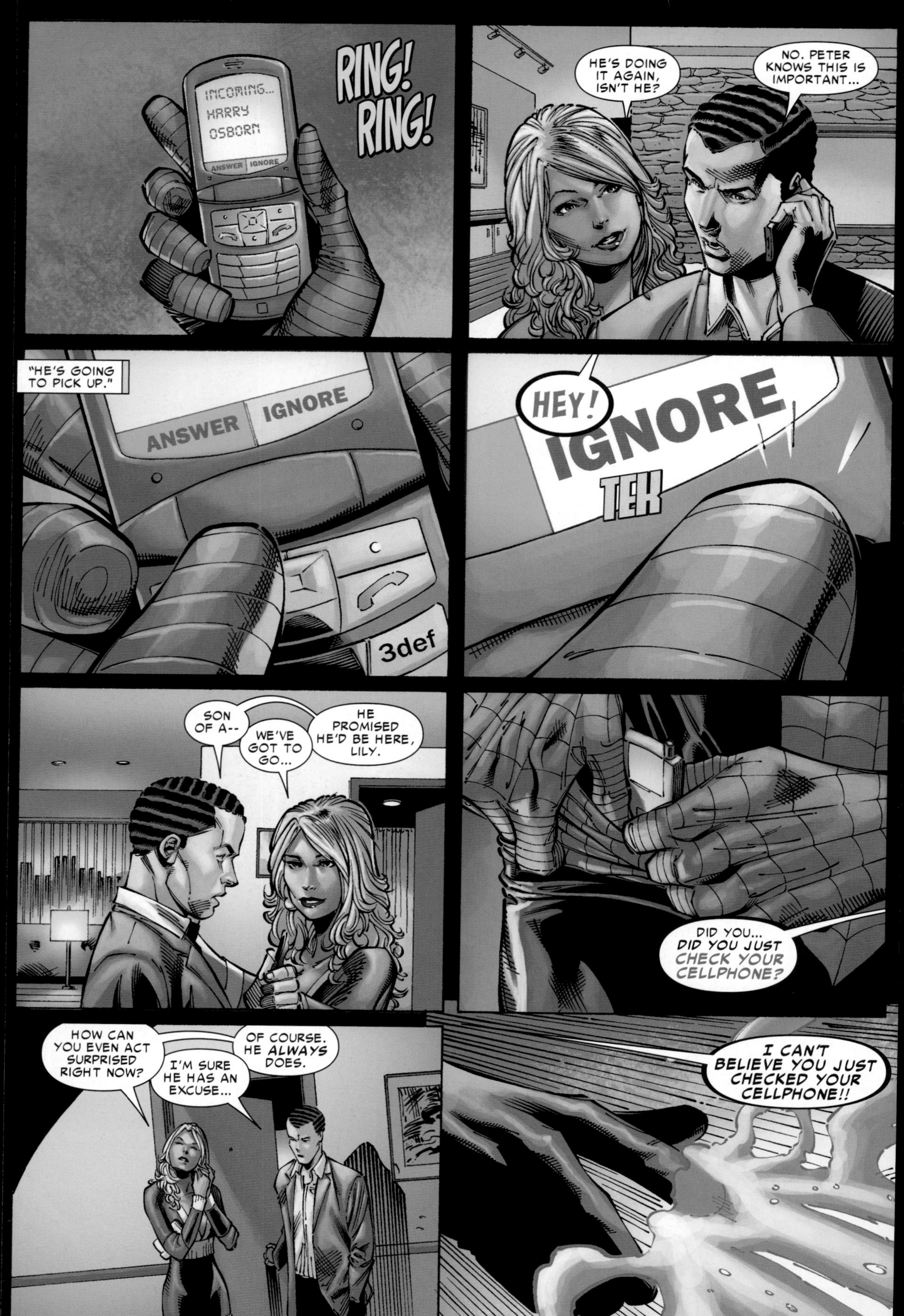
INCOMING...
HARRY
OSBORN
ANSWER IGNORE
RING!
RING!
HE'S DOING IT AGAIN, ISN'T HE?
NO. PETER KNOWS THIS IS IMPORTANT...
"HE'S GOING TO PICK UP."
ANSWER IGNORE
3def
HEY!
IGNORE
TEK
SON OF A--
WE'VE GOT TO GO...
HE PROMISED HE'D BE HERE, LILY.
DID YOU... DID YOU JUST CHECK YOUR CELLPHONE?
HOW CAN YOU EVEN ACT SURPRISED RIGHT NOW?
I'M SURE HE HAS AN EXCUSE...
OF COURSE. HE ALWAYS DOES.
I CAN'T BELIEVE YOU JUST CHECKED YOUR CELLPHONE!!

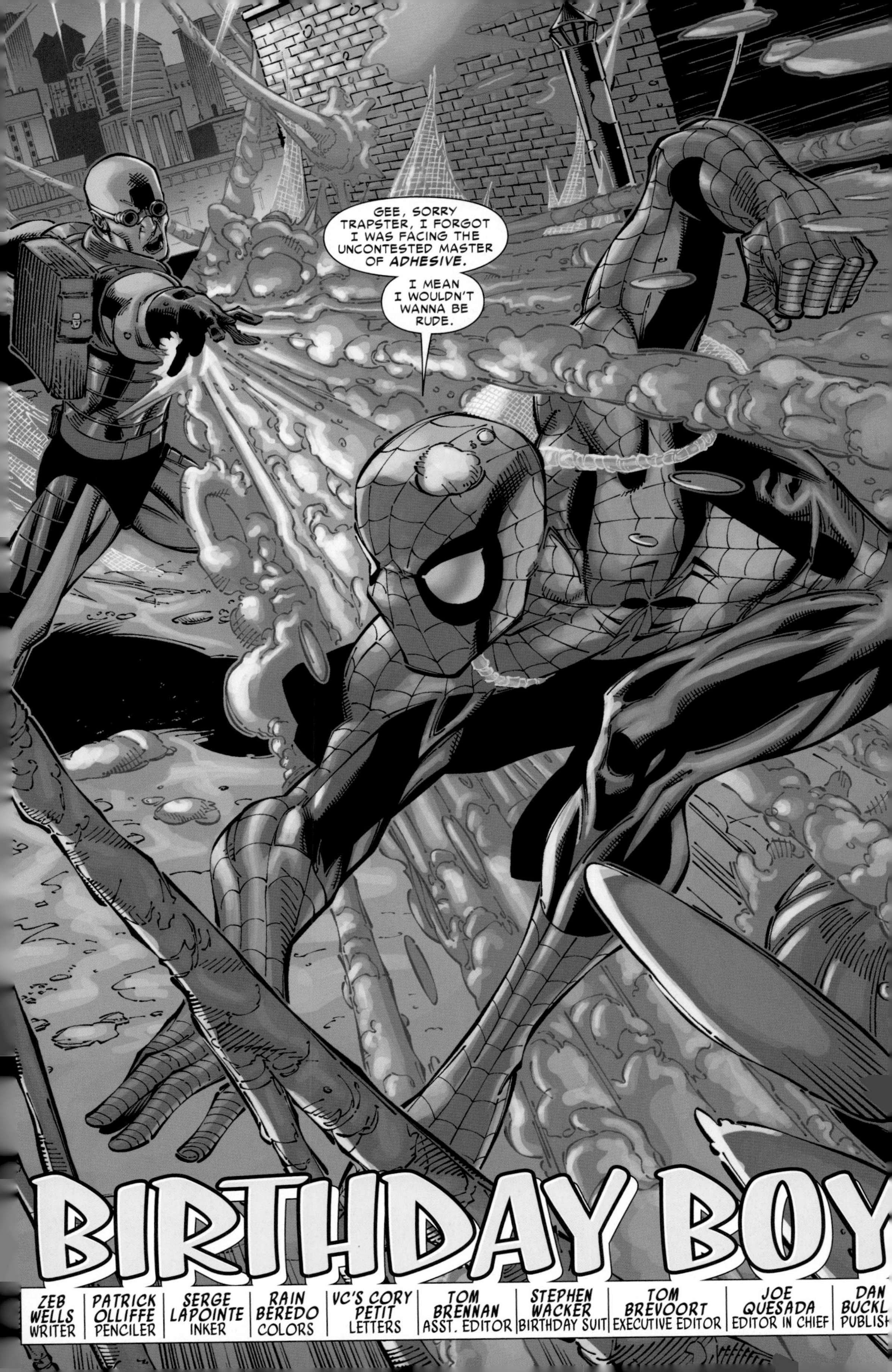
GEE, SORRY TRAPSTER, I FORGOT I WAS FACING THE UNCONTESTED MASTER OF ADHESIVE.
I MEAN I WOULDN'T WANNA BE RUDE.
BIRTHDAY BOY
ZEB WELLS WRITER
PATRICK OLLIFFE PENCILER
SERGE LAPOINTE INKER
RAIN BEREDO COLORS
VC'S CORY PETIT LETTERS
TOM BRENNAN ASST. EDITOR
STEPHEN WACKER BIRTHDAY SUIT
TOM BREVOORT EXECUTIVE EDITOR
JOE QUESADA EDITOR IN CHIEF
DAN BUCKL PUBLISH

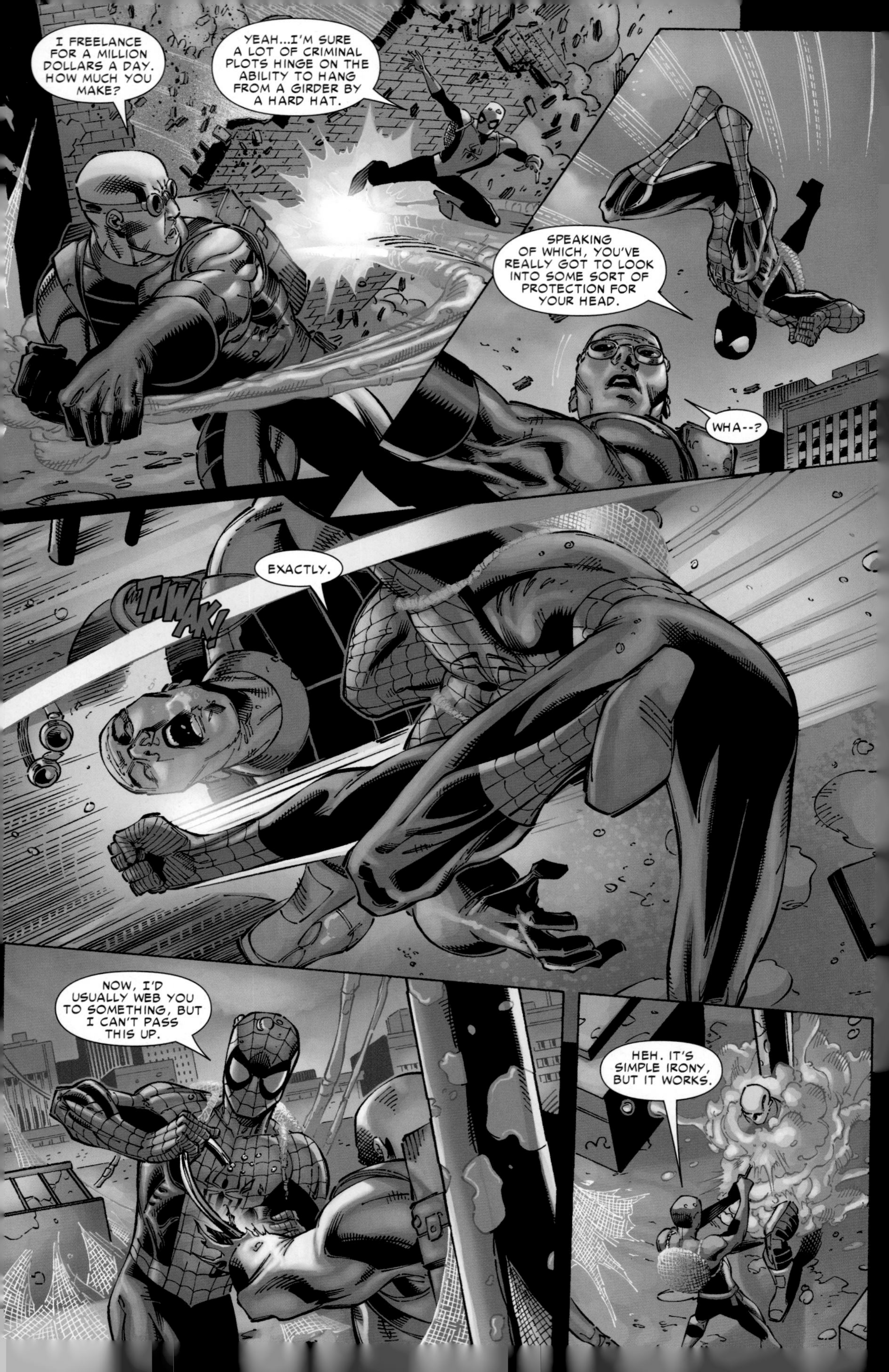
I FREELANCE FOR A MILLION DOLLARS A DAY. HOW MUCH YOU MAKE?
YEAH...I'M SURE A LOT OF CRIMINAL PLOTS HINGE ON THE ABILITY TO HANG FROM A GIRDER BY A HARD HAT.
SPEAKING OF WHICH, YOU'VE REALLY GOT TO LOOK INTO SOME SORT OF PROTECTION FOR YOUR HEAD.
WHA--?
EXACTLY.
THWAK!
NOW, I'D USUALLY WEB YOU TO SOMETHING, BUT I CAN'T PASS THIS UP.
HEH. IT'S SIMPLE IRONY, BUT IT WORKS.

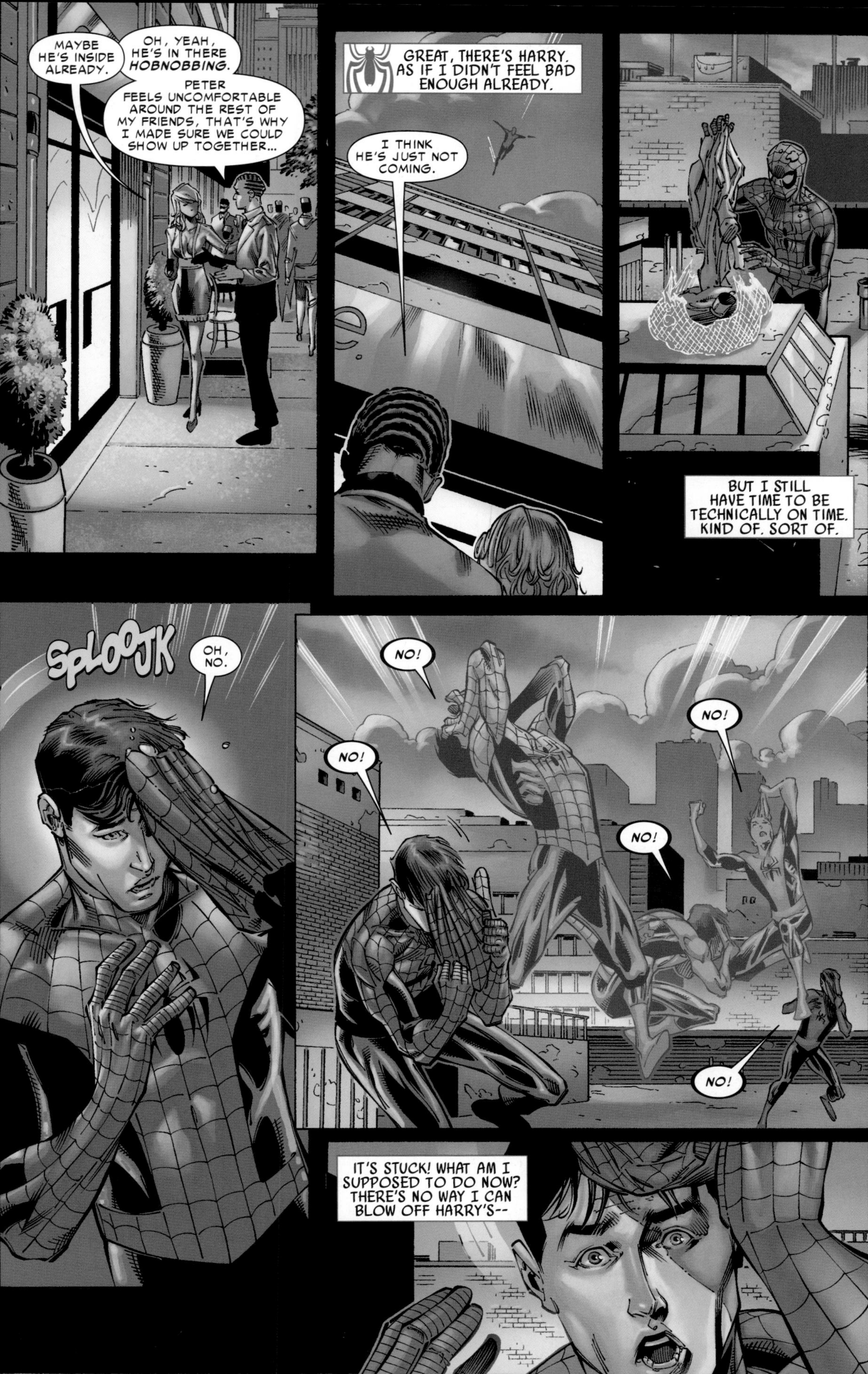
MAYBE HE'S INSIDE ALREADY.
OH, YEAH, HE'S IN THERE HOBNOBBING.
PETER FEELS UNCOMFORTABLE AROUND THE REST OF MY FRIENDS, THAT'S WHY I MADE SURE WE COULD SHOW UP TOGETHER...
GREAT, THERE'S HARRY. AS IF I DIDN'T FEEL BAD ENOUGH ALREADY.
I THINK HE'S JUST NOT COMING.
BUT I STILL HAVE TIME TO BE TECHNICALLY ON TIME. KIND OF. SORT OF.
SPLOOJK
OH, NO.
NO!
NO!
NO!
NO!
NO!
IT'S STUCK! WHAT AM I SUPPOSED TO DO NOW? THERE'S NO WAY I CAN BLOW OFF HARRY'S--

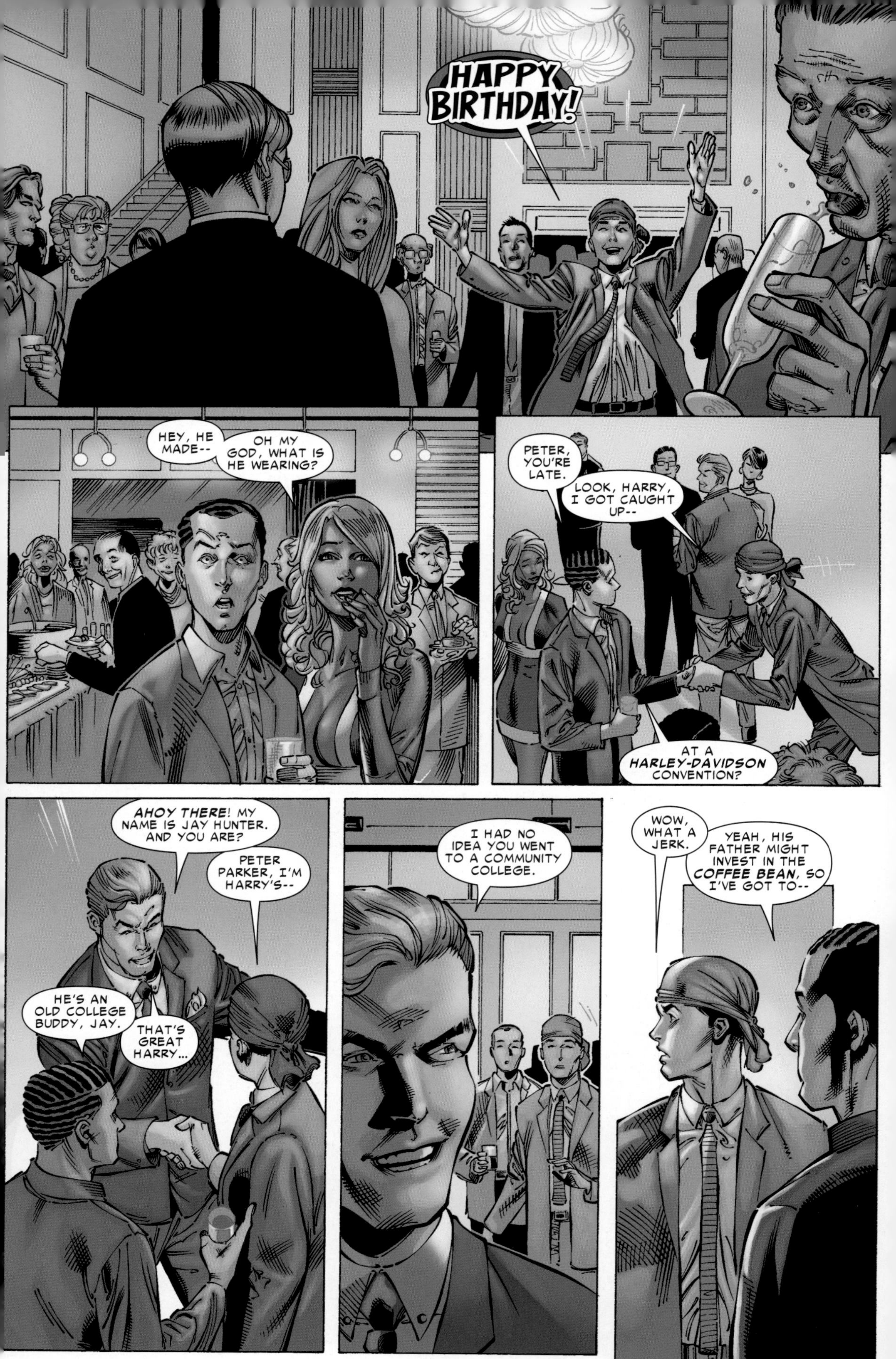
HAPPY BIRTHDAY!
HEY, HE MADE--
OH MY GOD, WHAT IS HE WEARING?
PETER, YOU'RE LATE.
LOOK, HARRY, I GOT CAUGHT UP--
AT A *HARLEY-DAVIDSON* CONVENTION?
AHOY THERE! MY NAME IS JAY HUNTER. AND YOU ARE?
PETER PARKER, I'M HARRY'S--
HE'S AN OLD COLLEGE BUDDY, JAY.
THAT'S GREAT HARRY...
I HAD NO IDEA YOU WENT TO A COMMUNITY COLLEGE.
WOW, WHAT A JERK.
YEAH, HIS FATHER MIGHT INVEST IN THE *COFFEE BEAN*, SO I'VE GOT TO--

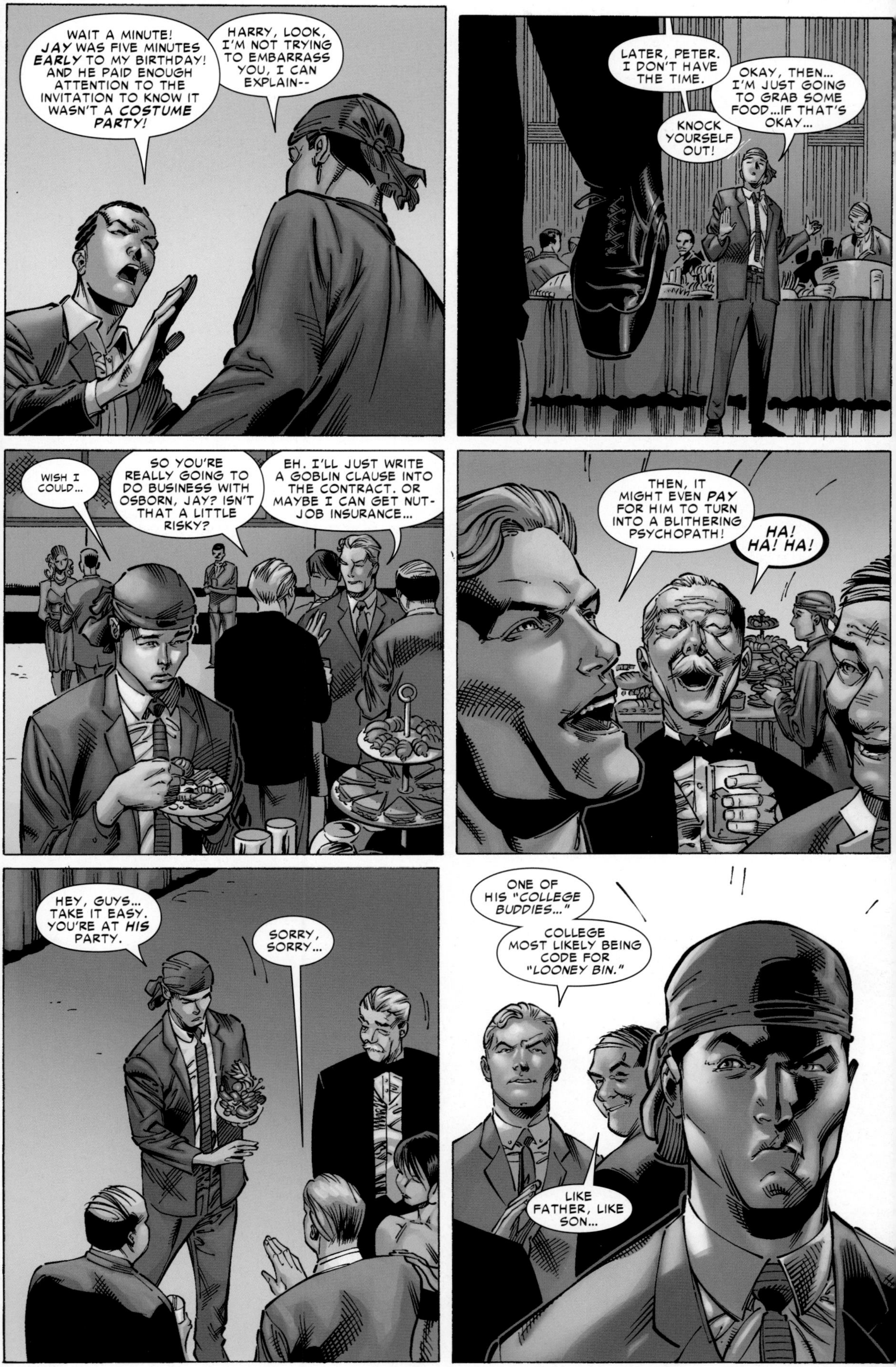
WAIT A MINUTE! JAY WAS FIVE MINUTES EARLY TO MY BIRTHDAY! AND HE PAID ENOUGH ATTENTION TO THE INVITATION TO KNOW IT WASN'T A COSTUME PARTY!
HARRY, LOOK, I'M NOT TRYING TO EMBARRASS YOU, I CAN EXPLAIN--
LATER, PETER. I DON'T HAVE THE TIME.
OKAY, THEN... I'M JUST GOING TO GRAB SOME FOOD...IF THAT'S OKAY...
KNOCK YOURSELF OUT!
WISH I COULD...
SO YOU'RE REALLY GOING TO DO BUSINESS WITH OSBORN, JAY? ISN'T THAT A LITTLE RISKY?
EH. I'LL JUST WRITE A GOBLIN CLAUSE INTO THE CONTRACT. OR MAYBE I CAN GET NUT-JOB INSURANCE...
THEN, IT MIGHT EVEN PAY FOR HIM TO TURN INTO A BLITHERING PSYCHOPATH!
HA! HA! HA!
HEY, GUYS... TAKE IT EASY. YOU'RE AT HIS PARTY.
SORRY, SORRY...
ONE OF HIS "COLLEGE BUDDIES..."
COLLEGE MOST LIKELY BEING CODE FOR "LOONEY BIN."
LIKE FATHER, LIKE SON...

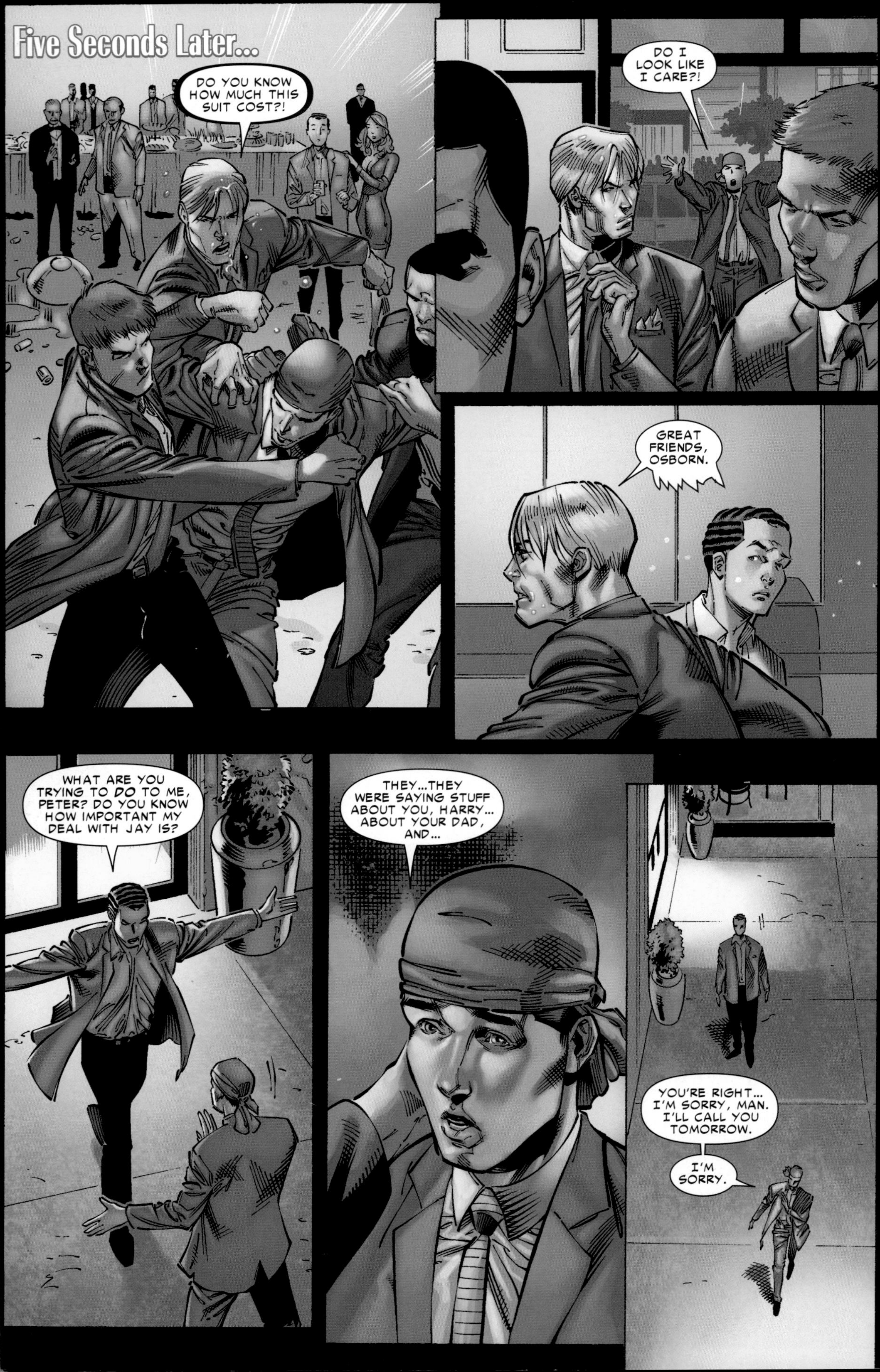
Five Seconds Later...
DO YOU KNOW HOW MUCH THIS SUIT COST?!
DO I LOOK LIKE I CARE?!
GREAT FRIENDS, OSBORN.
WHAT ARE YOU TRYING TO DO TO ME, PETER? DO YOU KNOW HOW IMPORTANT MY DEAL WITH JAY IS?
THEY...THEY WERE SAYING STUFF ABOUT YOU, HARRY... ABOUT YOUR DAD, AND...
YOU'RE RIGHT... I'M SORRY, MAN. I'LL CALL YOU TOMORROW.
I'M SORRY.

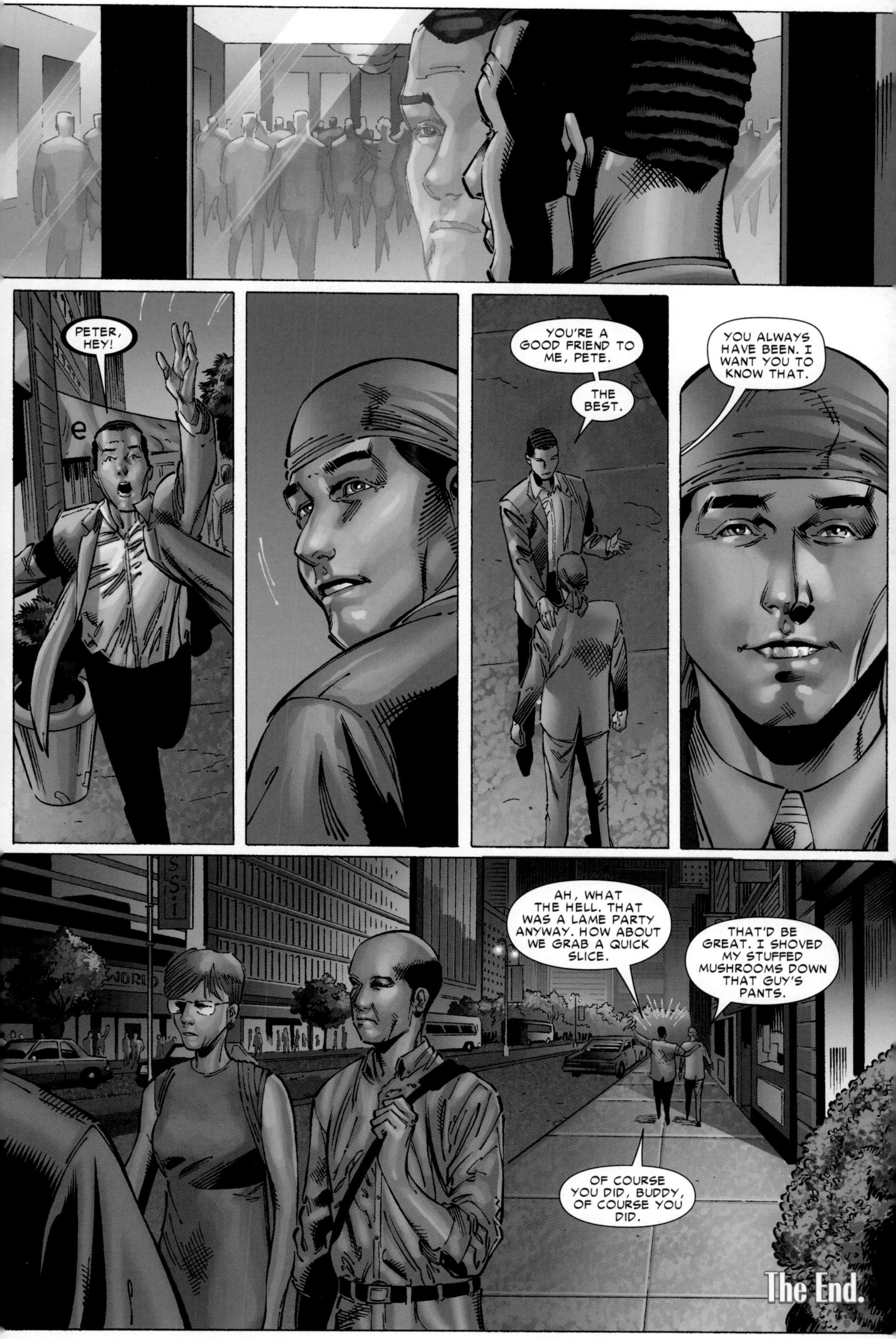
PETER, HEY!
YOU'RE A GOOD FRIEND TO ME, PETE.
THE BEST.
YOU ALWAYS HAVE BEEN. I WANT YOU TO KNOW THAT.
AH, WHAT THE HELL. THAT WAS A LAME PARTY ANYWAY. HOW ABOUT WE GRAB A QUICK SLICE.
THAT'D BE GREAT. I SHOVED MY STUFFED MUSHROOMS DOWN THAT GUY'S PANTS.
OF COURSE YOU DID, BUDDY, OF COURSE YOU DID.
The End.

AMAZING SPIDER-MAN #564

Bob Gale, Marc Guggenheim & Dan Slott

PAGE 1 (5 PANELS)

PANEL 1 Big panel. Low angle. Street-level. We're in the Bronx, in the shadow of the NEW YANKEE STADIUM. Yeah, there's a new one, apparently.

A tricked-out (see below) CONVERTIBLE SPORTSCAR is racing towards "camera."

The driver of the sportscar is OVERDRIVE, the super-villain who first (and last) appeared in *Spider-Man: Swing Shift*.

The exterior of the sportscar itself actually mimics Overdrive's look -- i.e., shiny BLACK armor plating (think Night Rider, Street Hawk, Airwolf, etc.), CHROME grill & accessories, with NEON GREEN piping and lighting. The interior should be BLACK leather with NEON GREEN piping.

TITLE & CREDITS at the top of the page:

THREEWAY COLLISION!

Above the sportscar (but below our title), web-swinging in hot pursuit, is... SPIDER-MAN!

SPIDER-MAN: Hey! Slow <u>down</u>, willya?!

SPIDER-MAN CAPTION: Why do these things always happen to <u>me</u>?

SPIDER-MAN: How can I pummel you senseless if I can't get my hands on you?

PANEL 2 Behind Spidey now as he swings after the sportscar, which is weaving in and out of traffic.

SPIDER-MAN: And you <u>just</u> ran a red light!

SPIDER-MAN CAPTION: <u>Of</u> <u>course</u> some homicidal driver would wanna play real-life *Grand Theft Auto* while I'm on my way to a job interview.

PANEL 3 The sportscar SKIDS past a MAN walking on the sidewalk. His face OBSCURED by the copy of THE DB that he's got his nose buried in. **(SW-This is Dexter Bennett, though we don't realize that until chapter 3)**

SFX: SKREEEEEEEEEEEEEEEE

PANEL 4 Spidey is somersaulting down on to the hood of the convertible now as it brushes past the man, blowing the newspaper out of his hands (though in such a way that we still can't see his face).

SFX: FFFFFOOOOOOOOOMMMMMMMMMMMMMMF

SPIDER-MAN: I'm gonna need to see your license and proof of-- Hey! I know you!

PANEL 5 New angle. Spidey's P.O.V.: Looking at Overdrive in the driver's seat.

SPIDER-MAN: Overdrive!

(CONT'D) I should've known. This little chase smacked of *déjà vu*.*

CAPTION: *Spidey first chased Overdrive in *Spider-Man: Swing Shift*.

(CONT'D) What do you mean you didn't buy it? It was *free*.

(CONT'D) What do you mean "and you want your money back"? Go back on the Internet, fanboy.

PAGE 2 (5 PANELS)

PANEL 1 Spidey is leaning forward, over the windshield, and tagging Overdrive with a punch across the jaw.

SPIDER-MAN: Speaking of <u>smacked</u>...

SFX: CRAK

PANEL 2 Overdrive, reeling from Spidey's punch is losing control of the car...

OVERDRIVE: Idiot, I can't--

PANEL 3 Big panel. Spidey is LEAPING out of the way as the sportscar careens out of control.

SPIDER-MAN CAPTION: Like I was supposed to know the guy can't take a punch <u>and</u> drive at the same time...

PANEL 4 New angle. We're with VIN GONZALES, in civilian clothes, pursuing the action on foot, CELL PHONE pressed to his mouth, as the sportscar FLIPS OVER, SOMERSAULTING through the air.

VIN: Twenty-Adam-Twelve, Fifteen-Baker-Nine

<<COULD WE GET PROPER NYPD RADIO TAGS?>>.

(CONT'D) Need ESU and medics down here ay-sap. Continuing to pursue on foot. Officer in civilian clothes.

PANEL 5 Back with Spidey as he fires his webshooters at the still-flipping car.

SPIDER-MAN CAPTION:I just know I'm gonna get blamed for this somehow...

(CONT'D) Even though it's kind of my fault...

SFX: THWIP

PAGE 3 (6 PANELS)

PANEL 1 Spidey is tugging <u>hard</u> on his webstrands (both fists), trying to stop the car's momentum.

SPIDER-MAN: GNNNGG--

PANEL 2 Aftermath. The sportscar is webbed up and safely stopped now, upside down in the middle of the street. Spidey is leaping towards it.

SPIDER-MAN: Please keep your hands and arms inside the car until the ride has come to a full and complete--

PANEL 3 Overdrive is LEAPING out of the car, tagging Spidey with a PUNCH to the jaw.

SPIDER-MAN: OW.

SFX: SHAK

PANEL 4 Spidey is spinning around, reaching out to catch the fleeing Overdrive, but SOMEONE is edging into panel, holding a REVOLVER.

SPIDER-MAN: (to Overdrive): Lucky shot!

OFF-PANEL SOMEONE: FREEZE!

PANEL 5 Spidey is wheeling back around to see that the person from the previous panel is Vin, holding his service revolver in a two-handed grip, pointed at Spider-Man.

VIN: On the ground!

SPIDER-MAN: Are you talking to me or the, y'know, ACTUAL BAD GUY?

PANEL 6 Spidey is leaping away, firing a web strand as he goes.

VIN: You're under arrest for violation of 6 U.S.C. § 558 and multiple counts of Chapter 40, Article 120 of the New York Penal Code.

SPIDER-MAN: You can't arrest me! I'm the good guy.

VIN: You're a vigilante and a serial killer and you have the right to remain silent. You have the right to an attorney...

SPIDER-MAN: Keep going. Don't let me stop you.

(CONT'D): Told'ja you couldn't arrest me...

PAGE 4 (6 PANELS)

PANEL 1 New angle. With Overdrive as he forces his way on to a YELLOW SCHOOL BUS. The short, van-like kind.

OVERDRIVE: Excuse me...

PANEL 2 Back with Spidey. Swinging in pursuit as Overdrive boards the bus.

SPIDER-MAN CAPTION: A school bus.

(CONT'D) He's getting on a <u>school</u> <u>bus</u>.

(CONT'D) Well, that's just dandy swell...

PANEL 3 In the bus. The BUS DRIVER stays at the wheel and Overdrive is kneeling down on the floor of the bus, pressing his palms to the floor. The SCHOOLKIDS are watching in amazement and awe. **(SW-Some kids should have NY Mets hats and jerseys and others should have NY Yankees)**

OVERDRIVE: Hang on to your seats, kids.

PANEL 4 Big energy effects are radiating out from Overdrive's hands.

SFX: SHHHHHHRRRRRRRRRRRRRRRMMMMMMMMM

PANEL 5 Spidey is swinging into panel in the foreground, while in the background, the school bus is MORPHING into an "Overdrived" version of itself -- i.e., the same sleek black look described above for the convertible, but applied, incongruously, to a school bus.

SFX: MMMMMMMAAAAAAAANNNNNNKKKKKKKK

SPIDER-MAN CAPTION: Holy Spit.

(CONT'D) I'd heard tell Overdrive's power was to "trick out" vehicles --

(CONT'D) (<u>Interesting</u> little power, by the way.)

PAGE 5 (5 PANELS)
PANEL 1 High angle. Spidey is DIVING towards the bus' REAR WINDOW.
SPIDER-MAN CAPTION: -- but you really have to see it in action to believe it.
(CONT'D) I've just <u>gotta</u> ask this guy how he does it.
PANEL 2 Inside the bus. Spidey is CRASHING through the rear window.
SFX: SKRASH
SPIDER-MAN: Just thinking outside the box here, but I was wondering if you might consider turning yourself in...
PANEL 3 Maintaining his momentum from the previous panel, Spidey is landing a punch across Overdrive's face.
SFX: KRAK!
SPIDER-MAN: I've got me a job interview to go to and you probably wanna save yourself some bodily injury.
(CONT'D) It's win-win.
PANEL 4 Overdrive is pulling out a HI-TECH GUN from his costume.
OVERDRIVE: I have a better idea.
PANEL 5 The gun is creating a kind of SONIC WAVE, which is propelling Spidey towards the back of the bus.
SFX: BOOOOOOOOOFFFFFF
SPIDER-MAN: THAT IS <u>NOT</u> A BETTER IDEA!

PAGE 6 (5 PANELS)
PANEL 1 Outside now. Spidey is exploding out of the back of the bus. In the background, we can spot the TAXICAB that we'll see Vin in later in this issue.
SPIDER-MAN CAPTION: And to think... for <u>this</u> I left a promising career in the world of <u>professional</u> <u>wrestling</u>.
PANEL 2 Back in the bus. Overdrive is standing over the terrified bus driver, who's half-way out of his seat.
OVERDRIVE: Mind if I drive for a bit?
PANEL 3 With Spidey now. He's leaping back in pursuit of the bus.
SPIDER-MAN CAPTION: Okay, let's think...
(CONT'D) How'd I beat Overdrive last time?
PANEL 4 Spidey LANDS on the roof of the still-speeding bus.
SPIDER-MAN CAPTION: That's right, I sent his car into the East River.
(CONT'D) PROBABLY WOULDN'T BE A GOOD IDEA WITH A BUSLOAD OF SCHOOL KIDS.
PANEL 5 Spidey, facing the rear of the bus, is firing his webshooters at something off-panel.
SPIDER-MAN CAPTION: So... Plan B.

PAGE SEVEN (5 PANELS)
PANEL 1 Back in the bus. Overdrive, still at the wheel, is reacting to the sight of Spidey PUNCHING THROUGH the windshield.
LEGEND: Two full canisters of web-fluid later...
SPIDER-MAN: Hi. I'm from Geico. Did you know you could save fifty dollars a month on car insurance?
SFX: SHRAK
PANEL 2 Spidey is reaching forward and GRABBING the gun Overdrive had used on him earlier.
SPIDER-MAN: Mind if I borrow this for a sec? Thanks!
PANEL 3 Spidey is FIRING the gun towards the back of the bus.
SPIDER-MAN: DUCK KIDS!
PANEL 4 REVEAL that the REAR DOOR of the bus has been completely BLOWN OPEN. Through the open gap, instead of street, all we see is WEBBING.
SFX: SHHHHRRRRRMMMMAAANNNNNNKKKKK
PANEL 5 Spidey is pointing to the rear of the bus.
SPIDER-MAN: Alright, kids! Abandon ship! I mean, bus! Abandon bus! Get outta here!

PAGE 8 (5 PANELS)
PANEL 1 The kids are now JUMPING through the gap into the webbing.

KIDS: Yeah!
(CONT'D) Cowabunga!
(CONT'D) Dude, nobody says "cowabunga" anymore.
(CONT'D) Spidey's the bomb!
PANEL 2 Outside now. REVEAL that Spidey has webbed up a huge BUBBLE OF WEBBING to the back of the bus. It's CATCHING the kids as they jump out the back of the bus (which we don't need to see in this panel).
SPIDER-MAN CAPTION: I <u>love</u> it when I'm this good.
PANEL 3 The weight of the kids holds the webbing bubble down as the bus continues its forward momentum, causing the bubble to DETACH from the back of the bus. **(SW-Spidey needs to be seen detaching webbing)**
SPIDER-MAN CAPTION: Happy -- and safe -- landings, kids.
PANEL 4 Back in the bus. Spidey is turning back around, towards the front.
SPIDER-MAN: Now that we have this moment alone...
PANEL 5 REVEAL that Spidey is looking at... *an empty driver's seat.* Overdrive is nowhere to be found.
SPIDER-MAN CAPTION: Funny. I remember this from an *Indiana Jones* movie...

PAGES 9 AND 10 (11 PANELS ON 2 PAGES)
Paolo, I didn't call the page break because I don't want to impinge on your outstanding sense of layout. I'm guessing you'd want to put 6 or 7 panels on page 1, so that you'll have more space for bigger images on page 2, but you're the artist! (And a damned good one!)
PANEL 1 ON VIN, OUTDOORS SOMEWHERE - DAY
We start medium close on Vin – he's wearing a lightweight button down Yankees jersey, open so we can see a T-shirt underneath, and a Yankees baseball cap. We're not sure where we are, other than being outside in daylight.
VIN NARRATION: "Why do these things always happen to <u>me</u>? First Parker ruins my morning…and then Spider-Man ruins my afternoon."
PANEL 2 FLASHBACK BEGINS. VIN/PETE APARTMENT - DAY
The apartment of Pete and Vin. Living room or kitchen. Vin is in T-shirt and jeans. I'm thinking he's leaning against a doorway, arms crossed and not happy – he's just overheard his roommate, Peter Parker (also dressed very casually) **(Put Peter in a New York Mets jersey)** finishing up call on his cellphone in hand. So maybe this is the doorway that leads to Vin's bedroom – Vin just came out and overheard Pete on the phone. Pete has a sheepish expression.
VIN: So I presume there's something you forgot to tell me, Parker…?
PP: Huh? Well…no…not really.
PANEL 3 Vin steps closer to Pete.
VIN: I heard you on the phone. A job interview in the Bronx this afternoon, eh? Photographers who make good money at the DB don't go out on job interviews in other boroughs. Unless it's because…
PANEL 4 Favoring or single on Pete. Busted.
PP: Right. Okay. I got fired. Two weeks ago.*
FOOTNOTE: *Which would 561 to us.
PANEL 5 Vin and Pete. Pete's dropped his head.
VIN: And you were planning on telling me this…when?
PP: Once I got another job.
PANEL 6 VIN: Lying to a cop. I don't need that from my roommate.
P: I wasn't lying. I was…withholding information.
PANEL 7 On Vin
VIN: Look, as long as you pay your rent, I don't care if you're unemployed. But for two weeks I've been giving you news tips, and you've been taking 'em, acting like you were covering stories, only actually you were just playing me. And <u>that</u> really pisses me off!
PANEL 8 Vin pulls his Yankees jersey and cap out of the front closet. His body language shows he's pissed.
PP: I'm sorry. I -- I didn't tell you because I didn't want you to think you had a deadbeat roommate.
VIN: Well, I do. And FYI – I'm taking my Dad to the Yankee game

today. And since you'll also be in the Bronx…?

PANEL 9 On Vin exiting – Vin should be in the foreground, Pete should be small in the background.

VIN: Stay far, far away from the stadium. I'd prefer not to see your face for the rest of the day.

VIN NARRATION: After coffee with my Dad, we headed over to Yankee Stadium…

PANEL 10 Across from Yankee Stadium. Vin (now with Jersey and cap) and his Dad (maybe dressed the same way) approach the stadium on foot.

DAD: All the games I took you to at this ballpark…and now you're taking me.

VIN: Maybe we'll see a winner for once.

VIN NARRATION: That's when I heard the tire screech…

SFX (small to denote distance): SCREEECH!!!

PANEL 11 Vin reacts to a tire screech -- and Spider-Man. This is Vin's viewpoint of Spidey on Overdrive's Sports Car. It shouldn't be too close because Vin is going to have to run to get there. (REF: Page 2, panel 3)

VIN: Spider-Man! Dad, duty calls -- I'll meet you inside!

DAD: But you're off duty! Call 9-1-1!

VIN: I _am_ 9-1-1!

VIN NARRATION: Spider-Man. He's always rubbed me the wrong way. It's the mask. Only a guy with something to hide wears a mask like _that_. He'd rather hide his face than _breathe?_

PAGE 11 (4 PANELS)

PANEL 1 Vin runs after the flipping Sports car. He's talking into his cellphone as he runs. (This is a different view of the action we saw on page 2, panel 4)

VIN (into phone): Continuing to pursue black convertible on foot. Off-duty officer in civilian clothes.

VIN NARRATION: I mean, I'm a crime fighter. But I don't hide my face or my name like a criminal. Or a coward. And I don't even have any powers.

PANEL 2 This is a different p.o.v. of the action from Page 3. Vin has his pistol drawn on Spidey, near the webbed black car. Ideally, we should also see Overdrive escaping.

VIN NARRATION: So if I can do it, Spider-Man can do it. But he wouldn't even obey the law and register. In my book, that means he's a bad guy.

VIN: You have the right to remain silent…

SPIDEY: Hel-lo-oh? McFly? I'm the _good_ guy and you're letting the bad guy get away!

PANEL 3 There's now a shimmering effect on the car as it begins to morph back to its original state – maybe we can do something along the lines of a Steranko op-art thing, but much cooler via computer assist.

Vin's head turns to see what it is – he's distracted -- Spidey prepares to take off…

VIN NARRATION: When I took a moment to check the car for injuries…

VIN: What the hell -- ??

SPIDEY: Thank goodness for special effects.

PANEL 4 Spidey bounds away, firing a webstrand – a different p.o.v. of page 4 panel 4. Vin has his gun pointing at Spidey but since this is a Bronx street, there are buildings and people around. Note: Let's try to not show the webbed transformed car here so we can save it for the next page.

VIN: Hey! Stop or I'll shoot!

SPIDEY: Told ya you couldn't arrest me…

VIN NARRATION: Spider-Man ran like hell, compounding his crime. Given the surroundings and proximity of civilians, I chose not to fire.

PAGE 12 (5 PANELS)

PANEL 1 Vin is on his cell phone again as he looks over the webbed car, which has changed back to a more ordinary looking red convertible, with dents and bondo. Any damage done to the car in the chase would still be evident. (In the background a WOMAN is coming out of a building toward a waiting TAXI.)

VIN (into phone): …caused by Spider-Man. Vehicle is now a _red_ convertible and has no occupants.

VIN NARRATION: Apparently the web-slinger had some criminal disagreement with Overdrive…

DISTANT SFX: SCREEECH!!!

PANEL 2 Vin sees the souped up black bus way in the distance (maybe it's a silhouette). Spider-Man is on the roof. (See page 7, panel 4)

VIN NARRATION: And it had yet to be settled. There was no way for me to catch them on foot.

PANEL 3 Vin runs towards that taxi, holding out his badge. The woman is getting in. The taxi driver, when we finally see him, should be JAMAAL, from ASM 558. The style of cab should match 558 as well.

VIN: Hold it, Lady! Police emergency! I need that cab!

LADY: Call your own cab, jerk boy! I'm not falling for that one.

VIN NARRATION: Luckily, I had no trouble finding a taxi.

PANEL 4 Vin yanks her out.

VIN: Don't mess with the law, lady. Driver, follow that black bus!

PANEL 5 Ext. The street – the cab speeds along. (Note – this could also be done as a very high angle shot, giving a view of a lot of geography, showing the black bus is a distance away.)

JAMAAL: You gonna pay me for this, right, Mister Cop? 'Cause you don't pay, I don't drive.

VIN: What, you think I'm a deadbeat?

JAMAAL: It happens.

VIN NARRATION: The driver was glad to help…

PAGE 13 (5 PANELS)

PANEL 1 In the cab. Vin leans forward. Let's make this a street with elevated tracks, a la French Connection, to give us some cool shadows.

VIN: Turn left at the light! We can cut 'em off!

JAMAAL: Sorry, man -- one-way street, that's against the law. Can't get citizenship if I break the law.

VIN NARRATION: …and more than cooperative.

PANEL 2 Vin, now getting more irate, shows Jamal his holstered pistol – Vin's not pointing it, just showing it…a veiled threat. Ahead, through the windshield, a pedestrian is crossing the street.

VIN: Is _this_ enough law for you?

JAMAAL: Okay, sir, whatever you say, sir.

VIN NARRATION: I had him take a shortcut…

PANELS 3 AND 4 EXT. STREET –

In turning the corner, the cab has a near miss with the pedestrian – it's the same guy who almost got hit in chapter 1, and will later be revealed as Dexter Bennett, but we don't see his face here – use the shadows from the elevated tracks to obscure his face, or compose so we only see the back of his head. (Maybe do motion blur or multiple image to show the close call.)

PEDESTRIAN: Watch it, it's a one-way street!!

VIN: Jeez, keep your eyes on the road!

PANEL 5 The taxi catches up to the stopped black bus – the shimmering effect tells us that it's about to change back into a yellow bus. (From this angle, we can't see the back of it, or the web bubble or Spider-Man.)

VIN NARRATION: We finally got to the bus. Overdrive had escaped, but I heard screaming kids in the back – and someone else…

WORD BALLOON FROM BEHIND THE BUS: And that, kids, was your preview of Coney Island's newest thrill ride…

WORD BALLOON 2: Let's do it again!

WORD BALLOON 3: Whoa, this stuff is _sticky!_

PAGE 14 (5 PANELS)

Paolo, these panel breaks and image descriptions are suggestions – please feel free to adjust things as you see fit to make the scene play. .

PANEL 1 Behind the now yellow, normal school bus. Vin draws on Spidey, who is making sure the kids are safe in the web net/bubble.

(Note – the kids are stuck to it.)

VIN: Freeze, Spider-Man! You're under arrest and you're not getting away from me again!!

SPIDEY: Told you before, Sherlock, I'm the good guy, so YOU give it a rest.

VIN: I'm warning you!

PANEL 2 Spidey raises his hands up.

SPIDEY: Look, Einstein, since when do bad guys stop what they're doing to make sure children are safe?

VIN: Since when do good guys fail to register and become fugitives wanted for multiple murders?

PANEL 3 Favoring Spidey and the kids.

SPIDEY: Point. Tell you what, let's take a vote. Hey kids, you want him to shoot me?

KIDS: No way! Kick his butt, Spider-Man! He's no cop, he's a b-hole! You rule!

PANEL 4 Spidey aims his webshooter at Vin.

SPIDEY: Aw, you lose. Gotta give my public what they want!

PANEL 5 Spidey webs Vin's pistol, to the cheers and delight of the kids in the web net/bubble.

(Steve – your call if we should have Spidey web Vin's entire right hand.)

SPIDEY: Now Mr. Can't-Tell-The-Good-Guys-From-The-Bad-Guys, be a Good Guy and keep traffic away from my fan club until that web net dissolves. An hour or so. I've got a perp to chase.

VIN NARRATION: Spider-Man used the kids as a shield to make good his escape.

PAGE 15 (5 PANELS)

PANEL 1 As Spidey swings away, Vin frantically goes to Jamaal, standing next to his taxi, pointing an accusing finger at Vin.

JAMAAL: You owe me fifteen dollars, man.

VIN: Not now! We've gotta go after Spider-Man!

JAMAAL: You are a deadbeat! No real cop would just leave kids in the street!

And Spider-Man is a good guy.*

*FOOTNOTE: Jamaal met Spidey back in 548. –Scorecard Steve

VIN NARRATION: I knew my first duty was to protect the kids, so I gave up the chase…

PANEL 2 The cab speeds off, leaving Vin with the kids in the web net/bubble. Vin is frustrated and ashamed.

KIDS: You suck, man! All Yankee fans suck! Get us outta here!

VIN NARRATION: …because sometimes you just know the right thing to do.

PANEL 3 Flashback ends: this has all been Vin's tale to the VETERAN UNIFORMED COP at the scene. There are 2 squad cars, and other cops are trying to free the kids from the web bubble.

VIN: And then you guys got here, and here we are.

VETERAN COP: Stick around, Rookie. The Captain'll need to hear your story.

PANEL 4 Veteran Cop and Vin.

VETERAN COP: And listen, Cowboy: you were off duty, you called it in, and that was right. But don't try to be a cop 24/7. It's a bad way to live. You'll end up with no friends, no family, no life. Ain't worth it.

RADIO FROM NEARBY CAR: "This ball might be outta here---"

PANEL 5 Close on Vin – much like the very first panel of this chapter. Maybe he shouldn't have left his Dad at the ball park.

RADIO: "It is!!! A-Rod hits a Grand Slam! It's Yankees 4 to nothing!"

VIN: Yeah.

PANEL 6 Ending shot of Dad at the game. Dad looks sadly at the empty seat next to him while everyone else is having a great time.

FINAL VIN CAPTION BOX: "I guess Spider-Man didn't really ruin my afternoon. I ruined it all by myself."

PAGE 16 (5 PANELS)

PANEL 1 Establishing shot, a hangar/warehouse by the waterside. It's about an hour after the events from the previous page. The warehouse is open on one side, leading out towards the docks and the back street. We can see a white, luxury limo and a neon-green

motorcycle nearby.

There are five small figures on the loading bay: MR. NEGATIVE, three of his INNER DEMONS, and OVERDRIVE.

OVERDRIVE is tied up on the ground. MR. NEGATIVE observes as his goons, the INNER DEMONS, go about beating the living hell out of OVERDRIVE.

The INNER DEMONS wear black suits and ties, white shirts, and dull, metallic Chinese demon masks (see ASM #547-548 for ref.). They are usually armed with hi-tech versions of Chinese martial arts weapons. This time, only one of them is armed. He is using an energy whip to beat on OVERDRIVE. The other INNER DEMONS join in by kicking him—or they could just stand around looking tough.

PANEL 2 We go in closer so we can now see a good shot of MR. NEGATIVE interrogating OVERDRIVE while his INNER DEMONS continue to whip and kick him.

MR. NEGATIVE seems very controlled and nonplused. As OVERDRIVE yells out in pain, MR. NEGATIVE seems to be paying more attention as to how clean his own cuticles are.

MR. NEGATIVE asks OVERDRIVE to give him a full account of HOW he failed his mission today.

PANEL 3 Cut to OVERDRIVE, he swears he'll tell MR. NEGATIVE everything! In the foreground, the INNER DEMONS break into frame from about the chest down. We can see their clenched fists—and the dangling energy whip—primed and ready to start laying into OVERDRIVE again if MR. NEGATIVE isn't satisfied with OVERDRIVE'S answers…

PANEL 4 Cut to EARLIER TODAY—as OVERDRIVE drives a pimped out, super MONSTER TRUCK towards the security gates of a small start up lab in the BRONX (something that is one step above a business that's run out of someone's garage—but with a little bit more security).

The MONSTER TRUCK has, of course, been tricked out FROM Overdrive's powers. Somewhere on the street, we should be able to see the NON-tricked-out version of the convertible that OVERDRIVE was driving on PAGE 1.

PANEL 5 Cut to INSIDE the LABORATORY. Two scientists (one's pudgy, the other's stringy—and both of them look like they're from the neighborhood) were working on their new invention, when suddenly…

…OVERDRIVE'S MONSTER TRUCK came bursting through their wall (and/or security gates from outside). The scientists yell and duck for cover as giant chunks of masonry go flying through the air.

PAGE 17 (5 PANELS)

PANEL 1 OVERDRIVE jumps out of the cab of the MONSTER TRUCK.

PANEL 2 CUT to a shot of OVERDRIVE'S hand as he steals the scientists' invention… It's THE SONIC GUN that OVERDRIVE used on SPIDER-MAN back on PAGE 6!

PANEL 3 As OVERDRIVE runs out the big gaping hole in the wall, he passes the MONSTER TRUCK. The truck is already returning back to normal—now that OVERDRIVE'S powers aren't keeping it "tricked out".

PANEL 4 Outside, OVERDRIVE jumps into that normal convertible…

PANEL 5 …and drives off in it—as his powers begin to convert it into the "tricked out" car we saw on PAGE 1.

PAGE 18 (6 PANELS)

PANEL 1 Back in the present—at the warehouse-- MR. NEGATIVE asks OVERDRIVE what happened next. OVERDRIVE tells him that everything was going great—until SPIDER-MAN interfered—AGAIN!

PANELS 2 THROUGH 6

These panels are highlights from the previous two stories, but drawn from different angles—favoring OVERDRIVE more.

PANEL 2 We see a new version of PAGE 3, PANEL THREE—where OVERDRIVE is leaping out of his webbed up convertible and punching SPIDEY in the jaw.

As he tells the story, OVERDRIVE makes it sound like he really let

SPIDEY have it.

PANEL THREE We cut to a shot from OUTSIDE the TRICKED OUT SCHOOL BUS as SPIDER-MAN crashes in through the rear window (from PAGE 5, PANEL TWO).

In narration, OVERDRIVE mentions how he commandeered another vehicle—but SPIDEY wouldn't let up!

PANEL FOUR We see OVERDRIVE using the sonic gun on SPIDER-MAN from PAGE 5, PANEL FIVE.

PANEL 5 We see how SPIDEY later snatched the gun AWAY from OVERDRIVE...

PANEL 6 ...and how, while SPIDEY was using the sonic gun himself, OVERDRIVE slipped out the driver side window and made good his escape!

PAGE 19 (5 PANELS)
PANEL 1 Out on the street, OVERDRIVE "clotheslined" a guy off of his neon-green motorcycle (the same motorcycle from PAGE 16, PANEL ONE)...

PANEL 2 We see a shot of OVERDRIVE getting on the motorcycle—while using his power to transform it into a new, tricked-out version.

PANEL 3 With the motorcycle completely transformed, OVERDRIVE tears through the streets—looking cool as all hell—and even popping a wheelie while he does it!

PANEL 4
As the tricked out motorcycle whhhhooooooossssshes through the city streets, it avoids traffic by swerving up onto the sidewalk—almost hitting a poor old man who has to jump out of the way! It's the same person who almost got hit in both the first and second chapters .

PANEL 5
In a match shot, we stay on the street instead of the motorcycle. As the old man gets up, not only can we tell that he's REALLY PISSED OFF—but we can finally, CLEARLY see that he's DEXTER BENNETT—owner of THE DB, New York's best selling tabloid!

PAGE 20 (5 PANELS)
PANEL 1 Back in the present, MR. NEGATIVE asks ONE simple question. Where is the SONIC DEVICE that he asked OVERDRIVE to steal for him?! OVERDRIVE thinks hard...

"By now?" he says...

PANEL 2 "...probably in a precinct's evidence room."

Cut to crime scene investigator, CARLIE COOPER'S hand (in a surgical glove) picking up the SONIC DEVICE from the floor of the school bus.

PANEL 3 We pull back to see CARLIE coming out of the back of the school bus (which is back to normal and NOT tricked-out). CARLIE is telling VIN that thanks to him and Spider-Man, this weapon won't be falling into the wrong hands.

VIN rolls his eyes, he wants to know *why* CARLIE had to put it that way?

PANEL 4 CARLIE tells VIN that she's proud of him—that he stepped up and went BEYOND his duty—like every good cop should.

"Tell that to my dad," VIN sighs.

In the background police teams are pulling apart SPIDER-MAN'S web-ball and are helping all the kids out. It's been an hour and the webbing is starting to dissolve. (One of the kids could be complaining that he has to use the bathroom—he held it in for a full hour!).

PANEL 5 CLOSE UP on VIN and CARLIE in a kind of *possibly* romantic moment.

"Actually," says VIN, "would you? Tell that to my dad?"

"So?" CARLIE tells him, "You want to take me to meet your father?"

"Yeah. If that's okay. Um... He's probably still at the game."

"Oh. There was a game today? No one told me the Mets were playing."

PAGE 21 (6 PANELS)
PANEL 1 Cut back to the warehouse by the docks. As two of THE INNER DEMONS drag the tied-up OVERDRIVE away, MR. NEGATIVE addresses him.

"That's twice you've failed me Overdrive. I will not tolerate a third time. Dispose of him."

PANEL 2 As one of those two INNER DEMONS throws OVERDRIVE into the trunk of MR. NEGATIVE'S white limo in the background...

...in the foreground, MR. NEGATIVE talks to his third INNER DEMON. He says that for their next move they'll have to figure out a way of liberating the sonic device from one of the NYPD'S storage rooms....

PANEL 3 CLOSE UP on MR. NEGATIVE and the INNER DEMON that he was talking to... suddenly MR. NEGATIVE is distracted by a sound from off panel...

"In the past," says NEGATIVE, "one of my operatives on the force, Detective Willowby, has proven useful in this type of—"

VRROOMM!!!

PANEL 4 We pull back as MR. NEGATIVE and his INNER DEMONS turn and watch as MR. NEGATIVE'S WHITE LIMO begins to morph and change into one of OVERDRIVE'S tricked-out vehicles.

"Where did you just put him?!" demands NEGATIVE.

"In—in the trunk of your... car," says the INNER DEMON who was last holding on to OVERDRIVE...

PANEL 5 Fully transformed into a super-black-tricked-out limo—with OVERDRIVE in the driver's seat, OVERDRIVE guns the car and takes off, while yelling, "So long, suckahhhs!"

PANEL 6 Standing on the docks, one of the INNER DEMONS asks MR. NEGATIVE, "What now, sir?"

"Now?" says NEGATIVE while pointing at the INNER DEMON who threw OVERDRIVE into the trunk, "Now I'd like you to dispose of HIM."

PAGE 22 (5 PANELS)
PANEL 1 Cut to SPIDEY swinging through the BRONX. He has all of his PETER PARKER clothes bundled up and crammed under one arm.

PANEL 2 Ducking behind some cover, he quickly changes back into PETER. Maybe there's still some time... to show up to a job interview an HOUR late.

PANEL 3 As PETER walks down the street towards his job interview... He pauses in shock as he sees...

PANEL 4 The lab from PAGE 16—with the huge hole in the wall and the monster truck sticking out of it. Outside, the two scientists are standing around looking quite upset.

PETER introduces himself as the potential new hire—and asks them what happened.

One of the scientists tells him that they're going to have to put that job on hold for a while. It looks like they're going to have to do some extensive remodeling first.

PANEL 5 CLOSE UP on PETE as he sighs and wonders how things could possibly get any worse.

PAGE 23
SW-Paulo if you need we can get you reference as to what the style of the "DB" newspaper is. It needs to be VERY sensationalistic)

CUT to the FRONT PAGE of TOMORROW'S DB. The headline proudly declares "DEXTER BENNETT TARGETED BY SPIDER-MAN"—with a big photo of an ACTION SHOT of the SPIDEY and OVERDRIVE in the school bus as it almost hits DEXTER BENNETT.

A secondary photo on the page should be a HEROIC headshot of DEXTER BENNETT—with a sub-article of why SPIDER-MAN fears DEXTER BENNETT and is trying to silence this proud beacon of truth!

A third photo should be of the small children being helped out of the web ball, with a caption explaining that in order to pull off this mad scheme—SPIDER-MAN was willing to risk the lives of YOUNG CHILDREN!

And, in a small inset article, it's mentioned that the Yankees played one of the greatest games of all times! "Something that had to be seen to be believed!" said David Gonzalez.

THE END